THE POLITICS OF
CRISIS-
MAKING

WORLDS IN CRISIS: REFUGEES, ASYLUM, AND FORCED MIGRATION
Elizabeth Cullen Dunn and Georgina Ramsay, editors

THE POLITICS OF CRISIS-MAKING

FORCED DISPLACEMENT AND CULTURES OF ASSISTANCE IN LEBANON

ESTELLA CARPI

INDIANA UNIVERSITY PRESS

This book is a publication of
Indiana University Press
Office of Scholarly Publishing
Herman B Wells Library 350
1320 East 10th Street
Bloomington, Indiana 47405 USA

iupress.org

Manufactured in the United States of America

First printing 2023

Cover artwork: Dima Nashawi, an artist, a clown, and a visual storyteller, who collects and reflects tales from Syria.

Cataloging information is available from the Library of Congress.
ISBN 978-0-253-06638-1 (hardback)
ISBN 978-0-253-06639-8 (paperback)
ISBN 978-0-253-06640-4 (ebook)

To Amal Turki Mohammad

CONTENTS

FUNDING ACKNOWLEDGMENT

I wrote the drafts of this book while working for the "Analysing South-South Humanitarian Responses to Displacement from Syria: Views from Lebanon, Jordan and Turkey" project (led by Professor Elena Fiddian-Qasmiyeh and funded by the European Research Council under the European Union's Horizon 2020 Research and Innovation Program, with Grant Agreement No. 715582).

NOTE TO READER

Transliteration: I transliterated the names of places, research participants, and organizations, as well as local idioms and sayings, by adopting simplified conventions for the Lebanese dialect. Following the rules of classical Arabic, when the article *"al-"* precedes a sun letter, it is assimilated into the latter. In transcriptions, I opt to reproduce the letter's oral assimilation (e.g., ash-Shiyyah rather than al-Shiyyah). I also use the Arabic rather than the English transliteration of Arabic names (e.g., Hasan instead of Hassan).

Language: I conducted all fieldwork in Levantine Arabic, English, and, to a smaller extent, Italian and French.

Anonymization and pseudonymization: Unless I received specific, official consent (or an explicit request of mention), all names of NGO practitioners, UN officers, and inhabitants of Akkar and Dahiye have been pseudonymized in compliance with the General Protection Data Regulations 2018 and in line with ethical clearance obtained from the University of Sydney at the outset of my doctoral fieldwork in 2011. Even though I had to comply with the recommendation of anonymizing refugees and ordinary local people in the effort to protect their identities, I personally disagree with this common academic practice when applied aprioristically: it is often a pretext to anonymize their contributions to our theorizations. Not only NGO practitioners, politicians, and UN staff should be able to decide how to be cited and evaluate protection risk.

External assistance and contributions: Luca Mazzali (Appears, maps); Matteo Mazzoleni (appendix); Dima Nashawi (book cover artwork); Armando Perna (photo resolution); Lorenzo Trombetta (historical and geographical doubts).

THE POLITICS OF
CRISIS-
MAKING

Introduction

"So you want to establish a non-governmental organization, collective, club or cooperative in Lebanon . . . That is great and terrible news."

(From Lebanon Support, *The Basic Guidebook for Emerging Collectives, Cooperatives and NGOs in Lebanon*, 2016, 1)

In 2003, while studying for my bachelor's degree in linguistic and cultural mediation, I worked at a social center for migrants in Monza, Italy, where I was in charge of legal assistance and job recruitment, food and clothing distribution, and cultural activity organization. One day, an Egyptian man entered the office and stated that he was looking for a job. I told him that there were currently no vacancies. He replied: "But I'm talking about the job you're doing. I studied law back in Egypt, and I can speak four languages fluently. How can I apply for your job?" This request made me question my position as a first-class citizen living in my home country and working as a provider, presuming that migrants and refugees could only be beneficiaries or recipients. I realized that the assistance I was giving could be better provided by immigrants themselves, particularly when the stated goal of the agency was to empower migrants and provide them with better living conditions. In this vein, I echo Abu Lughod's argument that studying others and their cultures will never provide us with an understanding of their whole way of life (Abu Lughod 1991); I endeavor to liberate the term "cultures" from predefined, identity-dominated semantics. I therefore refer to culture as a continuously evolving set of principles, behaviors, beliefs, and ways of caring that does not necessarily align with national, community, or religious boundaries (but can, indeed, emerge across such boundaries). In the same semantic endeavor, I write against identity-loaded "Culture" insofar as it tends

1

to "enforce separations that inevitably carry a sense of hierarchy" (Abu Lughod 1991, 138). In this book, I question hegemonic cultures of provision and what war, displacement, and humanitarianism mean experientially for war-affected people. The encounter above taught me that aid cannot involve unconditional acts of generosity without implications for interpersonal and intergroup power relationships. It also induced me to question standardized terminologies, such as "aid beneficiaries" or "aid recipients." While I failed to find alternative definitions in this book, I find it dutiful to emphasize how poorly they represent people affected by conflict and, above all, by the political management of the displacement that generally ensues.[1]

Eight years later, I crossed paths with a man named Wael in northern Lebanon. He was born to Syrian parents in a northern Lebanese village and only had a Syrian passport. Wael's family decided to return to Syria when he was seventeen. In April 2011, the Syrian government's shelling destroyed his house in the Hama countryside, in central Syria. Now in his forties, Wael is a Syrian refugee in Lebanon. He lives in a tent that he built on a plot of land he needs to pay rent for. When he returned to Lebanon to flee the conflict in Syria, what exactly did Wael lack to live as a local resident? How did he not have easier access to aid, and why could he not capitalize on a local network of people in the country where he was born and lived while in his teens? This encounter triggered my interest in how the emergency crisis discourse, rather than emergency per se, changes the ways in which individuals and groups understand themselves and relate to each other in settings marked by crisis. Likewise, I was distressed by the question of how the crisis discourse influences everyday living and the sharing of space and time with old and new social presences. Both of these encounters functioned in anticipation of how aid can change or shape social relationships—creating distance from or proximity to other individuals and groups—and the political organization of society. This book, a diachronic ethnography of humanitarianism in contemporary Lebanon spanning from the July 2006 War to the arrival of Syrian refugees from 2011, unravels the infinite complexity of the humanitarian experience, where aid provision, reception, and exclusion all create a space in which social groups, polities, and moral worldviews are continually made and unmade not only in response to crisis but, more importantly, to crisis management. With this purpose, I incorporate into my experience the infinitely vast polyphony of voices of displaced people and assistance providers I encountered across the southern suburbs of Beirut (in Arabic *ad-Dahiye al-Janubiyye*, which, throughout this book, I will refer to as Dahiye, as locally named) and in the Akkar region in northern Lebanon. In such a polyphony, the fictitious dichotomies of current humanitarianism inevitably emerge, including aid recipients versus aid providers, hosts versus guests, secular versus religious, and local versus international actors.

THE POLITICS OF CRISIS-MAKING

Whenever human-made conflict breaks out, it is indiscriminately identified as *the* cause of social and political transformation. The complicity of aid and service provision in compartmentalizing groups and cementing distances (e.g., Lebanese approaching their longstanding Syrian neighbors as refugees) in a society marked by crisis often remains unthinkable because the act of aiding displaced people is, to some extent, a self-evident act of humanity and generosity, especially when it speaks to universal morality (Belloni 2005). It is here that this book makes a critical intervention: while politics in Lebanon has proven all its brutality, humanitarian action is also likely to inscribe itself on the pre-existing ground of privileges, self-indulgence, and corruption of Lebanese and global politics. This book suggests that social, political, and moral distances within society are not determined by the occurrence of war and subsequent forced displacement, but rather produced by the way in which crisis is declared, talked about, and practically managed. This warns us against simplistic formulas (e.g., "caused by crisis") and claims that suffering, injustice, and deprivation mechanically derive from war and displacement.

In the past years, I have often found myself fighting the assumption that humanitarianism research is an armchair-based attempt at assessing humanitarian programs for displaced populations. This book does not—and cannot—offer such assessments because the humanitarian experience, made up of encounters, interactions, and imaginations, only partly shapes the lives of the people who helped me undertake this research. In fact, I do not view forced migration and internal displacement as mere *humanitarian* experiences. This book aims to highlight the infinitely variegated landscape of such experiences, including social, political, and moral distances between groups, and the enmeshment of the lives of refugees with those of locals—some of whom have experienced internal displacement. Focusing on people's response to international, regional, and local crisis management, this book questions mainstream forms of international assistance that place the "white savior's" knowledge and agenda at the heart of the humanitarian scene. I will navigate nuanced meanings of assistance and how they relate to issues such as neutrality, hospitality, professional authority, and international accountability. In this context, despite the variegated nature of hegemonic humanitarian interventions, such interventions, on the whole, still tend to prescribe cultural dominance.

There is a tendency to think of war and displacement as triggers of a universalized human condition, where people presumably experience similar ways of thinking and behaving. This book endeavors to reclaim and unroll such endemic peculiarities. The politics of crisis-making in Lebanon remains a long and complex journey of understanding. With humanitarianism offering only one observatory window—among many—into people's lives, my gaze moves from the individual to the collective, from the local to the transnational, and back again. I engage with aid providers, recipients, and nonrecipients, categories which are not always separate and distinct. With a focus on local and international assistance providers, forced migrants (Palestinians, Iraqis, Sudanese, and Syrians), and local internally displaced people (IDP) in Lebanon, I examine the period following the July 2006 War—also called the 33-Day War, which ended with UN Security Council Resolution 1701—during which the Israeli Air Force destroyed the southern suburbs of Beirut. My attention later switches to 2011–2013 and the large-scale arrival of Syrian refugees to the Akkar region in northern Lebanon, which became one of their main shelters. Reflecting on the politics of crisis-making subtends the intersection between the "politics of life"—casting humanitarianism as inherently political when it values segments of human life while devaluing others (Fassin 2007)—and the "politics of living" in and with humanitarianism (Feldman 2012b, 2018), which considers not only humanitarian practices but especially the "dynamics of being (surviving, claiming, acting) with and within it" (Feldman 2012b, 157).

Humanitarianism, a constellation of ways of practicing care and actors who at times identify themselves in ways other than humanitarian, does not mechanically produce any *typical* form of living. It is rather the official crisis discourse, the physical emplacement of new actors in the areas marked by crisis, and the idea that official humanitarian spaces are being created that reshuffle society at a political, socio-relational, and moral level. In this framework, protracted displacement is sustained by protracted, long-term humanitarianism, which produces the paradox of making crisis sustainable. The "things could be worse" mantra, which has characterized most of Lebanon's humanitarian history, has made us believe that the normal functioning of society and economy can only be based on making crisis to activate resources. At the level of global economy, the physical emplacement of humanitarian agencies in Lebanon employs large segments of the Western labor offer, whose contribution to local infrastructure and employment remains provisional and, as will be evident, structurally unjust toward local, refugee, and migrant human capital.

Based on a diachronic ethnographic investigation of the practices of local and international nongovernmental organizations (NGOs) and UN agencies in urban and rural environments from 2011 until today, I explore the humanitarian response to the short-term displacement of Lebanese and refugee residents during the war in July 2006 and the long-term displacement of Syrian refugees who coexist in Lebanon with the aging refugeehood of Palestinians, Sudanese, and Iraqis. Far from humanitarianism being an exclusive factor that manages individual and collective experiences of displacement, however, this book will show that aid is not only about policies to be implemented but also dominations to be resisted (Mosse 2006). I develop three frameworks of analysis to show how local and refugee populations respond to diverse modalities of crisis management: the politicization of aid, the ethnicization of needs and services, and humanitarian distances. These three frameworks inform how different groups respond to humanitarian presence (and absence).

WHAT FORCED DISPLACEMENT?

The aftermath of the July War is the empirical inception for this book, which examines the social atmosphere of Dahiye's response to crisis management, reception of temporary forms of humanitarian care, and resentfulness within the geopolitical scene. For instance, US-aligned regimes, such as Egypt, Jordan, and Saudi Arabia, publicly rebuked Hezbollah for kidnapping two Israeli soldiers and inciting the massive Israeli destruction of Lebanon in 2006. As a result of what was locally perceived as a lack of solidarity with the Lebanese predicament, resentment toward US-friendly political coalitions in the region and worldwide soared (Valbjorn and Bank 2012). Local resentment toward the international community also stemmed from the ineffectiveness of humanitarian action assisting the displaced during and after the war. Indeed, Israel was unwilling to grant safe passage to aid convoys (Quilty 2006, 87), and goods earmarked as aid were sold and started appearing in grocery stores (Quilty 2006, 88).

Hezbollah's pyrrhic 2006 victory was celebrated as a triumph in several parts of the region and world, increasing secretary-general es-Saiyyd Hasan Nasrallah's fame and making him the most popular Arab hero since Gamal 'Abd an-Nasser (Achcar and Warschawski 2007, 119). Nevertheless, the consequences of war included 1,300 civilian casualties, 4,409 wounded, 74 Hezbollah fighters killed, and almost one million displaced following the largest ever infrastructural destruction in Lebanon.[2]

While many refer to the July War as the war of Israel on Hezbollah, it affected many refugee groups in Dahiye, producing "overlapping refugeedom" (Fiddian-Qasmiyeh 2016). International actors tend to interpret crises as "unpredictable shocks" disrupting normal life, but they are a political construction (Calhoun 2004; Ophir 2010; Vazquez-Arroyo 2013). Crises, in reality, are rooted in colonial and geopolitical history, yet they are addressed as disruptive events. The politics of crisis-making in Lebanon, which this book unpacks at an inter- and intragroup level, has either fed into preexisting social, political, and moral cleavages or generated new ones. The continuity on which the workings of this politics are based enables such cleavages. Having developed an interest in crisis discourse and practice and what it does to people and human relations, I navigate crisis not only as a political construction but especially as a social one, where the humanitarian space ends up functioning as a local laboratory for longstanding claims and contestation. In this framework, what I call "compensatory humanitarianism" is neither legitimated nor able to act as a functioning state and heal old wounds.

Scholars of forced migration and humanitarianism have predominantly focused on distinct refugee groups in the Middle East (e.g., Allan 2013; Feldman 2007, 2012a, 2012b, 2018; Fiddian-Qasmiyeh 2014, 2016; Gabiam 2016; Hassan and Hanafi 2010; Knudsen 2018; Salih 2020; Sassoon 2009). I endeavor to consider the humanitarian experience in Lebanon across—rather than merely between or within—different social groups faced with diverse motivations to migrate and ways to cope with forms of hardship more or less related to conflict. In this vein, in Dahiye, I build connections between local experiences of internal displacement with the multiple forced migrations in the country. Likewise, the history of Akkar, although marginalized by state and nonstate development policies, is interrelated with the rest of the country and Dahiye. At the time of the July War, for instance, ammunitions and other weaponry would reach Hezbollah's headquarters from Syria through Akkar's Dabbusiye-'Abboudiye road because the Israeli Air Force destroyed two bridges in the summer 2006.

Examining the hindsight of long-term and the outset of short-term humanitarianism in Dahiye and Akkar respectively, the book sheds light on how humanitarian practice becomes articulated through forms of welfare and development. The field research points to the impossibility of separating short-term from long-term humanitarianism, revealing the irreducibility of the humanitarian-development nexus vis-à-vis the human experience. Looking at the intersectional nature of what I name "develop-manitarianism"— the entanglement of development and humanitarian governance—enables us to see different yet enmeshed temporal patterns and practices. The current develop-manitarian impetus frames development as a temporary nuance of an overarching humanitarian plan that dominates donorship until an urgent response to a new crisis is needed elsewhere. This book hopes to inform the cyclic boost and depletion of resources and how the lives of people—both aid providers and displaced people—follow such cyclic patterns of intervention.

In this context, the language of "catastrophe" overshadows the human agency engendering and managing it, while catastrophe, per se, only engenders destruction, injuries, and deaths. It is the politics of crisis-making, not war or human mobility per se, that inscribes forced displacement within a catastrophe rubric. In an environment of generalized political disaffection, the humanitarian tendency to address immediate needs and enact crisis-driven modalities of governance—namely "catastrophization" (Ophir 2010; Vazquez-Arroyo 2013)—consigns local and refugee populations to a violent status quo. Moreover, crisis-driven governance is based on "strategic indifference" (Norman 2020), where receiving states allow migrants and refugees in while tacitly delegating welfare provision to humanitarian actors. In this way, the receiving state exerts minimal resources while parading resilience during crisis. *The Politics of Crisis-Making* shows how these dynamics also apply to Lebanon, where the anesthetic power of humanitarianism blurs political etiologies and undermines the possibility of a functioning public state. However, the politics of crisis-making does not merely work through the state: importantly, it is amplified by diverse forms of assistance as well as other local and international power holders.

EPISTEMOLOGICAL REFLECTIONS

As my research travels from Dahiye's postwar humanitarianism to Akkar's relief provision for Syrian refugees, some epistemological observations are particularly necessary. Over the years, I consciously experienced parallelism between crisis-driven aid and crisis-driven research. As an ethnographer looking at humanitarianism, I chased worlds defined by crisis, shifting my gaze with the latest displacement and cycle of resources. When I migrated my research work from Dahiye to Akkar during 2012 (which was unplanned), I lost touch with the types and levels of aid provision available to refugees from Syria in Dahiye. Moreover, Dahiye became closely monitored after 2013, when Hezbollah's military intervened in Syria and subsequently began to deal with outbursts of violence from extremist groups. These difficulties made it unlikely to continue working in Dahiye and encouraged me to delve into "adhocratic" humanitarianism (Dunn 2012) following the new arrivals from Syria in Akkar. However, my personal relationships with people in Dahiye continued beyond the scope of my research, with my informal presence being more welcomed than my research questions. Thus, my ethnographic pathway from the southern Beirut suburbs to the North of the country follows, to a certain extent, the same problematic chronology of the politics of aid, deprioritizing long-term action to address new crises and cyclically depleting the resources previously destined to postwar development projects. This pathway entangled me in the uncomfortable ethics of research—questioning the humanitarian politics of temporality while acting similarly—and left me short of knowledge on the tangled connection between long-term humanitarianism in Dahiye and short-term relief in Akkar.

At the outset of my fieldwork in Dahiye, I noticed a lack of interest in discussing past emergencies, such as the July War. Meaningfully, after I shifted my research focus from Dahiye to Akkar, the same humanitarian and development actors that were reluctant to discuss the assistance they had provided in 2006 were eager for me to focus on their engagement in the new relief provision to Syrian refugees. I realized that the July War was an out-of-fashion topic exactly because of how the politics of crisis-making develops—between amnesiac strategies aimed at removing the political past and deafening focalization on an ahistorical tyranny of the present.

In discussing both Dahiye and Akkar, I talk of social groups while referring to social membership as a sociological marker that acquires a strictly contextual significance in the humanitarian experience. In this vein, national or community identity is not always a meaningful explanatory tool for local histories of vulnerability and cultures of assistance. This is especially the case for Syrian refugees, who are not compounded in well-bounded communities in Lebanon because of economic, political, and cultural disenfranchisement (Chalcraft 2006, 2009) resulting from the complex relationship between Lebanon and Syria since they became nation-states after the French colonial mandate. In this sense, communities, to me, still carry the burden of religious and/or ethnical predefinitions of groups and identities, rendering the research experience dangerously prescriptive rather than inductive and open-ended.

LEBANON IN THE GLOBAL HUMANITARIAN ARENA

Lebanon is not a signatory of the 1951 Geneva Refugee Convention; it is, however, the perfect example of a place that incubates long-lasting displacement and overlapping faces of foreign and "vernacular" humanitarianism (Brkovic´ 2017). When I started conducting field research in 2011, in the bosom of a rapidly changing regional scenario first applauded and then discarded as the "Arab Spring," most of the Arab world was witnessing popular uprisings and political protests aimed at overthrowing dictatorial regimes. Initially, Lebanon did not appear to be caught up in the regional whirlwind of change. This apparent calmness—*hudu' zaher*—led the Lebanese, who craved social change, to sarcastically describe the regional unrest as "the spring of others."[3] Even though the Lebanese did not officially join the Arab uprising, instability has characterized Lebanon's political history from the Lebanese Civil War (1975–1990)[4]—when aid was less internationally financed than it is now—to the Israeli invasions (1978, 1982, 1996), the July 2006 Lebanon-Israel War, the 2007 fighting in the Palestinian refugee camp of Nahr al-Bared and the subsequent destruction of the camp, and the so-called spillover of the Syrian crisis from 2011.

Between late 2008 and early 2009, humanitarian aid agencies moved within the Levant region from Lebanon to the Gaza Strip, providing relief to the Palestinian population that had endured the Israeli military's Cast Lead Operation. This type of motion is now happening with humanitarian actors and corridors moving from or downsizing staff in the countries neighboring Syria, which remain in dire need, and relocating to Ukraine in response to the Russian invasion in February 2022. The hypermobile character of humanitarianism engenders a Sisyphean cycle of resources and expectations, all of which merge into the discontents of modern and contemporary humanitarianism. Some humanitarian programs that commenced in Dahiye in 2006 continued after the war, at times developing into welfare assistance and, through territorial continuity, paving the ground to stronger political connections for future crises. The likely permanence of international humanitarian actors after crisis in Lebanon speaks to the wider tendency in Western humanitarianism to ensure organizational continuity in the areas of intervention. A tendency that scholars identified as emerging, along with the professionalization of aid, after the 1967–70 Biafran humanitarian crisis (Omaka 2016). Such permanence is in apparent contradiction with the abovementioned continuous motion of the humanitarian system, generating a hybrid world of policies and practices that rest on complex temporal circularities, where humanitarian practitioners tend to move while the agencies and organizations they work for tend to remain.

Different models of foreign aid intervention have been identified throughout the years. After the civil war, aid was sent to Lebanon primarily for reconstruction, and financial assistance became the main factor in foreign aid agendas throughout the 2000s. The July War diverted foreign aid to immediate relief provision and, again, reconstruction. Following the blast in Beirut on August 4, 2020, caused by large amounts of ammonium stored illegally at Beirut Port, destruction, homelessness, and impoverishment hit several neighborhoods, intensifying the financial crisis already aggravated by partial COVID-19 pandemic lockdowns in the previous months. Although many humanitarian actors were still present in the country during this timeframe, the August blast, as it has become called, led to a hybrid model of foreign care, ranging from financial support to reconstruction and relief provision, increasingly from the private sector.

WHAT HUMANITARIANISM?

Since the 1948 *Nakba*, the Palestinian refugee presence in Lebanon has been the protogenesis of prolonged displacement in Lebanon and the region. From 2003, increasing numbers of Sudanese and Iraqi refugees fled into Lebanon because of conflict in their homelands. What was initially designed as *ad hoc* humanitarian relief turned into welfare provision for refugees over time, as resettlement options looked unlikely; Lebanon seemed to have become the refugees' final destination, despite remaining a country of transit in international humanitarian law. While I was looking at the impact of long-term humanitarian programs and the "social afterlife" (Stoler 2013, 9) of the July War in Dahiye during 2011, the violence in Syria was escalating, and the Lebanese region of Akkar, which ranks poorest, became the primary destination for people fleeing Syria. The unfolding events induced me to investigate initial forms of short-term humanitarianism and observe how different these forms were to Dahiye.

As Lebanon's history is entangled with the politics of two leviathan neighbors, Israel and Syria, and has long been the theater for multiple proxy conflicts, navigating the humanitarian experience means considering Lebanon's relationships with regional and global actors. On the one hand, aid in Dahiye was monopolized by the major Shiite party, Hezbollah, and reinforced the party's social ethics, including or excluding residents from networks of support, recovery, and compensation measures after the July War. On the other hand, as Akkar witnessed the arrival of Syrian refugees fleeing violence and persecution, aid provision paved the way, with large delay, for international support to a broader local chronic predicament.

At the outset of my research, I aimed to understand what large-scale humanitarian assistance had left in postwar Dahiye. Had humanitarian projects turned into long-term development and more solid local welfare in the aftermath of war? Was Hezbollah's reconstruction policy as inclusive and participative as advertised by the party and certain international actors? How did the international financing of local welfare following the war influence outgroup and ingroup relationships?

As I redirected my gaze to the synchronous character of the humanitarian experience in northern Lebanon, I became interested in the transformation of Akkar into a humanitarian space and the emergence of a new refugee governance. Previous scholarship has shown how states of emergency are geopolitical strategies for attaining specific global achievements (Calhoun 2004). This book corroborates humanitarianism as an arm of global order, but, offering the complexity of the humanitarian experience, it also reveals that this cannot be the end of the story. As such, it examines the social, political, and moral responses to crisis management in a vicious environment where crisis is the *sine qua non* condition to survive or grow.

FIELD RESEARCH IN LEBANON

Humanitarianism has been viewed as a topic worth exploring ethnographically for the last two decades (Dunn 2012; Fassin 2007; Fassin and Rechtman 2009; Feldman 2018; Fiddian-Qasmiyeh 2014; Gabiam 2016; Pandolfi 2000a; Ticktin 2006). The ethnographic research included in this book is primarily based on my doctoral work between 2011 and 2013 in Dahiye and Akkar. However, I later integrated ethnographic data from more recent work on urban and faith-inspired forms of humanitarianism in northern Lebanon, which spans from 2015 until the present day. The foundational ethnographic work consists of in-depth interviews and extensive participant observation I personally carried out between September 2011 and November 2013 in Beirut's Dahiye—namely in Bourj al-Barajneh (outside the Palestinian refugee camp), Choueifat, Haret Hreik, al-Ghobeiry, Bi'r al-'Abed, ash-Shiyyah, Mreije, Laylaki, and Hadath—and the Akkar villages of al-'Abdeh, Bebnin, al-Bahsa, Bellanet al-Hisa, Wadi Khaled, and the city of Halba.

In Dahiye, my regular interlocutors comprised seventeen local families and twenty-five individuals. I also conducted interviews with sixty-eight practitioners working for UN agencies and NGOs[5] that had collaborated with representatives from the Lebanese Ministry of Health and Social Affairs and Dahiye's municipalities in the aftermath of the July War. In Akkar, I interviewed forty-three humanitarian practitioners working in NGOs and UN agencies[6] and one hundred forty Syrian individuals (including some from the same households) who had relocated from Syria to different villages in North Lebanon. Among the IDP of the July War and the refugees, I interviewed both people who had benefited from humanitarian programs and those who were excluded from or had shown no interest in such programs. Among those stricken by the July War in Dahiye, middle-class residents made up 60 percent of my research sample; working-class residents made up 40 percent.[7] The refugees I met across Lebanon predominantly belonged to the second category, with some important exceptions (especially among the Iraqi refugees I met). I find it particularly relevant to specify the refugees' social classes in response to the international media that overlook such information by referring to refugeehood as a one-size-fits-all definition of their life. It is equally important to highlight that I mainly happened to speak to economically vulnerable refugees because poverty concerns most refugee households in Lebanon and because I met many of my refugee interlocutors through NGOs that, by definition, aim to reach out to the most vulnerable. I selected my research interlocutors on a day-to-day basis, and I resorted to chain sampling (also known as snowballing) to find new participants. We met in informally organized settings, such as private houses and local cafés. Dahiye is generally a distrustful environment due to Hezbollah's anti-Western rhetoric. The party has implemented a state-like project of care and surveillance over the years. I approached locals with the conviction that they would not necessarily want to speak their minds about humanitarian and political matters during a crisis. Having prepared myself to be unwanted in Dahiye, where outsiders are usually received with suspicion or avoid the area *tout court*, and under the pressure of the academic institutions I was affiliated with, I developed mental red flags (Carpi 2020b) that marked boundaries I believed I should not cross to avoid any *faux pas*. In the Akkar villages, I embraced a transformative approach to research (Mertens 2005), as my active engagement in the provision of assistance to Syrian refugees was intended to be a form of *témoignage* (Redfield 2010) of the Syrian uprising and its subsequent repression by Bashar al-Asad's regime—an act of witnessing derived from a moral obligation to denounce suffering (Fassin 2013; Guilhot 2012a). My ethnographic gaze eventually transformed into active humanitarian work, and the spontaneous form of work I undertook helped me develop a more in-depth impression of the context. In the late stage of my doctoral fieldwork, frustrated and even exasperated by the rampant public rhetoric of neutrality of NGOs, I volunteered for the Syrian-led Committee for Syrian Refugees in Lebanon (financed by the former Istanbul-based Syrian National Council, the most overtly political of all actors). I also engaged in informal and small-scale forms of assistance, such as collecting items in Lebanon and Italy to distribute among families and households that had spoken about their needs. The Akkar experience, thus, turned my ethnography into advocacy, through which I intended to transform the public representation of Syrian humanitarian victims into political agents and rights bearers. That was my personal way of supporting the Syrian critical response to the international (predominantly Western) mode of operating, largely based on the principles of neutrality and impartiality.

BOOK STRUCTURE

This book, cognizant that humanitarianism cannot govern all aspects of individual and collective life, seeks to reveal what the chronic inception of catastrophization does to the lives of people, their social relationships, and their moral and political views. I explain how "the politics of crisis-making," which, to me, unlike catastrophe, is a more powerful reminder of emergency actors' role and responsibility in crisis, relates to such relationships and views in six chapters.

Chapter 1 introduces Dahiye and Akkar's political ecologies along with their "crisis inceptions" and how local societies and polities have responded to multiscale crisis management during conflict-caused displacement. I engage with a fluid understanding of displacement, whereby locals who did not physically migrate out of the country still have to deal with the official emplacement of the crisis. In this vein, displacement is not merely a humanitarian issue—as the crisis rubric wants us to think—but it entails class, race, and labor politics, all aspects that the humanitarian system does not aim to address yet acts on. Chapter 2 provides an overview of the main humanitarian actors I discuss in this book, ranging from the Lebanese government to local faith-based organizations (FBOs) and international nongovernmental organizations (INGOs). Chapter 3 discusses the politicization of aid and the humanization of politics in Dahiye and Akkar. Framing itself in the form of an urgent response to human suffering, Western mainstream humanitarianism casts itself beyond politics, decontextualizing displacement and disentangling it from the politics that created it in the first place. In mainstream humanitarian history—molded by the politics of the Swiss-founded International Committee of the Red Cross (ICRC)—depoliticization strategies have suggested that refugeehood is about biological needs rather than political rights, contrasting with regional actors (e.g., Gulf countries) that propose articulated forms of political humanitarianism. I engage with complex relationships between morality, neutrality, and politics, and how such relationships are deeply shaped by identity politics, leading to the full neglect of some Lebanese areas. Chapter 4 outlines how displaced people have responded to humanitarian logistics meeting needs and providing services on a national basis with modalities that can be defined as processes of ethnicization. I investigate the social consequences of an established ethnocratic system of provision in relation to Dahiye's low-income local residents and older Sudanese and Iraqi refugees, and in relation to Syrian refugees who, from 2011, relocated to Akkar. I discuss how the ethnicization of needs and services has evolved in recent humanitarian history. In chapter 5, I critically reflect on humanitarian lifeworlds in Lebanon, drawing on an economy of encounters and mutual imaginations of locals, refugees, as well as local and international practitioners. Defining Southism as a structural relationship that cements the Global South as the key symbolic capital of the Global North's empowerment, accountability, and capability, I discuss ways of thinking and behaving that characterize Lebanon's humanitarian economy. With the purpose of interrogating national and political geographies in the provider-recipient relationship, I forward a degeographized notion of Southism while attributing *ad hoc* relevance to nationality in the humanitarian field. Chapter 6 revisits the deceptive character of official emergencies vis-à-vis chronic predicament, which preexists the political declaration of crisis and the physical emplacement of the humanitarian presence. In this framework, a crisis-driven functioning of society and politics is produced by emergencization rather than emergency per se.

NOTES

1. As Arabic speakers made me notice over the years, the literal meaning of *mustafidun* (beneficiaries) often carries negative implications, as it can imply the act of benefitting from/taking advantage of a situation or a resource, which may happen at the expenses of others.

2. This destruction was a consequence of seven thousand targets hit by Israeli air strikes, two thousand five hundred bombardments from the Israeli Sea Corps, ten thousand combat missions, and two thousand helicopter combat missions launched over Lebanon.

3. The "spring of others" recalls the Lebanese narrative of the "war of others" forwarded by Ghassan Tueni (1985), a widespread post-civil war theory suggesting that Lebanon was simply a battleground of regional powers rather than a theater of civil war.

4. Lebanon was also affected during WWI, but hardly any attention has been paid to this prenational historical period that also caused human displacement and hardship. George Antonius estimates that 350,000 people succumbed to famine in Greater Syria. Based on German records, Linda Schilcher argues that the number was closer to 500,000 (Antonius, *The Arab Awakening*, 241; Schilcher, "Famine in Syria," 231; Thompson, *Colonial Citizens*, 27 in Tanielian 2017).

5. Among them, twenty-three worked for faith-based organizations (FBOs), forty-five for secular nongovernmental organizations (NGOs), thirty-eight for international nongovernmental organizations (INGOs), and thirty for local NGOs.

6. Among them, seventeen worked for local and Gulf NGOs, twenty for secular INGOs, and six for different UN agencies.

7. This is merely my personal evaluation of a large set of factors and living conditions, which, quantitatively, needs to be taken with a pinch of salt.

1 / The Politics of Displacement in Lebanon

Most foreign aid providers, such as INGOs and UN agencies, arrived in Lebanon to provide relief to the displaced after the 1948 Palestinian exodus (Nakba), which caused the displacement of 750,000 people, during the struggle over the end of the British Mandate in Palestine and the establishment of the State of Israel (Feldman 2018, 5). At that time, a large network of local providers was already responding to crisis. Many of these aid and service providers were faith based or faith inspired, while others were civil society organizations (CSOs). Local responses have sought to address the disastrous effects of human-made conflicts in disadvantaged Lebanese regions, such as Dahiye, throughout the twentieth and twenty-first centuries.

These local responses were hybrid interventions composed of aid provision, financial support, and postconflict reconstruction. Certain major urban projects ended up impacting the human geography of some Lebanese areas. Foreign aid interventions affected the Lebanese political and economic fabric to a great extent. The July War which caused a large-scale internal displacement as well as Syrian displacement after 2011 are only two examples of how heavily Lebanon's political economy was affected by endemic and external factors—in fact, on the one hand, Lebanon has historically been a target of Israeli attacks and, on the other, Syrian menial laborers were already part of Lebanon's architecture of labor during the twentieth century, way before the 2011 crisis.

Significantly, Malkki (1995, 507) contends that "development projects tend to see a whole world in a refugee camp," making no distinction between the living conditions of refugee groups vis-à-vis other forms of local vulnerability. This became evident in Dahiye, where it is possible to find many economically vulnerable Lebanese and migrant households. Looking at the presociology of the Syrian presence in Akkar, it is likewise apparent that even locals who did not physically migrate outside of Lebanon had to address the politics of crisis-making, developing organized and unorganized responses to displacement and, importantly, to crisis management. By this token, I view not only those included, but also those excluded from aid in both Dahiye and Akkar as fundamental actors of the humanitarian experience.

Most scholars trace the genealogy of assistance in Lebanon back to the legacy of the Ottoman administration (especially throughout the XIX and early XX centuries' forced migrations), which managed shelters for regional refugees through administrative decentralization strategies (Chatty 2013). Lebanon also hosted diverse groups of refugees at different times after the French mandate (1920–1943).[1] One important difference that marks Lebanon-based refugee groups is their Palestinian origin. Palestinians are assisted by the United Nations Relief and Works Agency (UNRWA), which was formally established in late 1949 (Feldman 2018, 9) and operates in the region in agreement with local governments. Non-Palestinian refugees are instead assisted by the United Nations High Commissioner for Refugees (UNHCR), established in Lebanon in 1964.

The Palestinian refugee group can be further broken down into three sub-categories (Doraï and Clochard 2007): first, those who have an identity card, especially if they migrated to Lebanon after 1948; second, those who acquired citizenship at a later stage (twenty thousand people during the 1990s); and third, stateless Palestinians who do not have documentation[2] and are not entitled to any Lebanese services. Throughout my fieldwork, I came across the largest groups of non-Palestinian refugees, groups from Sudan (nearly six thousand), Iraq (between thirty and sixty thousand), and Syria (nearly nine hundred thousand registered with the UNHCR as of 2022). Since the 1990s, smaller groups of forced migrants have come from Sierra Leone and Somalia (Doraï and Clochard 2007, 3).

Lebanon, as a nonsignatory to the 1951 Geneva Refugee Convention and the 1967 Protocol, is a transit country where forced migrants are de facto refugees who access UNHCR services exclusively because of bilateral agreements with the Lebanese government. Lebanon has not subscribed to the Convention, fearing alterations to its demographic composition from the 413,000 Palestinian refugees within the country. The official reason for not naturalizing the Palestinians is their right to return (*haqq al-'awdeh*) to occupied territories. However, yet there are no serious plans that would bring justice to four generations of displacement and statelessness (Salih 2020). In 1987, the Lebanese government canceled the 1967 Cairo Agreement that previously granted so-cioeconomic rights to Palestinians. The refusal to naturalize and nationalize Palestinians—*tawtin* and *tajnis*—was often reiterated by Lebanese politicians, like former president Émile Lahoud in 2003.[3] Nonetheless, Palestinians are the only official refugees in Lebanon. Other refugee groups—*laji'un*—are called displaced—*nazihun*—in official documentation.

In Lebanon, during the Iraqi refugee crisis, refugee matters relied on a mo-dus operandi based on the 2003 Memorandum of Understanding (MoU) be-tween the UNHCR and the Lebanese government. An appropriate MoU for the Syrian refugee crisis was pursued with the delayed enforcement of the Lebanon Crisis Response Plan (LCRP), first drafted in late 2014 (Boustani et al. 2016). As a result, Syrian refugees' permit to stay in Lebanon has predominantly been regulated by the Lebanese Residency Law, which requires periodical renewal (Janmyr 2016). However, while Palestinian, Iraqi, Sudanese, and Syrian refu-gees in Lebanon can supposedly access basic services or obtain resettlement from UN agencies, people who used to live in these countries affected by con-flict but did not own citizenship or other migrants, mainly from Southeast Asia and West and East Africa, do not classify for the refugee assistance regime in spite of living in dire conditions. The legal labeling system strongly impacts people's lives in Lebanon, giving rise to economic, political, and existential hierarchies inside the country. While some migrants' vulnerabilities are not ac-knowledged as issues that forced migration-related institutions must deal with, official refugees have to cope with a "disastrous policy of no-policy" (El-Mufti 2014). Indeed, regardless of their relationship with the UNHCR or UNRWA, refugees are unlikely to benefit from an effective protection regime; they are treated as illegal migrants and sometimes sentenced to imprisonment and de-portation. At present, the repatriation of Syrian refugees is a source of debate. Repatriation has been encouraged by the Lebanese government, especially by what is known as the March 8 coalition (including the Free Patriotic Movement of today's President Michel 'Aoun—Maronite Christian and born in Dahiye himself—the Amal Movement, and the Hezbollah Party, both representing Lebanon's Shiite demographic component), which, during a demonstration happened on 8 March 2005, has sought to mobilize Lebanese society in favor of the Syrian government's presence and tutelage of Lebanon after the civil war. The primary reason that is used to undergird *refoulement* has been the geographical extension of Syria and the safety of some regions no longer un-der the control of rebel groups. Some Syrian nationals are now being forcibly evicted from some Lebanese areas and repatriated, echoing past practices with other refugee groups, such as the Rwandans in Tanzania in the 1990s (Krever

2011, 599). Such pro-return voices have been countered by human rights activist groups and organizations like Human Rights Watch in Lebanon (HRW 2011), which broached the issue of Syria having welcomed Lebanese people fleeing war in the summer of 2006.

Beyond legal entitlements, some refugees do not register with the UNHCR out of fear of being intercepted by the police on their way to the UNHCR office (Dewachi 2017) and tend to lead their lives indoors. For instance, Syrian refugees consider UNHCR or Lebanese state institutions to be a *marja'iyya hukumiyyeh*, namely, a point of reference for the Syrian government to keep track of its citizens when they leave the country. In contrast, some of the Syrian refugees I met over the years preferred not to register because they could already rely on sustainable livelihoods and did not want to be classified as refugees out of dignity or political ideology (e.g., families who used to support the Syrian government but, yet, having worsening living conditions and personal security issues inside Syria).

With refugees facing deportation in Lebanon and worldwide, state and regional security have clearly trumped human security. Short-term displacement caused by Israel's war on Lebanon in 2006 and previous attacks[4] did not result in the same concern as the longstanding refugeehood of people fleeing conflict in Sudan, Iraq, and Syria, seen as "a new global danger of increasingly open borders" (Duffield and Waddell 2004, 24). In this context, humanitarianism has acted as damage control, sometimes challenging and other times supporting the Lebanese government's moves. For instance, UNHCR was asked to cancel the June 2014 Worldwide Refugee Day marches in Beirut to preserve public order.[5] Likewise, the government, especially starting in 2016, prohibited humanitarian agencies from prioritizing income-generating activities that would enhance refugee employment in Lebanon in order to counterbalance domestic unemployment.

Humanitarian actors have proven unlikely to enforce effective refugee protection. Lebanon does not have official laws that address the protection of refugees; therefore, some become easy objects of criminalization. Local municipalities have often resorted to self-made security measures, such as illegal curfews imposed on Syrian nationals (Mourad 2021), further challenging the role of the (tacitly compliant) state as the sole provider of security. In this complex framework, many humanitarian and development programs in Lebanon do not limit their actions to providing in-kind or cash assistance, but they also prioritize the inclusion of host communities and international goals, such as social cohesion and stability, by approaching self-reliance as a route to social integration and harmony. The Dahiye dwellers who were internally displaced people (IDPs) during summer 2006 and the refugee groups I met in Dahiye and Akkar benefited from disparate humanitarian programs. I will now illustrate the spatial and political histories of Dahiye and Akkar in an attempt to rebuild a sociology of international and/or local aid interventions—a sociology that can explain pre- and postcrisis societal and economic processes.

HUMAN MOBILITY AND URBAN GOVERNANCE IN DAHIYE

Throughout the nineteenth century, most southern Lebanon residents worked as peasants in a region that, with the formation of Greater Lebanon (1920) under the French mandate, remained marginalized in the national economy. This annexation stigmatized the South (Deeb 2006, 84) and, to some extent, worsened the conditions of Lebanese southerners, mostly holding a Muslim Shiite background. In the 1920s, migrants moved to Dahiye from Jabal 'Amel (the previous name for the mountaineous areas of South Lebanon) seeking to maintain their communal identity, rituals, and traditions. According to an elderly Ruwess resident,[6] Dahiye was beautiful at that time as "there were cacti [*subbar*] all around." These migrants made up 5 percent of Dahiye's total population, working as peddlers, shoe shiners, street cleaners, construction workers, newspaper distributors, and other types of unskilled labor (Kobeissi 2009, 1). Yet the departure of colonial powers in 1943 did not immediately empower the Dahiye migrants and, more broadly, the disadvantaged Shiite community in Lebanon.[7] With the 1948 Palestinian *Nakba*, the economic situation in the South worsened. Over the years, Lebanese services such as banking, tourism, and trade started to thrive, while southern agriculture saw a 50 percent decrease in Lebanon's agricultural exports, especially with the import of Israeli goods after 1983 (Saad 1996, 195). With national industrialization in the 1950s, the demand for cheap labor increased, so Shiite Lebanese workers moved from the South and the Beqaa Valley to Dahiye, making up 75 percent of the industrial workforce; other Lebanese Shiites followed in 1975 and 1976. Segments of them, expelled from East Beirut and the Bourj Hammoud neighborhood at the beginning of the civil war, looked for safety in the southern suburbs (Saad 1996, 195). After 1969, when the Muslim Shi'a Higher Council became operative and the Shi'a became autonomous from Sunni political dominance, the community produced an urban-based middle class. It was a new generation of political *élite* (Khazen 2000, 44), "the ascendant class seeking upward social mobility" (Kasfir 1979). In the 1970s, Dahiye also became home to Shi'a businessmen migrants who returned to Lebanon because of unfavorable conditions in West Africa (Petran 1987, 265). These businessmen had maintained ties to their villages and connected South Lebanon transnationally. Some families who had become economically empowered brought their wealth into the southern Beirut suburbs, abandoning the deprived South, where there was no state-led development (Norton 1985).[8] These historical processes underlie the class-defined diversity within today's Dahiye. The lack of state protection and care left room for local sovereignty of the two major Shiite parties, Amal Movement (in Arabic, *Harakat Amal*) and Hezbollah, which gradually overshadowed the presence of other political actors like the Communist Party (Jurdi Abisaab 2017). Overall, the living conditions of most Lebanese Shi'a previously based in the South remained the same in rural and urban contexts. The combination of poorer migrants and uncontrolled demographic growth made Dahiye a slum-like area lacking basic services. Today, one-third of Beirut's population lives in Dahiye, an area of 17 square kilometers (Harb 2010) and 586 hectares.

State neglect and legal chaos associated Dahiye with a homogenous Hezbollah-friendly political identity and a hotbed for Lebanon's rackets. While coastal Dahiye (*ad-Dahiye ar-Ramliyye*, "sandy Dahiye") is mostly Amal-oriented, Hezbollah predominates in the suburbs, more frequently associated with the stronghold of the Islamic Resistance (*ad-Dahiye al-Mazbuta*, "correct Dahiye"). The Dahiye municipal election victory by Hezbollah in 1998 can be regarded as a considerable change. Some areas, such as the district of al-Ghobeiry, passed from an Amal administration to Hezbollah, which accepted the presence of Christian mayors elected by ex-residents who had migrated to other areas.[9] This move helped build an anticonfessional reputation (Harb 2010), or confessional tolerance. The Hezbollah Party and its supporters see these southern districts as laboratories of inclusion and participation. The area is considered of Christian origin and, as I experienced during fieldwork, some Christian-led municipalities advocate for Christian revival in the suburbs against the international stigma that Dahiye is an exclusively Shiite, Hezbollah stronghold.[10]

A CYCLE OF RECONSTRUCTION PLANS IN DAHIYE

Al-'amal biruhiyat khidmat an-nas
wa al-muhafaza 'ala al-masalih at-tijariyya
li-ashab al-mu'assasat

Work in the spirit of serving people
and preserve the commercial interests
of the organizations

(*Waad's* motto 2006, author's translation)

As the July War attracted INGOs to Lebanese ground, most local dwellers viewed international humanitarianism as an opportunistic industry that had delayed its intervention until the entropic state of war had officially ended and urban infrastructure had completely been demolished. While today's "urban-humanitarian nexus" (Campbell 2016) was not as widely discussed in 2006, the July War became important for the increased urbanization of humanitarian action. Against this backdrop, in order to identify key humanitarian actors in Dahiye, I considered the most visible infrastructural and political actors in the urban space. Local residents steered me toward local initiatives, which, unlike INGO projects, continued long after the war. These local actors included NGOs, faith-based organizations (FBOs), local municipalities, and individual community-based acts of philanthropy.

In this complex context, Dahiye's municipalities seem to have played a large role in aid provision. However, their relationship with the central state has always been muddled and complex. It is worth noting that Lebanese municipalities do not generally benefit from financial autonomy as they depend on central government funding for housing and infrastructure (Harb and Atallah 2015). Furthermore, the Independent Municipal Fund, through which municipalities are funded on an annual basis, is often reported to allocate money unequally (Harb and Atallah 2015). While decentralization has, at times, been promoted by the government itself (e.g., Fouad Shehab's mandate during the 1960s), some international humanitarian actors reported it as a problematic humanitarian administrative strategy that tends to bypass governmental decisions.

External intervention projects in wartime and postwar urban reconstruction are fundamental in reshaping and enfranchising service-deprived areas like Dahiye. In the aftermath of the civil war, Lebanon's economic recovery was financed with foreign loans. The borrow-to-build strategy of the central state left the country indebted and the domestic economy stagnant. Dahiye underwent different stages of reconstruction in 1983, 1996, and 2006. The civil war cost US $14 billion in infrastructure damage. Poverty increased significantly during this time in Dahiye: in 1997, the annual per capita income was estimated at US $410, compared to the Lebanese average of US $2,970 (Deeb 2006, 173). During Rafiq al-Hariri's mandate in the mid-1990s, the state seemed willing to reconstruct the area, and the 1996 Elyssar Project saw roads and highways rebuilt and hospitals and schools reactivated. However, the project was not finished due to a financial shortage. State planning in Dahiye resulted in coercive and violent urban policies seeking to modernize the periphery (Fawaz and Harb 2010, 23). Bou Akar talks of "intricately planned" peripheries where "the dysfunctional qualities of urban infrastructure help political elites create the geographies of war yet to come" (2018, 34). The Solidère Project, financed by ex-prime minister al-Hariri, provided similar results. Despite the apparent polarization of Lebanese politics,[11] the ex-prime minister's real estate company was not opposed in Parliament by Hezbollah members. Corm (2006) notes that Hezbollah practically facilitated the evacuation of the Shi'a population from downtown Beirut, negotiating compensation with the residents. In privatizing Beirut's reconstruction (Balanche 2012), Solidère triggered hostility among the Shi'a who inhabited the *centre ville*, relegating some local dwellers to the Shiite-majority surroundings (e.g., the districts of Basta and Zuqaq al-Blat, north of downtown Beirut, and the Dahiye district of Hay as-Silloum). Dahiye dwellers usually interpret any form of state planning as threatening and suspicious (Fawaz and Harb 2010); Lebanese state agencies are biased against the dwellers and address them with hostility and violence (Fawaz and Harb 2010). During the July War, according to the perceived solidarity of Dahiye residents, the enmity of the state was a chronic contingency, and despite the official politics of liminality and neutrality (Carpi 2019), the state never hesitated to exercise violence and repression.

This series of unaccomplished projects is opposed to Hezbollah's promise (*waad*) made in postwar Dahiye. *Waad* was one of the largest reconstruction projects after the July War, with the philosophy of making the suburbs *ajmal min ma ken*, "more beautiful than how they used to be."[12] Similarly, the deputy mayor of Haret Hreik, Hajj Hatoum, saw the July War as an "economic opportunity" (*forsa iqtisadiyye*) to reverse urban destruction: "It was the first time that we employed such a large number of local professionals."[13] However, the delay of state funds and cash payments allocated to the Beirut peripheries was locally interpreted as a sign of longstanding unsympathetic state attitudes (Fawaz and Harb 2010). The foreign funding that arrived after the July War raised suspicion among local residents, and some Western states saw the main Lebanese Shiite party as a terrorist organization[14] and refused to provide any financial support. The people I knew in Dahiye recalled that a large section of the international community had denied help to Lebanon.

Despite Hezbollah's granular knowledge of the southern suburbs, strong service delivery, and longstanding ties with local society, some dwellers did not view the party as the only possible solution for Dahiye. For instance, an elderly shop assistant in the Dahiye district of Laylaki emphasized that "Hezbollah did a lot for us after the July War, but we didn't get the support of the state. All of this is pointless without an efficient state: Hezbollah can keep providing lots of things for us, but we'll see no real improvement here without state support."[15]

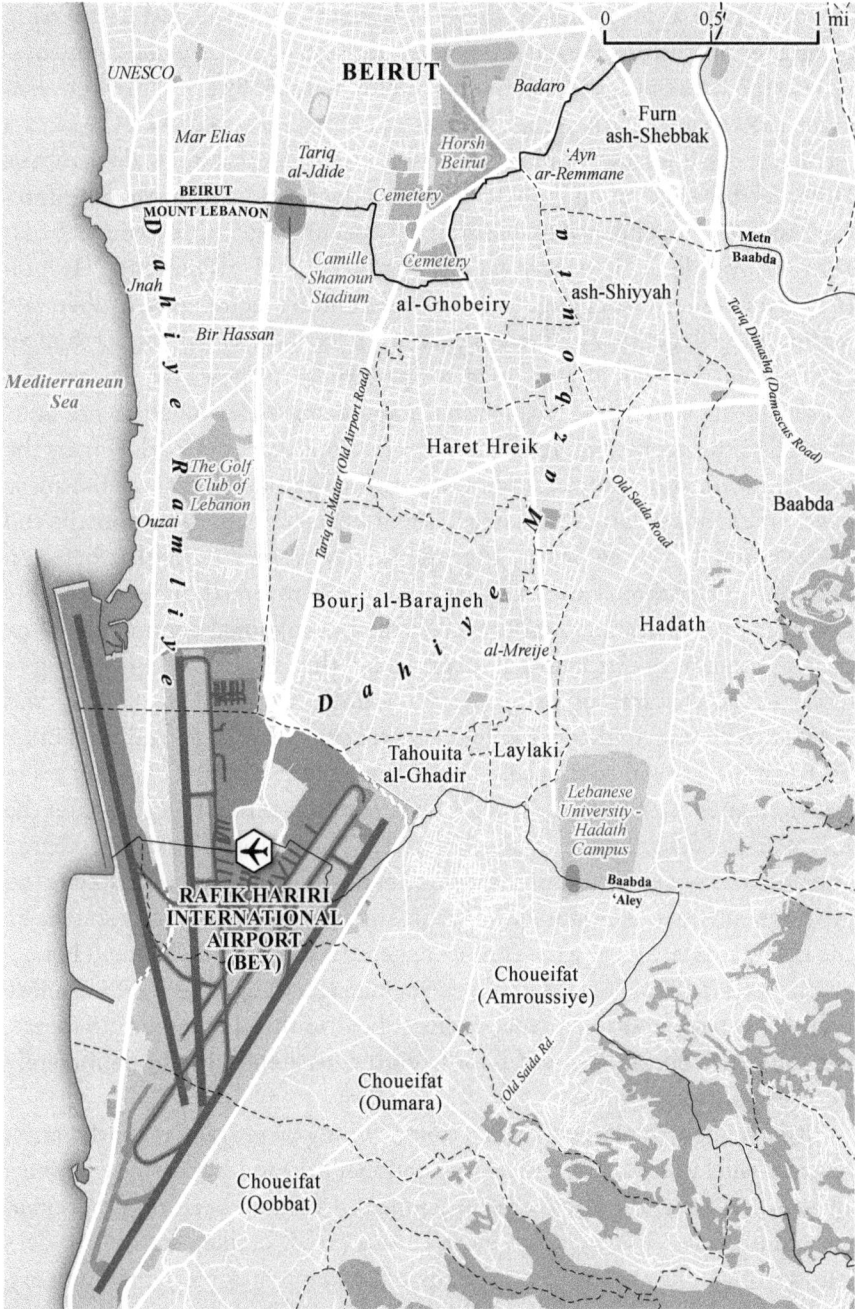

Fig. 1.1 Map of Dahiye. Credits: Luca Mazzali (Appears).

While it has been a common belief in Lebanon that the central state and Hezbollah are at loggerheads, they established an undeclared partnership during the postwar reconstruction, where residents gave financial compensation to the *Waad* project, which was paid for, in turn, by the central government (Fawaz and Harb 2010, 29). This dynamic, more widely, evidences a "strategic dissimulation" of Hezbollah with the central state (Calculli 2018). However, the state failed to remove the war debris quickly, further reinforcing residents' dependence on Hezbollah to secure housing in Dahiye (Hilal 2008, 71). While the Lebanese state participated in illegal building, Hezbollah "never requested a change in urban and building regulations, deliberately maintaining 'legality' as a favor it grants [to local dwellers], rather than an entitlement that would recognize people's right to the city" (Fawaz 2017, 1949). In this vein, some scholars have approached Hezbollah as not antithetical to the neoliberal order (Daher 2016; Bou Akar 2018, 102). During the July War, Minister of Social Affairs Nayla Mouawad stated that the Lebanese government hoped Olmert-led Israel would weaken Hezbollah before the end of the conflict.[16] Nonetheless, after the July War, the relationship between the state and Hezbollah became particularly controversial, appearing highly divisive and beyond the interference of the international community. During the conflict, the Lebanese state projected the image of being "willing to offer Lebanon to Israel on a silver tray"[17] in order to weaken Hezbollah[18] and seemed to play a paradoxical negotiating role between Israel and Hezbollah via the international community (Presidency of the Council of Ministers in Lebanon 2007, 44). The locals' negative perception of the state grew after the July War, and according to some scholars, the *Waad* project was implemented and financed not just without the government's help but despite obstacles the government created (Alamuddin 2010). The neutral positionality sought by the Lebanese state during the conflict engendered general discontent. For example, a Ministry of Social Affairs project manager[19] suggested that Lebanese politicians triggered an enhanced sense of cultural and religious difference, which, in her opinion, would have been inconsistent without deliberately divisive political actions.

In early 2000, foreign aid shifted from working on postwar reconstruction to addressing the country's increasing national debt and stagnating economy. In 2001 and 2002, the Lebanese government presented a reform program at two conferences—Paris I and Paris II—to avoid financial crisis. Funders transferred money to the Central Bank of Lebanon in 2006 (Baumann 2013, 142) and raised more than US $4 billion from international donors. Denouncing the suspicious use of international postwar funds, a pastry shop assistant in Dahiye's Haret Hreik complained about the decreased chance of receiving a state loan:

> Now, if you don't have a martyr or an injured person among your family members because of one of Hezbollah's wars, you are botched. There are charity services for special categories to show that the party is engaged and stuff like that. No one addresses the financial needs of small entrepreneurs like us . . . they organized Paris I, Paris II, Paris III,[20] and maybe there will even be Paris IV. They just do bourgeoisie meetings, showing off that they are commit-ted to improving human conditions, but they only want to fill up their pockets.

At the Stockholm Conference in August 2006, the international commu-nity[21] pledged US $900 million for humanitarian assistance and early recovery efforts, although only US $581 million was eventually paid (Collaborative Lis-tening Project 2009). In the 2008 framework of the Friends of Lebanon Confer-ence, funds were used to reconstruct basic infrastructure (electricity, power plants, water, and sanitation systems) and transportation systems (bridges and highways) and to support national security, administrative reforms, education, and the private sector. Furthermore, a Lebanon Recovery Fund (LRF) was established by the Lebanese government to reconstruct the country.[22] In this context, a Bi'r al-'Abed resident complained about the impossibility of receiving loans and the general economic situation: "Now the cost of living is too high. Do they think we're in Dubai? After the war, due to oil shortages, taxi drivers raised the ride fee from 1,500 LL to 2,000 LL. It didn't get back to how it was after that. Life became impossible."[23]

Similarly, a shop owner in Haret Hreik[24] expressed his disaffection and belief that "without these charity organizations, things would be better here. Everyone would finally get the same things." Yet there are several street signs, posters, and alms boxes in Dahiye's public spaces for raising funds for main-stream local charities. Khalil, a shop owner in Haret Hreik, emphasized that just because he displays an al-Imdad[25] charity box on his shop counter does not mean he intends to sponsor Hezbollah's NGOs: "My wife once went to their hospital, and they said they wanted to see the money first. And this is what they call philanthropy [ihsan]!"[26]

The reconstruction phase marked a major exchange of expertise between Dahiye's dwellers and local or international outsiders, who conveniently ac-knowledged local competencies. For example, the Best Practices UN Award for reconstruction efforts was awarded to the al-Ghobeiry municipality for its efforts in refurbishing and building infrastructure and providing social services (Harb 2010, 222). In the Waad project, Lebanese engineers and architects also

Fig. 1.2 Building in Dahiye damaged during the civil war. On its facade is a
picture of Hezbollah's leader, Hasan Nasrallah, who promised quick urban
reconstruction and a return to normal life after the July 2006 War. October 17, 2011.
Photo credits: Author.

played an important role. One of them, a Dahiye outsider, said he was strongly
encouraged to work for the project:

> I was initially skeptical about working with Hezbollah as I've always
> feared their weapons. Instead, I had the chance to see how well they can
> work [. . .]. Yet, the banks do not want to invest in their projects. For banks,
> it's like financing terrorism. With Hezbollah, I discussed similar problems, like
> the Palestinians that seized southern Lebanon, raped our land, and created
> disorder. Those memories still make people from the South shudder. This is
> why Hezbollah felt pressure to return people to their homes. This is great. We
> Christians had no one who could do the same for us: in 1967, before the civil
> war, Christian villages got demolished and no one rebuilt them.[27]

In urban Dahiye, after summer 2006, different forms of humanitarianism
were co-opted as a supplementary arm of reconstruction to reverse the Israeli
urbicide.[28] This co-option reiterated the selective nature of war destruction by
compensating those directly affected and, more broadly, conducting a "violent
reorganization of the city's spatiality" (Fregonese 2020, 142) that eventually

reasserted endemic inequalities. At the time of the July War, the NGO *Jihad al-Binaa*[29] played a key role in emergency relief provision. As one of its employees affirmed,[30] this NGO's humanitarian action and duty helped the Resistance in occupied regions. If Hezbollah proved to Lebanon that Israel could be "weaker than a spider web" (*awhan min beit al-'ankabut*),[31] it also proved that the party could efficiently provide immediate relief and rehabilitation. According to the local ethics of the Resistance[32] professed after July 2006, all Dahiye inhabitants (and not merely war combatants) were resilient during Hezbollah's struggle against the Zionist enemy. Before the ceasefire on August 14, 2006, *Jihad al-Binaa* was already present in Dahiye, visiting people door-to-door, assessing the damage in each apartment, and handing out cash compensation packets ranging between US \$10,000 and US \$12,000 for one year. People returned to their houses at great speed after the bombardments,[33] which helped the party maintain popularity and ensure the restoration of everyday life in Dahiye. It was amid international acclaim that local scholars and experts proclaimed, however, that the quick return to normalcy had prevented the party from enlarging green spaces and wisely redesigning Dahiye's urban space.[34] Furthermore, Hezbollah's haste in rehousing twenty thousand inhabitants in a one-hectare area did not improve health conditions; air sulfur levels were high as the dispersal of heavy airborne particles and pollution increased after building reconstruction, cleaning, collecting and transporting rubble, and increased traffic. As a result, asthma, cardiovascular, and respiratory morbidity and mortality increased in Dahiye (Makkouk 2008, 2).

When I first set foot in Dahiye in September 2011, the dust of ongoing construction work obscured the surrounding buildings. Mahmud, a resident from the coastal Dahiye district of al-Jnah, drove me around, having promised to take me on a Dahiye "wedding tour" (*fatlet 'arus*). With infallible memory, he told me what buildings were pulverized and when during July 2006, detailing the physical impact of war. The first attack on July 13, 2006, at six a.m., demolished the airport bridge (*jisr al-matar*) and "was heard by everyone in Dahiye." That attack reminded Mahmud of the 1968 Israeli attack on Beirut's airport. Mahmud said he was happy about Dahiye's reconstruction: "I like the colors and the style of the new buildings. We thank Iran for that." During our tour, he recounted the story of the martyrs printed on the street posters we came across, most of whom died for the Resistance against Zionism during the Israeli occupation (1978–2000). Mahmoud emphasized how nearly all of them were ordinary people who took up weapons for their families' survival.[35] He drove me through the suburbs with the pride of someone who resides in an area of urban improvement, complete with affordable vegetables and fruits, entertainment venues, crowded restaurants, children's playgrounds, hospitals, and schools.[36] Mahmoud wanted me to understand that he was not asking for anything but a quiet life: "We just want to live peacefully" (bas bedna na'yish ful). Today's proliferation of cafés, restaurants, amusement parks, and beauty shops[37] misleadingly points to a homogenous enfranchisement (Deeb and Harb 2012). The soaring prices of the housing market, monthly bills, and shopping areas over the last decade all position Dahiye closer to bourgeois Beirut neighborhoods.

The locals I met generally considered the 2006 victory a completion of reconstruction, compensation, and urban upgrading, not merely a fulfilled military effort. After the war, the memory of the enemy's defeat remained in the suburbs as the displaced quickly returned to their villages and saw their demolished houses rebuilt (Deeb and Harb 2012). After a general climate of chronic warfare, reconstruction and urban embellishment signified moral pride and material renaissance (Deeb and Harb 2012). At the same time, the postwar setting and reconstruction compensatory schemes gave rise to a wider socioeconomic gap within Dahiye. Refugee and migrant groups were further impoverished as a result of the continual neglect of vulnerable areas, such as the district of Hay as-Silloum or the slum of Hay al-Gharbe, located between the Palestinian camps of Shatila and Sabra (now considered a simple "gathering," tajammu'). These Dahiye districts have been historically neglected by the central state while hosting a heterogeneous population whose identity politics happen to be less functional to Hezbollah's agendas (see chap. 3). The destruction caused by war has brought the need for urban renewal, which has been largely monopolized from above. Scholars who have long worked on Dahiye believe that these historically marginalized suburbs were not involved in reconstruction projects under the pretext that the areas directly stricken by the Israeli Air Force needed to be rebuilt first.[38] Reconstruction thereby is hardly seen as an opportunity to rethink spaces where change would enfranchise marginalized communities. Such areas were practically cut out of the suburban socioeconomic progress that stemmed from the July War. In its aftermath, military success and speedy development were measured according to the same standards (Diamond 2010), whereas the July War relief provision redrew urban lines of inclusion and exclusion between local and migrant groups in Dahiye and among local citizens themselves. This motivated the local climate of decreasing consent toward Hezbollah's administrative policies, which I witnessed at the time of my fieldwork. For this reason, to some extent, some locals either welcomed or discarded my work as an inquiry into local dissent.

For Dahiye's residents, the July War came to signify what was lost and what was gained. The term "reconstruction" captures not only the repair and renewal of the urban environment but also the reasons behind who benefits and why, unavoidably generating social friction. Ranya's words exemplified how relationships between neighbors can be affected by compensation strategies causing different experiences of reconstruction: "The neighbor has always been close to Hezbollah; look at their door handle . . . It's real silver. Go to them and ask them why, after the war, they've been able to change all the furniture in the living room."[39] In this framework, reconstruction, humanitarian relief, and development, though based on distinct principles, all merge into the space of war.

CIRCULAR MEMORYSCAPES IN DAHIYE

During the Lebanese Civil War (1975–1990), according to longstanding local residents, Dahiye looked like any other community-oriented district in Beirut. In my everyday walks and talks through the southern suburbs, I realized that past battles, like those between the Amal and Hezbollah Parties in 1988 that resulted in two thousand victims, still mark Dahiye's spatial public memory. Public memory remains a fundamental part of Hezbollah's politics; the party depicted the July War victory as a victory for the whole Lebanese nation, not only Lebanese Shiites, similar to the defeat of the Israeli troops in South Lebanon in May 2000. International humanitarian intervention in the aftermath of the July War became inscribed within a preexisting Shi'a memoryscape that associated the postwar compensation system and public memorialization (Jelin 2007) with the rapid reconstruction of Beirut's southern suburbs.[40] Despite Hezbollah's several attempts to parade postwar party politics as national and inclusive, community belonging still survives. For instance, 'Ali, a Lebanese teenager from al-Ghobeiry, told me: "It's extraordinary. Now all of Lebanon owes its survival to Shiites. *We* won. *We* defended this country in the name of everyone."[41] In contrast, the municipal Hezbollah I dealt with during my fieldwork would not officially claim Dahiye as its own territory. The deputy mayor of Haret Hreik, *Hajj* Ahmed Hatoum, described Dahiye as an internally diverse reality, emphasizing to me that the southern suburbs do not belong to Hezbollah but rather that "Dahiye is like a rose, of which the petals are its different realities and the stalk is the Islamic Resistance."[42] The metaphor reflects the party's belief that the Resistance remains a unifying factor despite Dahiye's endemic diversification. In a sense, the Resistance emerged as a system of social ethics with which residents need to comply to have their suffering recognized in Dahiye's public space. During my visit to *Jihad al-Binaa* in Haret Hreik, a local engineer described the difference between the CIA's soft and hard powers to explain how the Resistance remains a necessary and deliberate common base for Dahiye's very existence:[43] "The best card we can play is soft power, deriving from our history and culture. The armed Resistance is a choice, but it adopts the language of necessity and defense [. . .]. The Resistance is like an aquarium. The fish are the core of the Resistance, and the water is the people. Israel always targets the fish, to finish them."[44]

In my everyday encounter with people in Dahiye, I realized there is no single narrative on the meaning of the Resistance, not even during the July War. Some segments of Lebanese society feel they were not targeted by the Israeli Defense Forces (IDF) and accuse Hezbollah of dragging the whole country into unjust power battles. In Lebanon, this brutal month-long war is considered the last installment in a long-running struggle that began in 1978, 'am ijtiah al-janub, the "year of the invasion of the South." Meaningfully, many local aid providers who experienced the July War contend that the thirty-four days of aggression, causing the death of twelve hundred Lebanese civilians and the displacement of nearly one million people, marked a watershed in national humanitarian and conflict history. Unlike the Lebanese Civil War, which was fought in everyday living spaces, the July War was fought with the Israeli Air Force's heavy shelling and Hezbollah's missiles. Targeting the Shi'a-dominated areas of the southern suburbs, South Lebanon, and the Beqaa Valley, the "spatial clarity of the attack" (Arif 2008, 676) became evident, as other parts of the city remained almost untouched.[45]

The war seemed to be a dramatic interruption of everyday life. It led to an estimated US $3.6 billion in unprecedented infrastructure damage, leaving 107 bridges, 94 roads, and 125,000 housing units destroyed or partially damaged. In the South, 80 percent of the villages were reduced to rubble. Losses to the local economy in the following three years were estimated at US $15 billion (Blanford 2011). Israeli air attacks pulverized the residential areas of 500,000 Lebanese residents and 15,000 houses; the headquarters of Hezbollah; their TV station al-Manar in the Bi'r Hasan district; and the *mujamma' ash-shuhada'*, where as-Saiyyd Hasan Nasrallah usually delivered his speeches. International humanitarian providers approached the crisis as an event or series of events that disrupted normalcy. Mariam, a Lebanese citizen who moved to Dahiye from the South after the July War, countered the logic of such event-driven relief: "Healthcare providers have addressed our psychological fears as though it were merely the bombing in the July War that made a difference to our miserable life in South Lebanon until 2000."[46]

From a local perspective, the July War occurred in a line of historical continuity, in which people live with a constant anticipation of violence—the idea that "war is about to ignite" (in Lebanese dialect, *bedda tulaa*)—making Lebanon's war a continuous living memory (Hermez 2017). As such, violence and war are a lifetime, not a one-off occurrence (Smirl 2015, 196). As Moghnie (2021, 10) put it, "the experience of *living in* violence, rather than encountering it, predicated forms of suffering that were not necessarily psychological or traumatic." On the one hand, those who experienced the war and felt targeted highlighted the brittle solidarity of outsiders toward war victims. On the other hand, some Dahiye residents I met blamed Hezbollah for the Israeli urbicide of the southern suburbs. Aid providers described the war as exceptional: "You did not need to worry about what neighbor could have turned around and shot you. In 2006, your fear was from the sky, not from people. Everyone in Lebanon was helping people who were coming up from the South [and] people were not worried anymore about the religious crossover. This consistently changed things emotionally and psychologically. You were angry at America; you were angry at Israel. If you were angry at Hezbollah too, you were more dismayed about how miserable Israel had rendered our lives in the twinkle of an eye."[47]

The local capacity to face and win war, provide services, reconstruct buildings, and restore normality was a fundamental factor of Dahiye's social ethos and South Lebanon's history of pursuing social justice and exorcizing public fear. In this sense, *Waad*, the promise, was aimed at managing future fears and protecting the party's constituencies. It is in this spirit that Layal from Haret Hreik argued: "As long as as-Saiyyd Hasan takes care of us, nothing bad will happen to us again."[48] Likewise, Husein from Msharrafiye affirmed that "As-Saiyyd Hasan never lies. Our life will not be jeopardized any longer," despite believing that war remains "almost a metaphysics of Shiite society," as Iranian scholar Farzin Vahdat has argued.[49] In facing the ontological determinism of longstanding violence, the promotion of ethical values and ideals, such as Islamic Resistance against the Zionist enemy, was meant to intensify the military and civil sense of agency. War victims perceived themselves as liberated from deprivation—*hirman*—and as part of a group where the survivor, the dead, and the wounded soldier contributed to local justice. Dahiye's dwellers associated the destructive July War with a dense past of oppression, letting crisis fall into the dimension of normalcy. This led to an outsider's misleading belief that "Dahiye's people are all ready to die."[50] In terms of the hyperbolic repetition of war and oppression, locals said they believe in destiny and were waiting for the next war. Souha', living in Haret Hreik, said she knew that war "will come soon, so we can just relax after that. It's already been five years since the end of the July War ... I'm developing anxiety while waiting." Ja'far, a Dahiye resident, was still living in the South during the summer of 2006: "During the bombings, we used to sleep in the corridor as it's said to be safer. After the war, my sister kept sleeping against the wall for another month. She was traumatized ...

I'm not sure whether we won't face another war. I don't care. Why should I? In the worst of cases, I just go back to sleep in the corridor!"[51] This account, loaded with sarcasm and suffering at the same time, does not necessarily speak to resilience or trauma, but it rather articulates a discourse that INGOs are unable to recognize (Moghnie, 2022). Ja'far's sarcastic awareness resonates with Najwan, an ash-Shiyyah resident, who powerfully recounted the ontological determinism of war in Lebanon: "I'm Lebanese . . . I can't do anything but choose which war I prefer. In this sense, the 2006 War was better than the civil war: the enemy came from outside, from the sky . . . at least there was no one shooting at you when walking to get some milk in your neighborhood."[52]

Similarly, Radwan, a shop owner in Hay as-Silloum, said: "I was born like this [pretending to hold a rifle in his hand], fighting against Israel, and I will die in the same way. It's our destiny." While actively opposing the Israeli army's futuristic logic of annihilation, Dahiye residents seemed to experience the 2006 attacks as a deterministic destiny of victimhood; a victimhood which had eventually redeemed itself. Although there was a bitter awareness that war lurked around the corner, some Dahiye dwellers preferred not to leave their homes during the Israeli bombings despite the leaflets (*manshurat*) dropped from Israeli planes warning about an imminent attack: "Within three damn hours, how can you wave goodbye to your belongings, your land, and your memories? You can maybe rescue your life by moving elsewhere, but I know of many people who refused to leave."[53]

DAHIYE'S SOCIAL IDENTITY

Dahiye's heterogeneity is due to its hybrid demography and endemic socioeconomic inequality. Poverty is diversely motivated—describing it as exclusively Shiite or Hezbollah-supportive is misleading. In this framework, Islamic Resistance has emerged as a moral sphere; the Resistance's discourse, which animatedly supported Hezbollah's victory during the July War, is deployed not only in military and political terms but also in terms of social ethics. The experience of war has given rise to a shared local membership, muddling the Freudian *Heimlich* (the familiar or intimate) and *Unheimlich* (the foreign and unknown to the insider)—a dyad which scholars often use to define the relationship between the Self and the Other (Bayeh 2015)—during postwar. The threat of the Zionist enemy has pulled together resistant subjects who were compliant with the local ethics of the Islamic Resistance but not necessarily active war combatants. During the war and later through recovery and compensation, the local residents' extent of compliance with official social ethics marked new lines of inclusion and exclusion. The movement was no longer solely the Islamic Resistance; in terms of ethical *milieu*, segments of Dahiye society may not have felt represented and were, therefore, forced to comply with the given standards, as happens in any system of values and beliefs. Without the idea of the Islamic Resistance, Dahiye, composed of several communal subjects and not just Lebanese Shiites, would face "symbolic death" (Hage 1996, 2). I asked the deputy mayor[54] of Haret Hreik what would happen if the threatening Israeli entity disappeared or stopped altogether, and he mentioned a renewed idea of the Resistance. Hezbollah was simultaneously boasting demographic and confessional heterogeneity, insofar as heterogeneity fulfilled the party's politics. On the one hand, Lebanese residents and Palestinian, Iraqi, Sudanese, and Syrian refugees have made Dahiye's local demography and polity diverse in a way that did not follow community lines. On the other hand, the southern suburbs were internationally depicted as Hezbollah's land or *Dahiyet al-Khomeini*, referring to the intimate bond between the birth of the Hezbollah Party and the Iranian Revolutionary Guards (*Pasdaran*). Outsiders tended to remind me of the "Iranization" of Dahiye. When I returned to Australia after my doctoral fieldwork, a colleague asked me whether I spoke Persian to interact with my field interlocutors. Such external stigmatization clashes with some residents' ideas and imaginaries. Husein, a local journalist, indeed told me: "I don't want Dahiye people to live like Iranians. In Iran, you cannot even shave and wear a tie."[55]

AKKAR: POLITICAL AND ECONOMIC INFRASTRUCTURE

Akkar was part of the North Lebanon governorate (*muhafaza*) until it became an independent governorate in 2014, according to the United Nations Office for the Coordination of Humanitarian Affairs (OCHA)'s databases. Home to five hundred thousand inhabitants, Akkar's population makes up nearly 20.5 percent of the entire Lebanese population. Akkar's society generally maintains a traditional sociocultural structure (Abi-Habib Khoury 2012, 25). While historians view the rural middle class that emerged among the Maronites of the mountains as merging tradition with modernity (Khater 2001), Akkar is often viewed by Lebanese people as primitive and backward. Constellated by hamlets, the regional political economy is characterized by feudal relationships (the *iqta'* system), where local state officials—*makhatir*—are from a traditional political elite whose support is based on allegiance to local ruling families. *Makhatir* are officially elected and coordinate with local municipalities, often acting as gatekeepers for INGOs that aim to deliver safe and rapid access to aid recipients in times of crisis. Local village leaders—*zu'ama'*—are usually members of prominent families dating back to Ottoman times. A *za'im*—local village leader—can be the client of another *za'im* higher up the local hierarchy (Gilsenan 1996), preserving a conception of social management that resonates with Tunisian sociologist Ibn Khaldoun's *'asabiyya*: the strength of the kinship system in an organized society where needs are met through personal relationships rather than through the state (Joseph 1997). These local lords were originally established by the Ottoman state with the rank of *pasha* or *bey* in the imperial hierarchy; they were usually of Kurdish or Turkman origin, not native to Akkar but treated as indigenous aristocrats by the French during the colonial mandate (Gilsenan 1986, 20).

Akkar has a 63.3 percent poverty rate, the highest in Lebanon, and the worst housing conditions after Hermel; some residents live in the same space as their cattle (Moushref 2008, 5). The majority of Akkar's villages receive electricity from Electricité du Liban, but some buildings are connected to the electricity grid. Despite its natural hydric resources, the region ranks lowest for accessibility to public water supply (Moushref 2008, 5). The arrival of humanitarian agencies after 2011 brought increased international attention to the area and contributed to reducing solid waste burning and dumps in the environment. Public transportation is scarce or unaffordable, and car ownership and maintenance is expensive, making schools and hospitals difficult to access. Fishing became more difficult after the July War because of Israel's sixty-day naval blockade and increased water pollution (Moushref 2008, 5). Local unemployment ranks among the highest in the country, and the commute to Beirut and Tripoli, where there are more job opportunities, is too expensive for some households. Furthermore, during the 2007 Nahr al-Bared siege (in which Fath el-Islam, an alleged al-Qa'eda offshoot, fought against the Lebanese Armed Forces and destroyed the whole camp), fishermen could not access the sea (Moushref 2008, 17). Healthcare is limited for most people as mobile clinics are expensive, with infant mortality rate being the highest in the country (48.1 percent). Health insurance only comes with military service, which occupies 14.8 percent of the male workforce (Abi-Habib Khoury 2012, 25), more than the trade sector.[56]

The effect of both conflicts on Akkar's infrastructure and labor economy was devastating (Moushref 2008, 18), yet the region was neglected by INGOs, which prioritized areas directly involved in regional wars. After the arrival of refugees from Syria and the subsequent closure of the Lebanese border (2014–2015) (Fakhoury 2021), traditional businesses, such as smuggling goods from Syria, were curbed or became unfeasible.

THE SYRIAN PRESENCE IN AKKAR: A PREREFUGEE SOCIOLOGY

"Every mayor of Akkar's municipalities had to pay lip service to the Syrian regime during the Syrian occupation of Lebanon," explained a Sunni *sheikh*[57] in the town of Halba. Throughout Akkar, local stories about oppression by the Asads are common (Hafez al-Asad from 1970 to 2000 and his son, Bashar al-Asad, from 2000). Before the 1559 UN Resolution of 2004, the Syrian regime kept more than twenty thousand troops and intelligence agents stationed around Lebanon, and in 1992, 1996, and 2000, the elected Lebanese Parliaments had Syrian-aligned majorities (Safa 2006, 27). In this climate of deep resentment, Hamed, from the small village of Bellanet al-Hisa, told me about the liberation from Syrian oppression in April 2005 (often phrased in Arabic as *az-zolm w ad-daght as-sury*): "I had never seen the people of my town so relieved."[58] After the Cedar Revolution (March 14, 2005) that led to the withdrawal of Syrian troops from Lebanese territory and broke out one month after former prime minister Rafiq al-Hariri's murder, the statue of Hafez al-Asad, erected in the 1990s in Halba's main square, was demolished by locals. Two elders in the border area of Wadi Khaled showed me where the center of the Syrian secret services used to be located (*markaz al-mukhabarat as-suriyye*). A shop owner in Halba emphasized that "everyone here has terrible memories; my father spent years in Asad's prisons, eating from the same dish where he was weeing."[59] Samir, in the border area of Wadi Khaled, contended that when Asad withdrew from Lebanon in 2005, "it was like a revolution. People began to communicate with each other in public. We had gotten rid of an atmosphere of terror."[60] Walid told me that he spent eight years in Hafez al-Asad's prisons for being an opponent during Pax Syriana (1976–2005 or 1990–2005, if only considering the postwar years).

The region shows the merging of Lebanese lives with Syrian lives and the fictitious yet crucial concept of national belonging. I have spent years traveling back and forth from this region and have observed that daily relationships, family ties, and a shared class-based economy of menial labor between Syrians and Lebanese Akkaris are stronger in North Lebanon than in other parts of the country, especially for people relying on rural livelihoods and/or of Bedouin origins. This is certainly not only due to geographical proximity to the Syrian border. As local historian Faraj Zakhour narrates (2005, 24–25), the Lebanese state's longstanding neglect of the region has meant that locals, especially in the border villages, have looked to Syria for basic services and, at times, a sense of national identity. 'Abderrahman, a Lebanese Bedouin from Wadi Khaled, felt both Syrian and Lebanese, although he did not have any relatives in Syria. He emphasized the hardships he and his family had faced in this border town, lacking education and health services. His parents would drive twenty minutes to reach nearby Homs for cheaper medical services.[61] Lebanese state neglect of Bedouin-majority border areas continued (Chatty 2011) after Bedouins gained Lebanese citizenship in 1994 (*tajnis*) during al-Hariri's mandate.[62]

In my first months of fieldwork in Akkar, people generally did not associate the Syrian regime with the Syrian people. Over a decade after the beginning of the crisis in Syria, Akkar's predicament, in the context of the deeper national economic crisis, is tangible and has morphed into a generalized antinewcomer rhetoric. This shifting collective attitude can be explained by a changing social identity that either inhibits or facilitates acts of assistance, feelings of solidarity, and support in emergencies (Levine and Manning 2013, 226–228). In Akkar, the widely advertised earlier hospitality toward and later rejection of newcomers both are an expression of a shifting social identity. This is an apparent contradiction that social psychologists have widely discussed (Tajfel 1978; Turner et al. 1987), showing how there is no linear temporality in accepting and then rejecting the Other and how, instead, the moment of acceptance complexly intertwines with the moment of rejection.

'Abbas, a hardware store assistant in Halba, described the years of the Syrian occupation of Lebanon, remembering how oppressive the atmosphere was when he was in his teens and reasserting the fictitious character of nationality: "We could not say anything about Syria, even in private conversations. We used to share the same fears with the Syrians. Once upon a time, we were the same people. Syrians are welcome here as well as Lebanese from other areas. I don't find anything natural in nationality."[63]

In this framework, local Akkaris, earlier Syrian migrants (mostly seasonal laborers), and Lebanese Bedouins all diversely suffered from state neglect. Despite a long history of sociopolitical mobilization, the region remained underresourced and lacked international attention, which was mainly focused on the occupied South. As a result of the Syrian flight into Lebanon, foreign humanitarian actors, in a first instance, exclusively addressed refugees' hardships. The conversion of the Syrian seasonal laborer—occupying the lowest grade in the labor economy—into a humanitarian victim triggered a local response to the official management of the Syrian crisis (see chap. 4).

THE ARRIVAL OF SYRIAN REFUGEES IN AKKAR

While regarding Syria as a model of stability and strong nationhood, the neighboring Lebanese found themselves dealing with the crisis of the Syrian Leviathan. If Lebanon embodies the Dionysian, with war scars and open wounds, Syria has historically represented the centralized, organized, and balanced Apollonian in the eyes of the Akkaris. Nonetheless, the living conditions of earlier Syrian migrants in Akkar were frightful and, for years, invisible to INGOs, UN agencies, and human rights advocates, as this region did not face an officially declared crisis directly concerning global geopolitics.

In December 2011, when my focus was still on long-term humanitarianism in Dahiye, refugees were coming from Syria to Akkar in larger numbers. Traveling by minibus from Cola station in Beirut to the northern city of Tripoli, two Syrian nationals complained about how difficult it was to reach NGOs via phone or using transport. When I became more familiar with the region and its recent history of aid reception, I realized that some families were unlikely to reach distribution spots independently. They missed deliveries of food items, medication, mattresses, diesel, and any other help they were entitled to receive. Not only was it difficult to pay for local transport, but some of them did not have access to mobile phones and therefore did not receive alerts about the weekly scheduled aid provision at the location nearest to them. Khaldoun, a Syrian refugee from a village in the Hama region, recounted: "I crossed the al-Kabeer River, fleeing the gunfire of Syrian army forces. I was wearing the same clothes as now. I only took my wallet with me. I don't have the means to get a phone now. INGOs should give one to me."[64]

Syrian refugeehood marks Akkar's history, a history that is largely made up of, but not reduced to, rivalry between local families and state neglect. Interestingly, the international community's attention barely focused on the arrival of international humanitarian agencies, leaving spectators with a sense that refugee newcomers were pouring into Lebanon; humanitarian organizations were presumed to be prepared and knowledgeable about what to do and how to act in a new region. The international humanitarian presence in Akkar was literally unprecedented. At an early stage, aid providers tended to neglect the longstanding Syrian-Lebanese relational history, which was as controversial as any nationhood, and ignore preexisting capacities for local stability and daily coexistence (ta'aiyush). The first humanitarian programs only addressed refugees in the framework of a chronically vulnerable region, so it comes as no surprise that my 2012 ethnographical material is marked by a gradual disruption of local empathy and informal arrangements of hospitality. Later attempts to fix such miscalculations of humanitarian programming came with scarce success and refocused on social cohesion in areas where humanitarian intervention had contributed to disrupting such cohesion in the first place.

Over the years, several early Syrian migrants abandoned Lebanon for safety or economic reasons. Despite decades of coexistence in the rural spaces of Akkar, the usual refugee-host relationship does not appropriately capture the connection between residents and the refugees from Syria. If local knowledge suggested that the past occupation of Lebanon by the Syrian army (1976–2005) marked the Syrian-Lebanese daily relationship, cheap Syrian menial labor cemented Syrian communities in a lower social status. Over 2012 and 2013, the increasing number of Syrian refugees in Lebanon was frowned on, as the crisis discourse had become official and began to populate the local and international media. In other words, the crisis discourse was making longstanding poor migrants more visible than how they ever used to be. At a grassroots level, I observed that more and more mental associations were made between Syria, meant as the regime (*an-nizam*), and Syria meant as the people (*ash-sha'b*). After relocating to Akkar, Ahmed, a refugee from Homs, was asked: "Why do Syrians complain about their state if education is free, at least?" In response, he emphasized the impossibility of receiving any kind of education other than that allowed and promoted by the Asad regime.[65] Likewise, Rabi' commented that some Lebanese were suspicious when he came to Lebanon and simply asked for aid. He was asked about the information sources in Syria that told him aid was available in Lebanon. His information sources were the bombs in his hometown and the feeling of not having a choice other than leaving.[66]

The history of border relationships shows a cycle of human expectation, especially between war-stricken Lebanese who sought refuge in Zabadani (the western Syrian border) in the July War and Syrian refugees from Zabadani who had previously hosted Lebanese families and relocated to Lebanon. Fouad, a Syrian refugee in the hamlet of Bebnin, resented having welcomed a Lebanese family into his house near Zabadani during the July War and not having received hospitality when geopolitics reversed their roles.[67] Yet the political grids through which refugeehood is produced and managed complicate the expectation cycle; some Syrian refugees resented even Syrian conationals who supported the regime in Syria, as "those kinds of refugees can easily find refuge in the shelters provided by Hezbollah."[68]

Even though these early episodes of local reluctance to host seemingly point to a never existing initial empathy, the socioemotional line departing from empathy and landing with rejection is the way most Akkaris I met across the years recount their relationship with Syrian refugees (see chap. 4).

THE EMERGENCE OF INTERNATIONAL HUMANITARIANISM IN AKKAR: MAKING THE CRISIS SUSTAINABLE

A somewhat dense network of local charities (church or mosque based) operated in the region for decades along with some political parties and local NGOs that, especially before elections, participated in the local provision of services. However, the vast majority of international humanitarian agencies did not arrive in Akkar until mid-2012. Despite the apparent absence of strong local powers comparable to Hezbollah, my research experiences in Akkar turned out to be as politically loaded as in Dahiye; some INGO practitioners viewed my presence as heavily political and viewed me as a critical inquirer threating their public reputation rather than an ethnographer and an independent aid provider (Carpi 2020b).

In December 2011, I first decided to focus on the border area where the refugees were coming. Indeed, many of the first refugees who fled from Syria initially chose to relocate to Wadi Khaled, an assemblage of villages extremely close to the Syrian border largely populated by Bedouins (*bedo*). When I visited the *wadi*, UNHCR had recently started their operations, whereas, according to the residents, NGOs funded by the Gulf and local charities had assisted Syrian refugees immediately after the first governmental attacks on opposition cities and towns in Syria in April 2011.[69] Most of the refugees who relocated to Akkar were from Homs, Hama, and the Damascus countryside.[70] At a later stage, people from Idlib and ar-Raqqa began to populate the villages I frequented (al-Bahsa, al-'Abdeh, Bebnin, and Bellanet al-Hisa in western Akkar), the city of Halba, and Wadi Khaled at the border.

Some of the refugees I met could be classified as situational (Kenyon-Lischer 2003), fleeing the shelling of their towns and villages or the demolition of their houses. This group was the largest among my interlocutors. Some refugees were political (Kenyon-Lischer 2003) and therefore more likely to fear persecution as public opponents of the regime, as they had been previously arrested or officially reported in Syria. Among the political refugees, some knew how to rely on political connections in Lebanon to cross the border. Others were associated with specific organizations that had promised to help them before they migrated. Migration was often motivated by preannounced offers of resources and based on family decision-making. For instance, I met Manial and her child in the municipality of Halba; originally from Aleppo, they had moved to Lebanon in February 2013 because her husband was working for a Kuwaiti organization that offered family health assistance and accommodation in Akkar.[71]

Some refugees did not want to register with UNHCR as they feared being sent back to Syria, where they might be tortured. Others, especially those in the first flow, simply did not know about the registration process: "At the beginning, there were very few services here. Information about registration was not as diffused as now," said Amal, a refugee from Homs.[72] According to a UNHCR officer in Akkar, "The majority of people who don't want to register are generally Alawites and Christians [religious communities generally believed to be closer to the regime in Syria] as they don't feel comfortable being classified as refugees. Others may not want to provide their details for some other reason; or, again, they may have relatives that support them and do not need protection."[73]

The stories I heard from refugees largely focused on how the refugees had to undertake an inhumane journey. A man from Homs told me his wife had to deliver a baby under a tree at a checkpoint: "Our loss of dignity started when we crossed the border." A woman from Hama recounted that she had to hide in her neighbor's truck to be sneaked past the Masna'a border (on the road from Damascus to Beirut) because she was undocumented.

While Gulf-funded NGOs and local charities prioritized cash to cover rent and medication for refugees at first, many INGOs and UNHCR refrained from rolling out cash-based programs and, instead, paid local families to refurbish old buildings to host newcomers. The longstanding kinship and societal ties, until then, had engendered a strong, informal local response to the crisis. This response resonated with other forms of hospitality and reciprocity during politico-humanitarian crises, such as that of the Kosovars in Albania (Nicholson 2017). In this context, international humanitarian agencies decided to pay local families to host the refugees from Syria for up to one year to preserve the temporal dimension of their stay, paradoxically making the crisis sustainable.[74]

When aid and service providers came to Lebanon to assist Syrian refugees, some of the charities that had previously worked in the region had to abandon ongoing projects and shift their operational agenda from development to relief work.[75] Local people referred to INGOs and UN agencies as a "new presence" that used to work in some areas of the North, but in smaller numbers. International humanitarian actors assisted the Syrian refugees by providing material equipment such as mattresses, heaters, and other winter tools. In the programs aimed at enabling local families to host refugees, relief material was distributed to local people, generating resentment among locals who were not selected as official hosts. At an early stage, international actors inflamed the situation by allocating the most visible equipment (e.g., household items, food vouchers, and survival kits) exclusively to Syrian refugees. Local resentment soon became tangible in the Akkar villages: "I think all these organizations came here because they're going to raise funding thanks to the war in Syria. Otherwise, they would not have lifted a single finger for us. Have you ever seen them around before?"[76]

Such words show how external interventions exacerbated the resentment of disadvantaged Lebanese who had never been beneficiaries of state social protection and suddenly witnessed their "guests" become legitimate recipients of international funding. In 2012, a UNHCR protection officer[77] reported that the number of programs addressing both groups were limited, while, in the same year, a protection officer at War-Child Holland argued that a number of programs already addressed the needs of Lebanese and Syrians.[78]

At the 2016 Humanitarian Summit, held in Istanbul, OCHA inaugurated the New Way of Working (NWOW) approach, introduced in the framework of the 2030 United Nations Sustainable Development Goals (UNSDGs) and

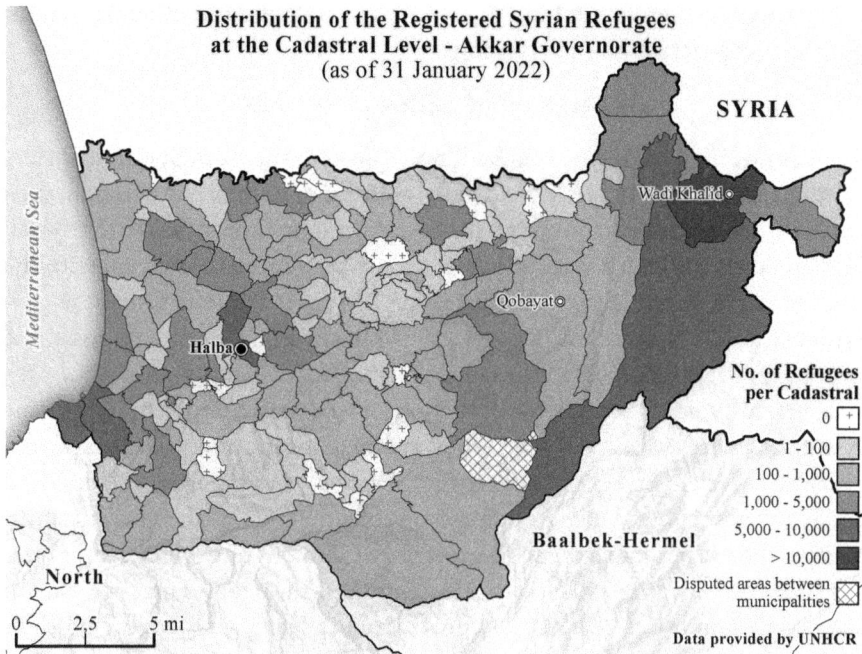

Fig. 1.3 Akkar's map of Syrian refugees registered with UNHCR.
Credits: Luca Mazzali (Appears).

based on the collective efforts of humanitarian and development actors. In the context of Lebanon, it meant promoting projects that addressed both Lebanese and Syrians. After then, humanitarian actors increasingly used inclusive rhetoric toward local host communities to handle and attenuate resentment among local inhabitants. It is now arguable that despite the initial neglect of local vulnerable people, humanitarian funding has been increasingly channeled into the Lebanese public service in an attempt to improve healthcare and infrastructures for local and refugee groups. Residents and Syrian refugees were often aware of such policy changes. Amira,[79] from Homs and now living in a tented settlement, affirmed: "After two years here, there is finally a mobile clinic I can benefit from." However, humanitarian programs certainly cannot sweep away years of state neglect. Greater awareness of the local capacity for cohesion and stability could have prevented the tension that discriminatory aid distribution triggered.[80] At the outset of the refugee flight, aid distribution was unconditional for Syrian nationals to avoid friction among them. The humanitarian discourse which emerged on aid provision to Syrian refugees in Lebanon problematically revolves around alleviating preexisting tensions in the country, therefore failing to identify the contribution of humanitarian policies and practices to such tensions.

The demographic changes in Lebanon that may ensue from Syrian displacement inside the country generate diverse political concerns. The nature of such concerns underlies the lack of unitary and systematic approaches to the Syrian humanitarian crisis. An institutional response only came in late 2014 with the first Lebanon Crisis Response Plan (LCRP) (drafted by the Lebanese government and UN agencies). Cognizant of the chronic Palestinian crisis, the Lebanese government refused to set up official refugee camps (*mukhaiyyamat*), stating that avoiding camps would encourage refugees to return to their home country and make their stay temporary. In the domestic political scenario, the polarized March 8 and 14 coalitions that, respectively, supported and opposed the Syrian government and its 1976–2005 "protection" of Lebanon (*al-wikala as-suriyya*) did not approach the issue uniformly. Opinions on refugee camps were very diverse within the same political orientation. The people I met in Lebanon seemed to support or oppose the construction of camps depending on their understanding of the Palestinian issue rather than their personal opinion of Syrian President Bashar al-Asad's politics and the Syrian revolution. Individual stances vis-à-vis the construction of camps also seemed to depend on the intention to undercut the scale of Syrian displacement, which, according to some views, could have been exclusively dealt with through kinship-based support, local hospitality, and charity initiatives. Overall, NGO practitioners I spoke to tended to see refugee camps as a factor of marginalization in Lebanese society.[81]

Haret Hreik's deputy mayor, from the Hezbollah Party, was against the construction of camps, stating that the refugees' living conditions were unacceptable and did not meet the cultural requirement of strict gender separation. He observed: "Women would be in close contact with men all the time, and this would not be culturally appropriate. In refugee camps, the degree of overcrowding is unacceptable."[82] Moreover, "we do not need separate spaces for Syrians or separate services. Whoever comes to Dahiye will get the same benefits as any Lebanese citizen. What is there for us will be there for them. What lacks for us will lack for them too." At first, a discursive strategy of concealing the scale of displacement to make refugees invisible dominated Dahiye's political environment. This political strategy of concealing newcoming refugeehood later became propaganda, hyping real numbers to show the strain under which the whole country, including Dahiye, was put.

Further evidence that political ideology on the Syrian conflict did not determine people's opinions on refugee camps was provided by the skepticism of the founder of the charity organization *al-Ayad al-Bayda*, headquartered in Fneideq (Akkar). As an anti-Asad philanthropist, he contended that the establishment of camps in Lebanon could cause severe problems by inciting targeted attacks by the Asad regime. Indeed, most of the camp dwellers would be Syrians from opposition-majority areas. According to an official at the Lebanese Ministry of Social Affairs (MoSA), it was instead more difficult to maintain security when refugees were displaced throughout the country.[83] His view echoed that of the UNHCR and INGOs, since the construction of official camps would help with the logistics of aid delivery.[84] Moreover, most foreign humanitarian actors affirmed that they were convinced the government's decision to avoid camps would be unsuccessful in making the refugee presence temporary. As a UNHCR officer argued: "All these people are spread out across Lebanon, and it's a big challenge for us. The more they are concentrated in a place like a camp, the easier it is for us to reach them."[85] However, most of the INGO practitioners I met thought that formal refugee camps might become a form of recognition of the Syrian uprising and repression in Asad's Syria and would therefore trigger instability. In this context, several INGO interviewees operating in Akkar complained about their difficult working conditions, denouncing the lack of engagement by the Lebanese government in assisting refugees in contrast to its humanitarian involvement in the July War.[86] Local NGO practitioners especially complained that the funds allocated for displaced Syrians throughout the whole region were inadequate.

The Kuwaiti Association argued that the official construction of camps was "not a real issue" as camps were being constructed throughout Lebanon despite the government's official stance.[87] The Kuwaiti NGO's Lebanese coordinator added that camps usually give rise to social problems such as insecurity, like in Turkey and Jordan (where the Syrian presence has fueled violent outbursts over the last decade); these views were thus mindful of the Palestinian experience in Lebanon. INGOs operating in the housing sector— especially the Italian Cooperation, the Norwegian Refugee Council (NRC), and the Danish Refugee Council (DRC) —had no other choice than to build shelters or refurbish abandoned buildings. "Informally, it's like we already have camps in Lebanon. The fact that they're not official tented settlements does not make a great difference," stated a UNHCR officer in 2012, echoing the Kuwaiti NGO's coordinator, a reminder of how the Lebanese government previously dealt with the Palestinian refugee issue in urban slums such as Tel az-Zaatar and Karantina.[88] Likewise, a Lebanese practitioner from the Qatari Initiative in Wadi Khaled confirmed that NGOs had had to tackle several problems inside institutionalized camps (as in the case of Turkey) and that camps were therefore not advisable in Lebanon:

> I believe the refugees' human conditions here in Lebanon are far better than in Turkey. In North Lebanon, we've shared our food [and] we've offered hospitality, even jobs, to our Syrian brothers. The construction of camps should not be our main concern: the sympathy toward our Syrian brothers and the intimacy of local people with the Syrians have been more helpful. There is no difference between Syrians and Lebanese. There have been mixed marriages and mutual relations between Akkar and Syria for a long time [...]. Camps would just improve the condition of the Lebanese who are now burdened with the need to offer long-term hospitality to the refugees; they would finally cease to share their beds and food, but camps would not improve the condition of Syrians at all.[89]

The practitioner's views seemingly echo Chatty's argument that the cultural value of hospitality in Arab majority societies, despite the lack of a legal framework for refugee protection, has enabled local acceptance of refugees, who are supported with cultural codes such as *karam*, the "duty to be generous" toward guests (Chatty 2017).

The majority of refugees worldwide now live in cities (Campbell 2016)—the humanitarian system has taken an urban turn since the beginning of displacement from Syria, and it is increasingly focused on urban-humanitarian coordination and collaboration. Camps can often turn into thriving cities, such as Yarmouk in prewar Syria and the Zaatari camp in northern Jordan. On the one hand, dismantling camps would be the first step against the displacement limbo (Dunn 2017, 210) through which protection is abdicated and the possibilities for resettlement nullified. On the other hand, camps are not built to rehabilitate life but to contain the displaced, dismantle their homes, and, at times, take back plots of land for the convenience of host governments (Dunn 2017). If the emerging urban-humanitarian nexus has encouraged policymakers and practitioners to consider preexisting urban infrastructures in areas of intervention, it has also created a seamless category of urban refugees who do not reflect the complex environmental circumstances in which refugees live outside of Lebanese cities (Carpi and Boano 2018). This seamless category has given rise to the misleading belief that most camps are located in rural areas in Lebanon, though such camps often share both a symbolic and practical continuity to the urban space (Schiocchet 2014).

In this continuous everyday exchange of goods and labor between refugees and residents, some prefabricated shelters, despite being unofficial camps, have slowly become proper districts. The Syrian tented settlements I first saw in the Akkar hamlet of al-Bahsa in January 2012 did not dispose of toilets. On one of my field revisits in 2015, thanks to the efforts of refugee inhabitants,

THE POLITICS OF DISPLACEMENT IN LEBANON

these settlements had become solid structures. Inhabitants had constructed streetlights next to the campsite to make the roads safer at night: "Thefts occur daily," warned Hussam, a Syrian refugee from Hama.[90] The cementation of refugee-fabricated tented settlements left me with the same numbed sense of chronic emergency as some of the spaces inhabited by Palestinians, Iraqis, and Sudanese I had met in Dahiye, whose lives were enmeshed in a sense of waiting and who made similar claims to a dignified life.

NOTES

1. Historically, the Middle East has produced the largest number of refugees, especially after WWI and the demise of the Ottoman Empire in 1919. At the end of 1991, 11.2 out of 16.7 million refugees emigrated from the areas between Morocco and Afghanistan and between Turkey and the Horn of Africa (Humphrey 1993, 2).

2. This group generally comprises those who were forced out of Jordan during Black September 1970 and those it was not considered urgent or necessary to register with the UNRWA and the Lebanese authorities during the Lebanese Civil War.

3. Published in *al-Ahram*, April 19, 2003.

4. Operation Litani in 1978 was the first Israeli incursion into Lebanon to occupy southern Lebanon. However, fighting with Hezbollah did not start until after the 1982 Israeli Operation Peace for Galilee and continued throughout the Lebanese resistance to Israeli occupation in the South.

5. Conversation with a Beirut based UNHCR officer, June 28, 2014.

6. Ar-Ruwess, October 2, 2012.

7. In 1945, the Lebanese government was described as being careless about the spread of cholera in the South as it did not send medical staff or medicine (Kobeissi 2009, 39).

8. The Lebanese government did not promote tourist activities or support agricultural production, the textile sector, or fishing in the South (Kobeissi 2009, 90).

9. In Lebanon, municipal candidates are only eligible if registered in a specific district—*qada'*—even if they have never resided there.

10. Interview with the mayor of the Hadath Municipality, February 3, 2012.

11. This polarization emerged in 2005 (Di Peri 2014). The March 8 coalition, led by an alliance between Hezbollah and General Michel 'Aoun—an anti-Syrian ex-general who left in exile in 1990 after the establishment of the Syrian protection of Lebanon—opposed the March 14 coalition, led by *al-Mustaqbal* (the party of Sa'ad al-Hariri, the son of Rafiq). Both groups sought to make Beirut representative of their own political orientation, organizing huge demonstrations in Martyrs Square in downtown Beirut. The demonstration calling for the Syrian troops' departure on March 14, 2005, was called the "Cedar Revolution" or "Beirut Spring" by Western media. The polarization worsened after the July War when, in May 2008, Hezbollah seized Beirut's airport and blocked the streets as a sign of protest against the

government's move to shut down Hezbollah's telecommunication network and remove Beirut Airport's security chief, Wafiq Shkeir, over his ties to Hezbollah.

12. *Waad* means "promise": the promise that Hezbollah made to "its people," that Israeli aggression and deprivation would be revenged through improving the old and redignifying the social environment destroyed by military attacks. Such a promise aimed to compensate for the previous promise given by Nasrallah about having a quiet summer—*al-wa'd as-sadeq*—"the sincere promise." The number of shops rebuilt was the same as before the war, and the opportunity to enlarge green spaces in Dahiye was given up in order to construct more commercial spaces (conversation with Dr. Mona Fawaz, AUB, December 1, 2011). *Jihad al-Binaa* blamed the government laws that allowed such a demographic density in Dahiye. Mr. Jashi, the general manager of *Waad*, said to researcher Nancy Hilal in an interview conducted on June 21, 2007: "*Waad* certainly can't enforce new laws" (Hilal 2008).

13. Haret Hreik, January 16, 2012.

14. The US administration defined Hezbollah as a specially designated terrorist group in 1995, a foreign terrorist organization in 1997, and a specially designated global terrorist group in 2001.

15. Laylaki, January 13, 2012.

16. Wikileaks cable, Beirut, July 21, 2006. Released March 15, 2011.

17. Conversation with Intisar, Haret Hreik, November 13, 2011, and with 'Ali, ash-Shiyyah, February 3, 2012.

18. At a speech on July 15, 2006, at the Beirut Grand Serail, Seniora called for national unity and blamed Hezbollah for the violence (Presidency of the Council of Ministers in Lebanon 2007, Appendix I: 2–3).

19. Interview, Ash-Shiyyah, October 30, 2011.

20. An additional US $7.6 billion was pledged at the International Conference for Support to Lebanon, or Paris III, in January 2007, to assist reconstruction and economic stabilization.

21. Major contributors to the reconstruction of Lebanon at Paris III included the United States, the European Investment Bank, France, the World Bank Group, the Arab Fund for Economic and Social Development, the Arab Monetary Fund, and the United Arab Emirates.

22. By July 2009, Romania, Spain, and Sweden had committed over US $45 million to the Lebanon Recovery Fund (LRF).

23. January 23, 2012.

24. February 2, 2012.

25. *Imdad* means "support." The NGO was founded in 1987, when the war between Harakat Amal and Hezbollah escalated, with the aim of providing social services to the poor and needy.

26. January 20, 2012.

27. Interview in Ashrafiye, Beirut, February 21, 2012.

28. The term "urbicide" was introduced by Polish lawyer Raphael Lemkin and recognized by the International Court of Justice in 1948. Stephen Graham (2003, 63) describes urbicide as a deliberate wrecking or killing of a city. The 2006 Israeli bombing of empty residential areas, where almost all inhabitants had been evacuated, reinforces the belief that the July War was carried out in terms of urbicide.

29. The name can be translated as "Holy Struggle for Reconstruction." Established in 1985 after a massive CIA car bomb in Bi'r al-'Abed aimed to kill the Shiite Imam Fadlallah, the organization was already active in rebuilding houses, rehabilitating infrastructure, and offering assistance to farmers. It was established as a branch of the Iranian NGO set up by Ayatollah Khomeini for Iran's reconstruction after the First Gulf War against Iraq. *Jihad al-Binaa* is partially in charge of garbage collection and electricity provision in Dahiye (Harb 2010, 112–115).

30. Conversation with a *Waad* employee, Haret Hreik, November 19, 2013.

31. From Nasrallah's official speech in May 2000, which marked the end of Israeli occupation of the South.

32. The Resistance is a long tradition in Dahiye, having been conducted in Bourj al-Barajneh during the Middle Ages against Prince Fakhreddine II, who wanted to implement feudalistic practices in the area (*Waad* official website: www.waad.org.lb).

33. In 2009, the Higher Relief Council under the Lebanese government reported that 774,184 displaced persons have returned to their homes since August 14, 2006.

34. Conversation with staff member of the American University of Beirut's Reconstruction Unit for Dahiye, December 16, 2011.

35. For instance, respected martyr 'Imad Fayaz Mughniyye was unknown before his martyrdom by a CIA car bomb in the Damascus countryside in 2008.

36. The residents of the mainly Christian district of 'Ayn ar-Remmaneh used to go to ash-Shiyyah, predominantly Shiite, to buy cheaper fruits and vegetables. Shiites from ash-Shiyyah, in turn, used to go to the Christian area to buy affordable Western-style clothes (interview with a Ministry of Social Affairs representative, October 30, 2011).

37. Charity organizations also invested in the local reconstruction market. *Al-Mabarrat* Association, originally serving the poor and orphans, opened a popular restaurant and hotel complex called *as-Saha* Traditional Village on the airport highway outside Bourj al-Barajneh.

38. Interview with Mona Fawaz, Professor of Urban Planning at the American University of Beirut (AUB), December 1, 2011.

39. October 2, 2011.

40. In February 2009, *Waad* had already rebuilt 95 percent of damaged houses (Al-Harithy 2010, 43).

41. Al-Ghobeiry, October 19, 2011.

42. Conversations with *Hajj* Hatoum in January 2012, September 2012, and February 2013.

43. Political scientist Joseph S. Nye explains the concepts of soft and hard power (1990).

44. Haret Hreik, November 19, 2011.

45. The locations of the Israeli attacks included some areas outside of Hezbollah-run neighborhoods. A bridge in Akkar on the way to Halba, known to be the physical passage of military support from Syria to Hezbollah in Lebanon, was demolished, as were other infrastructures in North Lebanon. TV antennas in Jeita were also destroyed, according to the local residents I met in winter 2007.

46. Msharrafiye, October 21, 2012.

47. Interview with US aid provider Mar Mkhayel Annahr, Beirut, February 21, 2012.

48. Interview with Layal, Haret Hreik, January 11, 2012.

49. Lecture held at the University of Sydney, June 7, 2012.

50. Conversation with Lebanese citizen. Hazmiyye, Mount Lebanon's district, October 3, 2011.

51. Hadath, February 28, 2012.

52. Hamra, March 3, 2012.

53. Msharrafiye, November 28, 2012.

54. January 26, 2012.

55. November 28, 2011.

56. Trade sector: 14.3 percent; education: 8.4 percent; industry: 8.4 percent; construction workers: 8.2 percent; transport and communication: 6 percent (Abi-Habib Khoury 2012).

57. January 13, 2013.

58. January 5, 2013.

59. January 12, 2013.

60. Interview in Wadi Khaled, December 27, 2012.

61. January 26, 2012.

62. Bedouins living in this region were neither Lebanese nor Syrian until the naturalization law was enforced by Rafiq al-Hariri in 1994. During the first postwar government led by the assassinated PM, groups such as Syrians (over 42 percent), Palestinians (16 percent), stateless people like Kurds and Arabs of Wadi Khaled (36 percent), and other migrant groups (6 percent) obtained nationality, especially if they had a Sunni Muslim background that would preserve the confessional balance of Lebanese demography.

63. December 29, 2012.

64. Interview in Wadi Khaled, January 30, 2012.

65. Halba, August 28, 2012.

66. Al-'Abdeh, August 29, 2012.

67. Bebnin, August 25, 2012.

68. Bebnin, August 27, 2012.

69. Interview with the Qatari Initiative, Kuwaiti Funds Association, and Dar al-Fatwa, Tripoli, December 2012.

70. The UNHCR website that indicates refugee demography in Lebanon can be found here: https://www.unhcr.org/lebanon.html.

71. December 8, 2012.

72. The associate protection officer at UNHCR-Qobaiyat—interviewed on November 11, 2012—stated that UNHCR had started registering refugees in the Tripoli district in August 2012. At that time, it was the only registration spot in North Lebanon. Mobile registrations between Tripoli and Wadi Khaled began later in the year since many refugees could not easily reach the Tripoli office due to health or economic reasons.

73. Associate protection officer at UNHCR-Qobaiyat, December 11, 2012.

74. Interview with an aid worker at an Italian NGO, Qobaiyat, December 14, 2012.

75. Among them was Taiba Association, a Saudi NGO in Halba that redesigned its programs to meet the needs of Syrian refugees (interview, December 14, 2012). Most faith-oriented organizations based in Akkar had previously assisted orphans and vulnerable locals. Many of them ended their programs in Lebanese communities to cope with the costs of the Syrian mission, which had become a priority for foreign donors (mainly Qatar, Kuwait, and Saudi Arabia). Some of these NGOs had been created *ad hoc* to provide support to Syrian refugees while waiting for the departure of Asad's regime.

76. Interview with a Lebanese resident, Halba, October 4, 2012.

77. Interview, UNHCR Protection section, Qobaiyat, December 11, 2012.

78. Interview, October 29, 2012.

79. Al-Bahsa, January 10, 2013.

80. The fifteen years of civil war, quick turnover of local and foreign humanitarian workers, and scarce attention given to maintaining records often make humanitarian agencies unable to identify so-called local capacities.

81. Interview with Acción contra el Hambre, January 11, 2013.

82. Interview, February 6, 2012. As a further reason for opposing the construction of camps, *Hajj* Hatoum stated there was still a small number of Syrian refugees in Dahiye compared to areas in Lebanon "where these people feel more comfortable in political terms," implicitly recognizing that Hezbollah's political opponents would not seek assistance from them.

83. Interview in Badaro, Beirut, February 18, 2013.

84. Interview with five aid workers at Save the Children-Sweden, UNHCR, and the Danish Refugee Council (DRC), Qobaiyat, December 14, 2012.

85. Interview with UNHCR's associate protection officer in Qobaiyat, November 12, 2012.

86. For instance, in an interview (February 4, 2013) in Tripoli, the president of the General Committee of the Islamic Organizations in Lebanon (*al-I'tilaf*) pointed out that EU states intervened in the Syrian crisis because of the Lebanese

government's lack of engagement and refusal to name the displaced (*nazihun*) "refu-gees" (*laji'un*).

87. Interview, Tripoli, January 14, 2013.
88. Interview with UNHCR's associate protection officer in Qobaiyat, November 12, 2012.
89. Tripoli, December 18, 2012.
90. Al-Bahsa, February 20, 2013.

2 / Lebanon's Assistance Landscape

The landscape of aid provision in Lebanon is a complex constellation of faith-based, secular, local, and international assistance with diverse political and humanitarian purposes. On the one hand, formal FBOs[1] often benefit from migrants' remittances and other individual private donors, enjoying greater financial independence from governments.[2] In the current global humanitarian scene, religion is indeed considered a strategic factor in localizing aid provision (Kraft and Wilkinson 2020). This belief is not occurring by chance—NGOs in Lebanon have often been founded by poets, intellectuals, professors, and journalists who are mainly secular and are, therefore, believed to be elitist (Karam 2006, 51). As a consequence, the social impact of secular actors is often believed to be smaller than that of religious organizations (Jawad 2009).

On the other hand, international aid provision is not a homogenous apparatus; it adopts diverse ways of thinking and practicing assistance. As a complex assemblage of different cultures of assistance provision, international aid provision is not necessarily antithetical to local humanitarian structures and networks. Likewise, secular and faith-based NGOs are not always distinguishable from one another, especially in the Akkar context. Some secular NGOs do not reflect the religious orientation of most of their staff. The latter is a decisive factor in capturing the organizational philosophy of action. Similarly, it is not easy to draw a boundary between international and local organizations; the lines of separation can be set according to the source of the funding or the nationality of most of the staff. UN-Habitat Beirut, for example, has local staff members while its operational agenda and funding are foreign. However, I also interviewed members of NGOs whose staff was international but funding was locally generated.[3] With this in mind, I decided to embrace self-definition as a founding criterion to classify the humanitarian actors included in this book and, during my fieldwork, this criterion reflected the provenance of funding. I have never intentionally stretched the "humanitarianism" label too far, instead trying to reflect these diverse actors' self-determination. My belief is that, at some stage, this terminological discussion becomes a sociolinguistic debate on what humanitarianism—as a word and an actual economy—makes people lose and gain.

The aid I familiarized myself with in Lebanon was largely formal and organized, though smaller and more spontaneous forms of individual assistance were still mentioned by people in Dahiye and Akkar. I let myself be guided by my interlocutors to identify the forms of aid in place; in Dahiye and Akkar, I interacted mostly with refugee groups who had very little economic capacity. Therefore, during 2011 and 2012, I did not focus on sizable forms of refugee-refugee assistance in my field sites (see Khalili 2006 on Bourj al-Barajneh's Palestinians hosting displaced Lebanese in 2006 and Fiddian-Qasmiyeh 2016 on the arrival of Syrian and Palestinian refugees from Syria in the Baddawi camp and her broader conceptualization of "refugee-refugee humanitarianism").

HUMANITARIAN GOVERNANCE AND LOCAL SOVEREIGNTY

Even though Dahiye and Akkar present different spatial and political economies, the role of the Lebanese government during crises in each site is comparable. After the July War and throughout the Syrian humanitarian crisis, local municipalities played a role in responding to displacement and demographic change. Most municipalities aimed to enlarge their service provision, becoming more financially independent from the central government and relying on structures of intermediation with external donors, such as the Municipal Assistant and the Local Development Office (LDO). These new figures attempted to enhance coordination between INGOs, local authorities, and the Union of Municipalities to maximize and harmonize municipal efforts. Nonetheless, during the years of my fieldwork, I realized how thin and scattered coordination was. Moreover, municipal employees, residents, and refugees often stressed to me that local power was concentrated in the hands of local state officials (*makhatir*), in accordance with—or, at times, at odds with—the local village leaders (*zu'ama'*) and municipal authorities, with important contextual nuances in each site.

The role of FBOs in Dahiye was peculiar because Hezbollah's NGOs—some of which had mother institutions in Iran (e.g., *Mu'assassat al-Shahid, Mu'assassat al-Jarih*, and *Mu'assassat al-Imdad*) but had adapted to the Lebanese context (Fawaz 2005, 248; Catusse with Alagha 2008)—made up a large part of local relief delivery. Foreign aid providers in Dahiye encountered a centralized form of local state in charge of projects and organizations operating in the suburbs. If many practitioners often suggested that aid provision across Lebanon remained at the mercy of local authorities, who stifled aid delivery in a patron-client societal structure, INGOs and the UN agencies in Akkar increased local sovereignty to a certain extent. INGOs initially contacted local power holders to bypass the central government,[4] but local authorities complained about INGOs exercising territorial sovereignty without consulting them. Such intricate relationships often made the philology of funding and distribution difficult to navigate. INGOs and UN agencies were considered resourceful and able to reach the largest number of refugees in the region with their service provision, while local charities had been relying for years on diasporas' remittances and other private donations by individual philanthropists and were generally believed to have a smaller capacity. This was the case of several local NGOs, local charities funded by Arab countries in the Gulf, and municipal services in Akkar, which covered a smaller area than the INGOs. Indeed, Lebanese NGOs are mostly financed by international donors (74.2 percent) and, to a lesser extent, by the private sector (19 percent) and private endowments (43 percent) (Daou and Ghazal 2020, 51).

With the arrival of Western humanitarian agencies, Akkar, a region historically dominated by fragmented forms of statehood, became populated by foreign technocrats who tended to roll out standardized humanitarian projects. When the global humanitarian agenda turned its focus to localization efforts after the 2016 World Humanitarian Summit, foreign aid providers began to rely on local power holders as gatekeepers but mostly failed to learn from local capacities and knowledge. INGOs, unable to quickly access local and refugee populations due to their scarce knowledge of local infrastructural history, needed to link up with local power holders. As a result, local power holders acquired a form of moral acknowledgment by acting as key intermediaries for the international humanitarian system in the region. The fact that some of these were not accepted locally and were at times even considered dangerous to the local population resonates with studies conducted on NGOs with negative views on local leaders who are likely to be community elders demanding respect, inclusion, and accountability (Dunn 2017, 157). The involvement of the *makhatir* was needed initially: it became coated with humanitarian afflatus and, therefore, was seen as a moral and human involvement through collaboration with foreign humanitarian actors. However, as Syrian displacement continued, both Akkar's governor and Halba's mayor (February 2017) pointed out that most INGOs instrumentalized local power holders to subject them to INGO interests. In turn, INGO practitioners contended that their challenge was gaining access to people in need and increasing their knowledge of a region they barely knew. Many also confirmed that they rarely reported to local authorities on what they were doing and what effect they were having, as they did not want to become involved in domestic politics (Carpi and Boano 2018).

In a nutshell, in Dahiye, the sovereignty of international technocracy was temporary and selective because it needed municipal approval, and local service provision ended up thriving to some extent because of international funding and training. Akkar, instead, became the land of international technocracy, where informal power holders became conveniently vested with international humanitarian legitimacy to ease the job of INGOs. After an initial phase of neglecting local authorities, INGOs eventually had to deal with them due to global pressures to include local actors and implement capacity building with local institutions. As will be evident (see chap. 3), however, international technocracy in Dahiye should not be mistaken for undiscussed, permanent sovereignty. In fact, Lebanese state institutions benefit from the rapid mobilization of international resources during a crisis, with liminality being the unspoken behavioral politics of the Lebanese state. In this sense, I view liminality not as inactive passiveness but as the specific character of the state's agency (Carpi 2019). The state adopts liminal politics in times of crisis, while in practice, myriad (in)formal, contradictory, and multiscalar powers interact to shape and rule life on the ground (Fregonese 2020). The official neutrality politics of many humanitarian agencies in Lebanon satisfies the existential need of the Lebanese state to maintain domestic stability. This political position was officially marked by the 2012 Ba'bda Declaration, where Lebanon underscored its neutrality toward the Syrian conflict. However, as outlined in Dahiye's urban history and Akkar's hamlets, this apparent liminality is operationalized either through acts of repression or violent neglect of disadvantaged and impoverished people.

THE LOCAL ORIGINS OF ORGANIZED ASSISTANCE PROVISION

The origin of humanitarianism more broadly has long been debated among scholars. Some have investigated it as rooted in Christianity, adopting a secular and secularist discourse over time (Fassin 2011), while others identify it as Islamic Shiite acts of assistance with a universalistic purpose (Mostowlansky 2019). This tension emerges whenever attempting to pin down the origins of humanitarianism in a specific context. More than the question of what can legitimately be called "humanitarian," the historical thread of local, regional, and transnational assistance provision within Lebanon is influential in understanding the interplay of different cultures of assistance. Scholars have identified modern humanitarianism as a moral vessel in which the politics of foreign presences, like that of the United States, may be placed (Watenpaugh 2015, 56). While not all external aid in the region should be associated with such forms of colonialism, a significant number of international resources support the colonial sentimentalism of "bringing good" to the Middle East (Ibid.). Nonetheless, such colonial sentimentalism is heterogeneous across different foreign powers; for example, as Watenapaugh writes (2015), Levantine diasporas in the United States advocated for Arab independence from Ottoman power through relief advocacy. Several INGOs continue the colonial tradition today, reproducing ex-colonial agendas and drawing on older forms of the Global North's missionary charities that think of suffering in the Middle East as a plague to be addressed by making religious minorities (e.g., Armenians and Assyrians) the deserving recipients of humanitarian responses. In part, humanitarianism should be disentangled from its colonial framework; it has been formed historically by multiple realities of managing crisis at a local level and should not be reduced to an object of the Western humanitarian agenda (Watenpaugh 2015, 3). Yet, it is possible to identify some longstanding relationships between key figures of Lebanon's history and foreign regions, which, over the last two centuries, invested in development and humanitarian aid in Lebanon. For instance, Mount Lebanon's Druze Emir Fakhreddine II went to Tuscany in exile in the first half of the seventeenth century (Makdisi 2000) after having created an alliance with the Medici dukes, who wanted him to back their crusades in the region. Tuscany (where the headquarters of Oxfam-Italia and other agencies are located) has been an active development and cooperation actor since older times, developing their humanitarian side of operations in Lebanon after the civil war.[5]

Associations have seemingly flourished along kinship and political lines in urban Lebanon since the second half of the nineteenth century. The conception of associative work has changed throughout the years (Karam 2006), and its goal has switched from charity and benevolence to social justice, participative citizenship, and administrative and development decentralization in favor of rural areas (Karam 2006). As Khater noted (2001), the Lebanese diaspora was instrumental in developing the Lebanese middle class, and philanthropic activities were the main material source that arose from migrants' funding.[6] Such diaspora-funded assistance was also a sign of civil resistance. Civil associations in Lebanon are considered places to reconstruct the political (Karam 2006, 24), proposing alternative agendas to confessional communities and the central state and presenting themselves as mediators of different and controversial interests. The sphere of civil associations in Lebanon, called the "third system" by Kamel Mohanna, leader of Lebanese NGO Amel (Karam 2006,

67), is collocated between state and society and has gradually expanded since the 1990s. Consequently, public policies in Lebanon have made room for associations' interventions to cover the demand for sanitary and social services (Karam 2006).

In this context, Lebanese civil society organizations (CSOs) play a prominent role in the Middle East, acting as cutting-edge advocates of human and political rights, gender parity, and economic enfranchisement. The definition of "civil"[7] in Lebanese history occupies an intermediate space that is neither confessional[8] nor affiliated to militias. More broadly, civil society is indeed described as a social segment that interacts with the state, influences the state, and is distinct from the state (Fisher 1997, 447). In the Lebanese context, NGOs are civil actors generally seen as less bureaucratic, more flexible, and more effective than states and as meeting grassroots needs, being less politicized, and doing good (Fisher 1997). NGOs are often used in volatile states as alternatives to development or as a tool to put peace-building strategies in place (Wildeman and Tartir 2014).

Local and international NGOs generally play a large role in delivering social programs to areas historically neglected by the state, such as Akkar and Dahiye in the Lebanese setting. Delving into the local origins of assistance in Lebanon, social movements form the very core of welfare and relief provision across the country. Concerns about eradicating poverty and inequality are often the principles of such variegated and domestic cultures of assistance. Civil society actors that represent an accountable alternative to the state without being in the position to replace it constitute one of the most important deadlocks of Lebanese politics. As social movements have mobilized worldwide to implement different aspects of social justice (Daehnhardt 2020, 59), some scholars have identified an inherent association between "social movement" and "mobilization" (Almeida 2019). Against this backdrop, foreign aid interventions in Lebanon throughout the twentieth century have largely molded the domestic scene by imposing the scission of assistance from justice and from domestic politics as a bargain for international funding. Among active civilian circles, this has led to the widespread idea that NGOs anesthetize political transformation in Lebanon.

More broadly, an NGO in Lebanon comprises any form of human collectivity and international or domestic action, including social welfare services, development support organizations, social action groups struggling for justice and structural change, groups providing legal or communication support, party-funded political action groups, and social movements composed of several NGO coalitions (Karam 2006). In Lebanon, NGOs do not originate from state hegemony (unlike in Arab states such as Syria, Egypt, and Libya) and have not even posed a challenge to the hegemony of already fragmented state institutions and atomized states (Gilsenan 1985, 397). It is believed that social causes and human rights are determined less by rules and more by communal relationships (Joseph 1999, 311).[9] Some Lebanese NGOs are the emanation of Lebanese political elites and ex-warlords (e.g., the Lebanese Welfare Association for the Handicapped of Randa Berri, Nabih Berri's wife from Harakat Amal) still involved in the state today. Political activism or commitment to a specific party is associated with access to social assistance (Cammett 2011) insofar as power is exercised through networks of clientelism. Indeed, electoral politics is only one of several modes of political competition: *mafatih intikhabiyya* (electoral keys) are prominent individuals who mobilize voters in rural and urban areas during election time (Cammett 2011, 76), largely through the provision of social welfare or the renovation of roads and public spaces (e.g., *tazfit al-intikhabet*, retarmacking roads in electoral times, is a popular saying in Lebanon). Exploiting the underdevelopment of Lebanese public welfare institutions, social welfare is the card played by some political parties to keep the loyalty of their constituencies.[10] In times of stability, CSOs play a more vital role than the state in development activities, capacity building, credit schemes, and providing basic services usually guaranteed by the state. However, the lack of democratic governance and reformed laws have caused NGOs to struggle to be efficient in their service provision (AbiYaghi and Yammine 2019). The Lebanese state is said to finance half of the schools and hospitals in the country, and the remainder are run by nonstate actors, such as charity organizations or political parties with sectarian orientations (Cammett and Issar 2010, 390) that rely on the politics of scarcity—namely, rewarding or denying benefits to citizens neglected by the state. The emergence of selective forms of social assistance results in an uncoordinated constellation of privatized welfare regimes (Cammett and Issar 2010, 390).

In Lebanese history, only one law regulates the associative sphere at a domestic level: the 1909 Ottoman Law, partially inspired by the 1901 French Law, enacted after the Young Turks Revolution in the wake of the Ottoman *tanzimat*.[11] Article 13 in the 1926 Lebanese Constitution also guarantees the right to create associations and, since 1900, Lebanon has had between five and six thousand local NGOs (Daou and Ghazal 2020, 45). Before the first constitution, active social spaces for religious communities were created during the time of *Mutasarrifiyya* (a state-like political entity born in 1861 in the aftermath of the Maronite-Druze clashes that ended in 1915). In this framework, Western welfare provision was already active in the Lebanese social sphere before World War I. In 1913, France ran over one hundred social centers and two hundred twenty schools in Syria and Lebanon (Karam 2006, 47). In this context, local associationism in the Levant is also a legacy of colonial history and interrelations between Syrian and Lebanese territories before their parti-tion (enacted with the 1920 San Remo Agreements). Religious organizations and missionary groups in the Ottoman era were key providers of social welfare to local populations (Fawaz 1994, 135; Chatty 2017). Sunni communities ran welfare institutions, and Christian communities had long-established church-based social services. During the French mandate (1920–1943), the Lebanese welfare regime was not centralized, which curbed the strength of state-run social safety nets after national independence. The government mandate of Fouad Shehab (1958–1964) is generally narrated as a remarkable period of re-forms and the development of the National Society Security Fund—*ad-Daman al-Ijtima'iy*—a new financial source for the health sector.

After the beginning of the civil war, the role of existing associations be-came the provision of relief to the displaced, injured, and homeless. Assistance was mainly given by ingroup members, reinforcing endemic solidarity and increasing the legitimacy of relief providers that greatly contributed to civil resistance during the Lebanese Civil War through their collective work. The constant state of emergency meant that long-term planning was postponed for immediate provision of humanitarian aid. Social, cultural, and economic development projects also faded into the background; for example, nineteen as-sociations were created with the specific aim of resisting the war (Karam 2006, 60). Nevertheless, following Karam (2006), CSOs and local NGOs struggled to obtain administrative autonomy due not only to corrupt local power holders who could guarantee quick access to conflict-affected populations but also to their necessary allegiance to foreign donors. A continual state of emergency became the norm, as did the need for huge material assistance, further tying the preexisting constellation of local relief actors to INGOs and UN agencies. Moreover, the affiliation of some organizations with civil war militias strength-ened to the extent that it reduced relief to the humanitarian wing of political projects (Karam 2006).

Judging one another on moral grounds was an in-war strategy used to dis-enfranchise political rivals throughout the July War and the Syrian humanitar-ian crisis in Lebanon. In this framework, Karam (2006) emphasizes how sev-eral organizations started working only in areas politically marked by militias and ousting service providers that addressed outgroup members in need. In this regard, he provides important examples. The Lebanese Social Movement (LSM),[12] self-defined as secular and politically neutral, was ousted from the suburb of al-Jnah on the southern coast of Beirut in the mid-1980s by the politi-cal forces of Harakat Amal and Hezbollah, which ruled the urban coastal areas (Karam 2006, 62). In the 1970s, several organizations such as Caritas-Liban,[13]

Amel Association,[14] Imam Sadr Foundation[15] (the social forerunner of the assistance section of Harakat Amal), and the Secours Populaire Libanais (created by Lebanese Communist Party sympathizers)—all of which Karam (2006) analyzes in depth—formed a core of strong social work providers in Lebanon. Most relief organizations were founded by people in the south of the country. This contributed to uneven NGO intervention between northern Lebanon and the South, which underwent financial and human hardship during the Israeli occupation (1978–2000). In the meantime, during the Pax Syriana years (1976–2005), Hafez al-Asad's regime supposedly had to protect Lebanon and prevent postwar tension; according to the locals I met throughout the years, this was one key factor that hampered economic development and the flourishing of CSOs in northern Lebanon.

The civil war dismantled state welfare institutions (Traboulsi 2007). It was only after reconstruction in the 1990s, the increased presence of INGOs in Lebanon due to Israeli occupation of the South (e.g., the 1996 Qana massacre), and the July War in 2006 that local community leaders became professionalized and began accessing international partners and funding channels. NGOs became increasingly competitive, and the state remained one of several actors contending for power (Trombetta 2014).

Historically, community self-organization can be traced back to the Ottoman *millet* system (Chatty 2013, 2017). In this context, family associations are peculiar, as their main goal is to help each other and poorer members of kin groups (Joseph 1999, 300). The presence of such communities rescaled political and social life around geographically bound spaces. In this diversified and vibrant Lebanese ecology of care, a burgeoning associationism gained momentum and became enmeshed with various forms of humanitarianism to alleviate ingroup suffering. As there are several communities—not merely defined by religious belonging—there are also several types of assistance within the same community, reflecting multifaceted projections of good societies (Barnett 2011, 223–32).

LOCAL FAITH-BASED ASSISTANCE IN DAHIYE

In order for the suffering to end,
you can contribute to
construction and giving.

(Author's translation from Arabic.
On a charity alms box in a Dahiye pastry shop)

During my time in Dahiye, I became familiar with Lebanese Shiite FBOs. In Lebanon, FBOs are believed to mobilize resources with greater ease in times of conflict. Although I failed to obtain interviews with practitioners from most Hezbollah-founded organizations, such as *al-Jarih* and *al-Imdad*, I talked to the staff of Hezbollah-led municipalities, which have acted as key service providers during conflict. Dahiye's FBOs were the service providers most familiar to locals when I would ask for street directions. Hezbollah-run organizations and Imam Mohammed Husein Fadlallah's FBOs were also mentioned locally as frontline assistance providers during the July War because of their historical proximity to locals and their needs. I interviewed staff from the Imam Sadr Foundation, which is headquartered in Tyre and later opened a Dahiye branch; *al-Mabarrat* Association,[16] founded by as-Saiyyd Mohammed Husein Fadlallah, and its subbranch *al-Hadi* in Dahiye; and *Jihad al-Binaa*, one of the largest NGOs run by Hezbollah.

My interviews with local FBO staff in Dahiye indicated that these organizations primarily act on cultural and moral principles and ensure the unity of the Muslim community (*Ummah*). Their antithetical position vis-à-vis the international system was often mentioned when stressing the importance of enhancing autonomy to reduce local dependence on exploitative Western donors. Such antithetical positioning was not exclusive to Dahiye: some FBO practitioners in Akkar also mentioned the need to protect their villages from Western ideologies.[17] Nonetheless, residents did not always appear to prefer community-provided services to INGOs or UN agencies. This does not imply that assistance compatible with religious and cultural values was not preferred, if available. However, most of the FBOs did not address their communities on an exclusive basis. Notably, Dahiye's FBOs promoted a political and cultural agenda where being tolerant and inclusive of non-Shiites was considered a local value. As Mona Fawaz stresses (2005), such organizations end up excluding the chronic poor, among whom are also ingroup Shiite members who simply do not feel represented by the hegemonic *civitas*. This diffused local disaffection was tangible toward both secular and faith-based actors in Dahiye. For example, Dahiye's residents frequently contested Hezbollah's services and defined them as politicized and corrupt, replicating their disaffection toward the central state. Critical voices were particularly melancholic about as-Saiyyd Fadlallah's organizations and views. To me, this suggests an important nuance in local aid provision and the heterogenous "Shiite way" of managing charity work. As a consequence, Fadlallah and Hezbollah emerged as the two main politico-moral forces in the aid landscape. Both Fadlallah—considered *marja'iyya*[18]—and the Hezbollah Party acquired increasing legitimacy from the 1980s onward, although the two sides were initially at loggerheads with each other.[19] Nevertheless, social change and struggle against imperialism[20] have been the cornerstones of both Hezbollah's and Fadlallah's thinking. Their assistance provision, in general, is strongly shaped by the Shiʻa religious cosmology of martyrdom and the struggle against injustice symbolized by the battle at Kerbala (680 AD). Charity is correlated with justice—charity is the response to immediate needs driven by benevolent action, while justice more specifically calls for the transformation of structures that incubate impunity and lack of dignity. For the Shiites, Kerbala is a historically recurrent event (Deeb 2009, 247) that reminds them that people should always have the spirit of revolution against oppression. This principle constitutes the bedrock of Shiʻa mobilization in Lebanon (taʻbiya). Ignoring this complex interrelationship between aid, morality, politics, and justice, some scholars have depicted Shiʻa service delivery as a mere political strategy to turn public compassion into political consent (Ajami 1986; Roy 2009). Rather, aid provision in times of conflict builds on a history of welfare provision that forms a constitutive part of today's social ethics in Dahiye. Uncertainty and the continuity of suffering are inherent to the existential approach of Shiʻa assistance providers in wartime and in times of stability. Volunteering and employment are seen as contributions to the development of the whole Shiʻa community. Working for a welfare organization brings Zeinab,[21] a holy figure in Shiite theology, into the present (Deeb 2009, 250). In this sense, assisting is endemically understood as resisting the cyclic crises that have hit Shiites in regional history (Ibid.).

Local FBOs tend to counter the emergency-driven culture of INGOs, highlighting the importance of continual assistance in times of conflict and stability and boasting increased technical and infrastructural capacity.[22] Nonetheless, the residents I encountered were ambivalent toward local FBOs. On the one hand, FBO charity work was compared to international aid as equally unable to eradicate the causes of chronic poverty and local injustice. As Mohammed, a Dahiye inhabitant, contended: "Local aiders often end up expanding the political constituency of the party that supports them, that has founded them, or promoted them."[23] On the other hand, while Dahiye's residents viewed INGOs as problematically enhancing the victimhood of some social groups in Lebanon by electing them as the only deserving individuals, Fadlallah's and Hezbollah's organizations made people feel like political actors,[24] resistant de facto citizens rather than objects of charity, unfolding the poietic function of charity over human life.[25] Fundraising material of the al-Mabarrat Association says: "Our organization was destroyed by Israel. We will continue, more committed, to doing good." The local inspiration for doing good means guiding individuals, irshad.[26] Such explicitness is traditionally banned or discouraged in Western organizations even though, over the last three decades, they have converted relief work into an instrument of conflict resolution and social transformation.

Providing a further nuanced understanding of community care, Maliha as-Sadr, at the helm of Early Child Intervention Lebanon (ECIL), emphasized[27] that *insaniyye*—which I functionally translate as humanitarianism—triggers social empowerment by supporting equality within Lebanese society. In this vein, the very goal of Shi'a charity work cannot and should not dismantle such work, dealing positively with recurrent exposure to war. Humanitarianism promoted by Western organizations ideally demands withdrawal from the territory of intervention as soon as domestic stability and sufficiency are achieved. The reality is an intensifying Western search for organizational and territorial continuity to maintain the political connections and consent useful for effective aid provision in the time of crisis. These different foundational principles around humanitarianism are often emphasized by local aid providers. The manager of the Research and Development Department at the Imam Sadr Foundation described international aid as outcome oriented rather than process focused: "NGOs that aim to engender change within society should focus on the process of their action and the encounter with their beneficiaries, rather than assessing material results."[28] Providing social services for the local community is inevitably part of a longstanding process. It is the struggle against Israel—not a war to kill, but a war for the right to exist, as often voiced in Nasrallah's speeches. Hope-driven policies steeped in religious beliefs, in this case, do not merely provide people with dreams of a better life, using religion as a tool to secure political quietism in everyday practices. According to my FBO interlocutors, they can also give people a proactive political and religious link with the future where hope, within a given geopolitical context, evolves from an intimate emotion into a conscious and realistic proposition.

DAHIYE'S MULTIFACETED "HUMANITARIANISMS"

Fadlallah and Hezbollah set up differently principled relief provisions in the 1990s. Fadlallah's *al-Mabarrat*'s practitioners considered themselves members of the international aid scene and reiterated their willingness to work with INGOs and foreign institutions. Hezbollah's municipal mayors criticized this openness, viewing it as mere commodification[29] in the framework of broader criticism toward INGO work and Western donorship. In this respect, the deputy mayor of Haret Hreik, one of Hezbollah's municipalities, said that donors in the July War rarely grasped local priorities: "Their main focus was on providing psychological assistance. That was not really the issue. Apartments were destroyed, buildings damaged, and women needed specific help. So, the problem is that INGOs don't fund and work for the things we really need. Humanitarian services do not take to changes. But if you really want to give something, help with money for housing, furniture, and infrastructure. From the outside, little money came with this purpose."[30]

A third important Shiite actor was the Imam Sadr Foundation, where a project manager contended that cooperation with INGOs was important because Lebanese NGOs need international visibility to thrive. As international funding primarily shows up in times of emergency, crises are key to local NGO survival.

Another peculiarity of Hezbollah's and Fadlallah's aid work was their approach to beneficiary communities. Al-Mabarrat promoted a cross-community vision in Dahiye, arguing that their services included all Lebanese communities. Nevertheless, they recognized that only a small number of people from non-Shi'a communities accessed their services, owing to demographic changes in the area since this FBO's foundation. Likewise, the Imam Sadr Foundation was created in the 1960s before the civil war and "used to address anyone in the South, where Christian Maronites, Christian Orthodox, and Armenians were far more numerous."[31] The deputy mayors of Haret Hreik and al-Ghobeiry (in November 2011), both from the Hezbollah Party, did not conceal the selective character of their services in times of stability, primarily addressing Lebanese Shiites. During the July War, the party became a compensation provider for any community in Dahiye. According to the local residents I interviewed, the political party has since placed particular emphasis on maintaining a postconfessional profile. Municipal actors highlighted the endemic nature of postwar reconstruction and the fact that people returning to their homes represents a victory regardless of the community they belong to.[32]

During the July War, some local secular NGOs acquired great visibility within the Dahiye public space, although through a different politics of care. In contrast to the cornerstones of Shiite assistance work, the leader of the Amel Association mentioned the necessity of cultivating responsibility in Lebanon by charging the beneficiaries for required services (when possible) to discourage aprioristic charity. "Amel acts as the feet, not the head, of our society," he contended,[33] in contrast to al-Mabarrat's concept of guiding individuals toward a moral life. Amel emerged as a catalyzing force for preexisting civic dynamism by defining itself as an apolitical organization and delegating politics to society. From this perspective, Amel aimed to accelerate and support people's actions and translate public ideas and intentions into real change. Amel's leader[34] argued that his NGO promoted a culture of rights—thaqafat al-huquq—against the backdrop of community-oriented Lebanese society. Reconciling the secular perspective with that of Shiite charity work, Zahir

Jalul,[35] from the municipality of Bourj al-Barajneh, spoke about the desire for a culture of humankind—*thaqafat al-insan*—in Lebanon. In this sense, acts of assistance mean individual commitment to the Resistance and being there on a continual basis (indeed, *shahid* is a martyr and, literally, a "witness" who follows continuity and regains human agency through the act of witnessing despite the humiliation and suffering that war can cause).

Years of Israeli attacks and local strife have led to an increase in informal care set up by residents, usually Dahiye businessmen from a variegated local middle class, frequently associated with Hezbollah's networks. I met some of these businessmen after the July War; they regularly distribute clothes, furniture, and money to vulnerable locals "for the Islamic value of doing charity as it's written in the Holy Qur'an," according to Hasan, a businessman from Haret Hreik.[36] "Some people became homeless in the July War, but orphans are always around in Dahiye. You always have a reason to help until the time these people will be able to empower themselves," he said, using the Arabic expression *yaksab ajar al-ma'ida*, meaning "until the time one can earn his own living." These small, vernacular acts of assistance reinforce a type of private welfare provision, culturally expressed by religious obligations. After the July War, this phenomenon brought a mixed laissez-faire economy for local businessmen and incentivized an aiding-purchasing-selling chain: wholesalers would donate some of their items to the local needy rather than selling them and make subsidies for the extremely poor without generating long-term sustainability. The Lebanese state's ceding of welfare to the local religious domain encouraged the colonization of the public by the private (Makdisi 1997). Charity and local entrepreneurship merged in postwar Dahiye's moral sphere.

THE LEBANESE GOVERNMENT'S HUMANITARIAN AGENDA

If the Lebanese government's response to the July War was described as hands-off by Dahiye's residents (Carpi 2019), its response to the Syrian refugee crisis was locally perceived as highly controversial. Although Lebanese minister of social affairs Wa'el Abu Fa'ur demonstrated flexibility in terms of humanitarian approaches,[37] others, such as minister of the interior Marwan Charbel, displayed reticence and racism toward the Syrian newcomers by repeatedly suggesting the closure of the borders starting in 2012. On a similar note, in September 2013, energy minister Gebran Bassil, affiliated with the Aoun-led Free Patriotic Movement (FPM),[38] called for the denial of entry to Syrians and the deportation of those inside Lebanon.[39] The early response remained fragmented and informal and lacked systematic coordination. Initially, the Lebanese government adopted an incoherent set of border management policies, seemingly wanting to keep the borders open and facilitate the temporary accommodation of Syrian refugees (Fakhoury 2021, 263).[40] However, for legal reasons, the government regarded the Syrians as temporary residents and used the term "displaced"—*nazihun*—rather than "refugee"—*laji'un*. An official from the Ministry of Social Affairs, Makram Malaeb, openly declared[41] that the Lebanese government's intention was not for refugees to feel comfortable but rather to encourage them to resettle elsewhere or return to Syria in "safe conditions."

Reflecting the private sector's growing involvement in humanitarianism since the 1990s—especially following the Indian Ocean tsunami in 2004—the government increasingly drew on support from the sector and international aid to cope with the demands of the situation.[42] Relying on external resources while denying the scale of the Syrian crisis was the state's strategy for maintaining stability and coping with the crisis. Despite its reputation for being unable to maintain stability[43] and weak and absent in the Weberian definition of state power (Mouawad and Baumann 2017), the Lebanese state has actively sought to build accountability over the years by guaranteeing cooperation with humanitarian agencies and openness to foreign aid actors. Lebanon's geopolitical order has become the common interest of local politicians and the international humanitarian order (Hoffman and Weiss 2017).

State politics regarding the Syrian crisis has certainly been the subject of debate. Local aid actors from the Lebanese March 14 coalition tended to sympathize with the Syrian opposition and sometimes ended up serving in Gulf-funded or other local NGOs. 'Azza Adra, the administrative chief of the local NGO *Akkarouna*, argued that the Lebanese government had provided much more assistance and funds in the aftermath of the July War than for the Syrian cause.[44] The apparent neutrality of the state toward the Syrian conflict, in this political environment, was often perceived as a *tout court* alignment with the Syrian regime.[45] The High Relief Council, presided over by the prime minister and made up of members of various government ministries, was tasked with conducting damage assessment and channeling foreign aid; however, it ended its financial assistance due to lack of financial resources. This was a recurrent theme in the aid discourse of NGOs funded by Arab countries in the Gulf assisting Syrians in Akkar. This "transnational governance" (Hannerz 1996, 6), composed of clan leaders, local *makhatir*, foreign governmental providers, UN agencies, and local and international NGOs in Akkar, came to reshape the region's transborder politics.

Since 2015, political rhetoric has revolved around the need for refugees to return to Syria, as seen in the proposal of Antoine Chedid, Lebanese ambassador in the United States:[46] "Lebanon cannot bear this burden; refugees should go back to Syria and resettle." Making people return to Syria by building more camps inside the conflict-ridden country, "which is eighteen times bigger than its Lebanese neighbor," Chedid stressed, is a strategic way to redomesticate the conflict and its consequences for the region—and a quick alternative to opening foreign borders to the displaced, a move deemed less appealing to global political actors.

INTERNATIONAL AID IN LEBANON

Overall, the civil war and subsequent chronic uncertainty contributed to the loss of a great number of archives, information, files, and, according to aid professionals,[47] to blurring the memory of who exactly intervened, where, and when. During the first period of my fieldwork, it was evident that tracing the historical stages of international aid provision in Lebanon is a real philological challenge. "Undoubtedly, the farther you get from the end of a war, the less you can find," told me Patricia Nabti, who long engaged in volunteering activities in Lebanon.[48]

During the civil war years in Lebanon, international humanitarian relief operations intensified but had different purposes. The longest-serving NGOs that aimed to save lives and provide relief were the Red Crescent, the Lebanese Red Cross, the International Committee of the Red Cross, and the United Nations Children's Fund (UNICEF). In 1978, the United Nations Interim Forces in Lebanon (UNIFIL)[49] was created to deploy international peacekeeping forces in the South along the Blue Line separating Lebanon from the Syrian and Israeli military (see Meier 2016). UNICEF renewed its mandate with the July 2006 War. However, I am, in this book, primarily concerned with international, regional, and local actors providing in-kind and cash assistance. The aid providers working in Lebanon during and after the 2006 War were both international (e.g., Save the Children, Terre des Hommes, Oxfam, UNICEF, Caritas, Christian Aid, Islamic Relief, USAID, NRC, DRC) and local NGOs (e.g., Amel Association, Najdeh). Activist collectives included Relief Center Sanaiyeh, later named Zico House, which became the base for the *Samidun* group. This group was not only a relief group but also a political part of the Resistance movement, combining efforts toward liberation of the Occupied Palestinian Territories and Lebanon from Israeli occupation (Lavalette and Levine 2011). Hezbollah's NGOs,[50] the *al-Mabarrat* Association, and the Imam Sadr Foundation were also highly involved. I interviewed only those who worked during the July War in the Beqaa Valley and the South and were still present in Dahiye.

After the Ta'if Agreement (1989) ended the civil war, the Lebanese government expressed its willingness to cooperate with the international community and attract as much foreign assistance and investment as possible to avert the looming financial crisis.[51] In the early 2000s, the focus of foreign aid shifted from postwar reconstruction to Lebanon's national debt, which had contributed to massive economic stagnation (Corm 2006), making relationships with outside donors particularly sensitive. Another international intervention in Lebanon was foreign investment in the reconstruction of the Nahr al-Bared Palestinian camp after the fighting in May 2007 (Knudsen and Hanafi 2011). The Lebanese government, the UNRWA, and the Palestinian Liberation Organization (PLO) requested US $328 million at the 2008 Vienna Donors Conference for the reconstruction of the camp, but only 37 percent of the funds were eventually pledged for that purpose. During my visit to the camp in November 2011, there still were temporary shelters and destroyed buildings, suggesting an important difference between the July War and foreign interests attached to other conflicts.

The July War marked a watershed in Lebanon's humanitarian history because it requested particularly large amounts of international aid. In the framework of continual crises, the Lebanese government has used international assistance and investments to mobilize resources while playing a negligible role in running healthcare institutions and maintaining infrastructures.[52]

Although the July War involved outgroup assistance on a large scale, according to most of my interlocutors who worked in Dahiye, it did not result in long-term societal changes, as preexisting forms of community-oriented assistance were continued afterward. As a scholar and practitioner affirmed:[53] "In the few years since the war broke out, we've seen everyone going back to their own community once again. Unfortunately, the tendency to create one's own family tree of organizations is still ongoing."

In this sense, local aid providers crossed community boundaries to provide services based on need rather than community belonging during the July War, but in the aftermath of the conflict, every group seemed to have gone back to its "safe haven."[54] Nonetheless, local and international solidarity was used as a rhetorical instrument in postwar speeches. It is at this point that the frequent international humanitarian narrative of being able to provide something *super partes* emerged against the backdrop of a divided local fabric (see chap. 5).

The postwar narratives populating the southern suburbs appeared in stark contrast with the ephemeral presence of international aid. In a bid to express harmony with the Lebanese who had not been directly affected by war, some war-stricken people expressed pride in having defended Lebanon against the common enemy because Hezbollah's army—referred to as "theirs"—was the only one in the whole country able to do so. Other Lebanese confessional groups, such as Maronite and Orthodox Christians, were sometimes viewed by Dahiye's Shi'a residents as groups who had cooperated in relief efforts, providing aid and assisting the displaced by means the Shiites had learned over the years.[55] Especially in spaces visually marked as Shiite, I perceived a strong public ethic of collectivity continuously reinforced by language used on local signs, in speeches, and in slogans, such as "Let's protect our safety together" (*nahmiluha al-amana ma'an*) at the entrance of the *al-Mabarrat* Association, or the as-Saha Restaurant on the airport road: "We love living together" (*nuhibbu an na'iysha ma'an*).

Against such collective rhetoric during and after the July War, Hezbollah delivered a Manichean view of the conflict. The party publicly talked about NGOs and governments as being either with or against it, a polarization that—as will be evident later—some humanitarian actors tended to discard to uphold a neutral and impartial logic of intervention. Moreover, in a bid to remain impartial and apolitical, some INGOs refused to provide aid in war-stricken areas where the Hezbollah Party was in charge, as it was classified as a terrorist group by some Western states (e.g., the Belgian and Canadian governments).[56]

A 2009 Listening Project report gives nuance to how international assistance should be thought about and formulated. The report proves that response to crisis management was different in all geographical areas in Lebanon. The inhabitants of areas occupied by Israel and subjected to several wars, such as the Beqaa Valley, South Lebanon, and southern Beirut, tended to relate international assistance to the relief provided in the aftermath of these conflicts and, similarly, during the 2006 reconstruction. Instead, people in Mount Lebanon and Akkar associated international assistance with government services (Collaborative Listening Project 2009, 6), as the state tended to provide services with the support of international actors. Interestingly, to the older Iraqi and Sudanese refugees I met, international assistance signified a decreasing number of NGOs providing assistance, while, as discussed by Feldman (2012b), Palestinian refugees tend to attribute international assistance and policies to the UNRWA and other specific Palestinian-focused INGOs.

INGOS, UN AGENCIES, AND HUMANITARIAN DISCONTENTS

In Dahiye, local FBOs had greater public visibility than other providers, while most of the aid agencies that enjoyed special visibility on Akkar's public signs were funded by countries in the Global North. Among the INGOs, the UNHCR coordinated all international humanitarian assistance. The UNHCR turned into a "mobile sovereignty" in terms of service provision (Pandolfi 2000b), but in our meetings between 2011 and 2013, UNHCR staff often spoke of the difficulty of improving aid services due to the legal constraints of their mandate in Lebanon. These limits were most frequently mentioned when projects failed, when staff could not gain people's trust, or when they had to justify operational flexibility. For example, a UNHCR practitioner in Qobaiyat (Akkar) told me it was increasingly challenging to uphold the legal procedures when dealing with refugees:[57] "For humanitarian reasons, we often find ourselves in the position of bypassing legal areas to be able to provide health and protection to irregular or undocumented Syrians in Lebanon. Sometimes preserving the dignity of people implies we go lawless."

However, inefficiency on the ground was caused by several factors that could not be reduced to legal mandates. While operational flexibility was emphasized as an important characteristic of the UNHCR's way of working, INGO practitioners were also required to institutionalize mistrust toward locals. A UNICEF practitioner who worked for the campaign for vaccination and school material distribution for Syrian and Lebanese children vented his frustration on the subject:[58] "I was told we should not give extra resources to the Lebanese government, even when we have them, because the government will sell the surplus to get more money. Corruption is widespread, and I just have to abide by our old rules."

Mistrust was sometimes accompanied by the self-criticism of being solipsistic. A practitioner from the World Food Program (WFP) recounted that he was disappointed in how his organization pretended to value critical feedback and complaints about its programs:[59] "I don't think we really act differently from the Lebanese state. Asking for feedback about our services is just a political strategy to show that we negotiate projects, but, as a matter of fact, we eventually do whatever we like, whatever the local feedback is."

Notably, in the Akkar villages of al-Bahsa, al-'Abdeh, Bellanet al-Hisa, Wadi Khaled (an area including 23 villages), Bebnin, and the small city of Halba, neither local authorities nor Syrian refugees said they had been consulted about the primary needs in their localities. Many refugees would not have prioritized food like oil, bread, and milk; "the WFP keeps boasting about the availability of more and more quantities of bread," a Syrian refugee man contended.[60] Most of the refugees I spoke to stressed that their greater need was medication, especially for chronic disease, the cost of which was unlikely to be covered by the UNHCR.[61] At the same time, medical infrastructure in the Akkar region was insufficient. Amal, in al-Bahsa, suffered from a wasting disease; 'Alia, in Wadi Khaled, suffered from slow blood circulation; *Hajja* Rana, living in Bebnin, needed to expel bile liquids from her spleen every two days and had to go to a hospital forty kilometers from her home for treatment with no private means of transport available.

Another priority for refugees was money for rent, which they argued was never a factor in INGO and UN policies in the first few years of the Syrian crisis. Most of the Syrian refugees I met in the North between 2011 and 2013 rented apartments or built tents on rented land, paying between US $50 and US $100 per month depending on the size of the land. In all cases, they needed to buy furniture and electricity without external support. Some refugees had connections in the resettlement area and were able to rent a place at a convenient cost. Some refugees owned homes without a kitchen or bathroom, services that INGOs, such as the NRC,[62] helped to build at a later stage. In Wadi Khaled, I visited a thirty-square-meter flat where three families were living with thirteen children. Fatuma, from Homs, reasserted rent and medication as primary needs and approached me as if I were an INGO representative, embodying the international community in her eyes, as often happens (Gabiam 2016): "I came from Syria to get packages of bread in Lebanon [sarcastic tone]. I don't give a damn about bread; it's just 2,000 Lebanese lira! I don't want to be given a grain of hope [see fig. 2.1 below]. I can still pay for it. Why don't they provide medicines and cash for rent instead? I share a small room with a family of nine people. Our conditions are inhumane. But you guys provide what is easier for you."[63]

With similar resentment, Hadi, an engineer from Hama living in al-'Abdeh, questioned the ethics of emergency that barely kept people alive and confronted me about the benefit of my research project: "I don't want aid. I don't want anything. We want to be able to go back. I don't even know why you came here . . . You're not going to find anything close to the truth because in this war, everyone has become a liar. For sure, many of us tell you we don't receive anything at all, but they lie. You're paid to ask questions, and you'll be paid for this research. We'll stay here instead until things get sorted out at your [the international community's] convenience."[64]

Indeed, many refugees saw aid actors as a coalition of interests (Collier 2000) that, regardless of official neutral politics, were a key part of the war scenario. Unlike the present moment, when Lebanon is in dire straits from food insecurity and severe currency inflation, and refugees need items such as food, the refugees I interviewed between 2011 and 2013 affirmed they were used to taking what was given, without it necessarily addressing their real needs. Despite this, the WFP developed[65] new methods of food distribution by relying on international partners throughout Lebanon.[66] The fact that basic food items like bread and clothes were offered to me several times as a gift of hospitality to welcome my visit[67] sheds light, to some extent, on the mismatch between actual needs and standardized assistance. 'Aiysha,[68] from Raqqa, was eager about having received three bottles of oil in the same week.

Fig. 2.1 Bread provided to Syrian refugees on a weekly basis by the Mercy Corps in Wadi Khaled (Akkar). December 29, 2012. Photo credits: Author.

In contrast, her neighbor Nour,[69] from Homs, complained that they had received no food at all the week before as she was late in finding out where the oil distribution would take place in Halba: "My mobile was broken, and no one told me about the oil distribution."

From late 2011, as INGOs began to implement programs in the region, Akkar seemed to become a chaotic land of random aid provision. I met recipients who benefited from more than one provider at once, whereas other families nearby were cut out of the aid system, experiencing what Feldman calls identity "traumas of category change" (2012a). It often happened that access to new resources in the area was guaranteed to the same groups of beneficiaries and failed to reach others.

From the perspective of many INGO practitioners, the expansion of outreach was at the mercy of local gatekeepers (e.g., the local *mukhtar* and *mandub*). However, on a visit with two INGOs working in Halba in February 2016, practitioners acknowledged that, to carry out needs assessments over two years, they had been relying on the UNHCR central database, presumably containing the names of the most vulnerable families. A door-to-door strategy to improve outreach had never been put in place. Lack of coverage induced some refugees to relocate elsewhere. In addition to job opportunities, as typically happens in receiving countries (Shearer 2000, 191), the emergence of particular spots of aid distribution influenced multiple relocations of Syrian refugees throughout Akkar, further isolating some refugee settlements from livelihood hotspots.

Syrian refugees often provided dense critiques about the mismatch between everyday needs and the assistance provided. Mohammed,[70] from Deir ez-Zor, denounced the fact that "humanitarian workers are mostly foreigners and can get their houses paid for, while we're dying in the tents that we built and pay for ourselves." Farah,[71] from Homs, expressed mistrust and a sense of helplessness by saying that "the best blankets are the ones that the INGO staff keep for themselves. We're given the worst stuff; we're worth nothing to them—just like the stuff we're given." Her words convey the sense of nothingness that aid triggers in displaced people (Dunn 2014), produced not merely by violence and displacement but also by care, such as the cheap materials provided by humanitarian enterprises (Dunn 2017, 111).

With the arrival of Syrian refugees, Lebanon's economic landscape became particularly layered. It became a land of increased cash mobility (Ashkar 2015) and a more vibrant labor market for local middle classes employed in local and international NGOs. Foreign practitioners in Akkar also sought properties, cars, and other everyday services. Such economic neodynamism in areas of humanitarian intervention typically contributes to the living conditions of a few individuals who already own labor capital before the crisis and are ready to sell it (Anderson 1999). For instance, a DRC practitioner[72] reported that their emergency relief (e.g., mattresses, baby and food kits) was purchased locally, except for kitchen tools that were imported from Pakistan. Some INGO practitioners, contrarily, mentioned wanting to economically help the areas where they intervened while complaining about the waste of resources and episodes of looting by Syrian armed groups. As a foreign practitioner recounted: "Once, in Wadi Khaled, we saw a truck coming into Lebanon from the border, taking the aid kits we had just prepared, and then leaving again toward the border. Local people told us they were affiliated with the Free Syrian Army, which struggles to get resources in Syria and tries to control goods in border areas to sell them and purchase weapons. Aid is not for fighters; we should check on our warehouse better."[73]

In Dahiye, a solid network of local services made temporary foreign providers appear as tourists of war and passersby. International humanitarian assistance in Akkar, in contrast, was not perceived as an outright political intrusion but rather as an opportunistic response to the Syrian conflict, where labor capital owners could benefit from the crisis while the most vulnerable were burdened with further hardship. However, refugees did not exclusively emphasize the political meaning behind assistance and the achievement of political rights: the cases of Dahiye and Akkar point to the importance of addressing refugees' "humanitarian rights" (Feldman 2018).

LOCAL AND REGIONAL FBOS IN AKKAR

The vast majority of local (predominantly Sunni) FBOs that engaged in humanitarian work for Syrian refugees were already established welfare providers before the Syrian crisis, generally working with the Lebanese poor and orphans.[74] FBOs and other entities such as *Dar al-Fatwa* allocated only 30 percent of their own services to the Syrian humanitarian crisis between 2011 and 2013.[75] In Akkar, I noticed that attitudes toward local organizations were ambivalent, and FBOs were often accused of corruption. For example, according to a resident from Halba,[76] "No one here stole as much as the Islamic organizations. And I say that as a Muslim . . . This region would have been wealthier without them." In the North, local FBOs mostly worked independently and did not coordinate with INGOs, UN agencies, or any local secular or faith-based NGO. Another Halba resident observed:[77] "Everyone provides whatever they want and whatever they can: there's poor mutual consultation, and we face continuous overlapping in service provision. You'll learn that this place is chaotic with no order." These words echo Dunn's conceptualization of aid adhocracy as chaos, consisting not only of technical failures but also resulting from the rationalizing practices of humanitarian bureaucracy (Dunn 2017, 90).

Twenty-two Islamic FBOs in the country provided aid during the July War; they were members of the Coalition of Islamic relief organizations—*I'tilaf*—founded in 2006 under the name Association of the Islamic Union (*Jamiy'at al-Ittihad al-Islami*). These FBOs had been in the region since the 1990s,[78] and some even since the aftermath of the French mandate. The fact they were considered local does not capture their hybrid nature, as some employees were Lebanese nationals and some regional donors (e.g., Kuwait, Qatar, and Saudi Arabia) did not give up their agendas, philanthropic ideologies, or geopolitical designs.

Importantly, the term "INGO" today tacitly signifies "Western." While several of the NGOs responding to the July War and the Syrian crisis were, indeed, founded and financed in the Global North, labeling them all as "international" makes them indistinctive. With this in mind, I have labeled Gulf NGOs "regional" to distinguish them from other foreign intervening actors. The position of such regional actors is peculiar because they are not associated with other international aid providers. Indeed, some Lebanese practitioners working on behalf of Gulf donors contended that some of them encouraged freedom of action in terms of what areas to target and how to establish beneficiary categories, create "modes of ordering" services (Janmyr and Mourad 2018), and decide what types of relief to prioritize. Moreover, some charities had been established long before the Syrian crisis and were simply supplemented by Gulf donors when a new emergency was officially declared. A Kuwaiti FBO practitioner viewed the Syrian crisis as "only a single event in the history of our social services in the country."[79] By a similar token, Sheikh ʿAbd-al-Qader Mohammad az-Zaʿbi, the leader of *Dar al-Fatwa* in Akkar, argued during our interview that INGOs were always more resourceful but did very little in the region. "Our continual efforts to improve the region when there were no refugees have never been properly funded."[80] The vast majority of INGOs said they started the Syrian response in mid-2012. In contrast, most Islamic FBOs argued that they had started assistance programs a few weeks after the Syrian protests in spring 2011 and were extending their already established welfare in the region.

According to Syrian refugee beneficiaries, INGOs and their (mostly secular) local partners tended to establish a fixed day during the month to distribute aid kits, whereas local and regional FBOs tended not to have a fixed schedule and location, following a randomized pattern of aid provision.[81] From the perspective of *Dar al-Fatwa*, whose representatives I spoke to four times over a decade, the primary motivation for a randomized pattern of provision was to follow up only with selected beneficiaries due to the limitation of funding. I met two sheiks in Akkar who were charity leaders in al-Bireh and Fneideq, and both highlighted the inadequacy of resources given the scale of the crisis. They were unable to enlarge their recipient group beyond the scope of their mosque goers and direct networks. This tendency at times suggested a deliberately unambitious approach to outreach, as contended by the leader of Saudi FBO Taiba in Halba:[82] "Everything works better when you select your aid recipients on objective criteria, and then you simply need to carry on your project until the end with no risk of having to shut it down due to a sudden shortage of funds. This policy assures our accountability to beneficiaries."

In this regard, both locally and regionally funded FBOs overtly affirmed that they did not aim to enlarge their scope of intervention, recognizing, to a certain extent, their entanglement in the longstanding patron-client networks of local welfare. With the advantage of hindsight, I can affirm that many of these FBOs, such as Taiba, also shut down at a certain stage. It was common also among INGOs to open and shut programs according to the most urgent needs, calling to mind Western empires that abandoned colonies when they became too costly (Calhoun 2004, 379). While locals and refugees voiced their sense of being abandoned and trapped in both Dahiye and Akkar due to continued instability and intermittent humanitarian care, on my visit to Halba in May 2019, the belief that the UN was the only agency "living up to the humanitarian promise thanks to their infinite economic resources," despite the moral and political resentments and the logistic chaos that this book tries to dig into, was widespread in some Syrian informal tented settlements (ITS), as the UN still guaranteed aid regularly a decade after the start of forced displacement from Syria.

NOTES

1. The term "faith-based" refers to NGOs that explicitly rely on a specific religion to set out their principles. However, faith is only one facet of a broader religious identity. Jawad classifies these NGOs as religious welfare (2009, 65). Nandy (2002, 61–62) differentiates between religion as ideology, a (sub)national identifier of populations protecting socioeconomic or political interests, and religion as faith—a way of life, an operationally plural tradition.

2. Such funds are also obtained from *al-khoms*, the Shi'a charity, and *az-zakat* (almsgivings), which aim to promote equality by redistributing wealth from the rich to the poor. Christian organizations rely on similar sources of funding. In Islam, voluntary contributions—*sadaqah*—are welcomed. According to the Holy Qur'an and the Prophet's *ahadith* (the sayings of Mohammed), they are a means of escaping Allah's punishment and provide necessities to the poor.

3. The Amel Association, Caritas-Lebanon, and Kafa Association, all of which are headquartered in Beirut, count many internationals among their staff.

4. Interview with INGO practitioner in Halba, December 12, 2013.

5. Interview with project manager of Oxfam-Italia. Forn ash-Shebbek, Beirut. October 1, 2011.

6. Lebanese migrants have financed hospitals, schools, orphanages, roads, and infrastructure during the world wars, the 1950s earthquake, the civil war, and the July War. In 2001, Lebanon ranked seventh in the top ten countries receiving workers' remittances, following India, Mexico, the Philippines, Morocco, Egypt, and Turkey (Hourani 2007, 5).

7. In Arabic, *madani* indicates something related to civil society but specifically connected to the urban sphere; *muduni* means civic but not necessarily *ahli*, local or domestic (Karam 2006, 90).

8. For example, the Lebanese Social Movement—*al-Harake al-Ijtima'iyye al-Lubnaniyye*—constitutes an archetype of aconfessional civic activism in the Chehabist era (mandate of Fouad Chehab, 1958–1964). Founded in 1957 by Greek Catholic bishop Grégoire Haddad, the movement was considered progressive and open to all communities.

9. Patrilineal religious identities are institutionalized as political identities. To gain access and representation, citizens are expected to belong to a religious community (Joseph 1999, 312).

10. The aim of political parties can go beyond elections; for instance, financing a particular kind of educational system is an opportunity to forge a socialization process that will encourage individuals to support a certain understanding of national history and political ideals (Cammett 2011).

11. Reforms took place between 1826 and 1834 in the territories of the Ottoman Empire. The Law of Associations 1325 was issued in Lebanon in 1909 (Lebanon Support 2016).

12. The LSM had been in al-Jnah since it created a dispensary for the displaced in 1977.

13. Founded in 1972 by a Jesuit father from South Lebanon, it enlarged its scope of intervention at the beginning of the civil war.

14. Created in 1978 by a group of doctors after the Israeli Litani Operation in the South.

15. Created in 1963 in the wake of reforms promoted by President of the Republic Fouad Chehab.

16. Fadlallah, known for having issued modernistic *fatwas* at al-Hasaneiyyn Mosque in Haret Hreik, founded the *al-Mabarrat* Association in 1978 to provide education for orphans, a dispensary, and other services. Not all these facilities were originally funded by Iran, as is often believed (Harb 2010, 45).

17. Halba, Akkar, December 14, 2012.

18. A *marja'iyya* is a religious Shiite institution. Hezbollah independently follows the Khomeini doctrine under *wilayat al-faqih*, which represents the fusion between religion and politics. At the end of all eras, the twelfth hidden Patron of Time— *Mahdi – sahib az-zaman*—is believed to come back to liberate the Shi'a from oppression once and for all.

19. Acts of vandalism against Fadlallah's properties occurred in Dahiye prior to the Shiite cleric's positive relationship with Hezbollah (Harb 2010, 44).

20. Such political orientations resulted in the attempted assassination of the Shi'a cleric on March 8, 1985, in Bi'r al-'Abed (Dahiye). The attempt was conducted by the CIA under the United States' preemptive counterterrorism program. The car bomb caused eighty casualties and wounded two hundred.

21. How Lebanese Shi'a women look at this figure is culturally nuanced and therefore different to the Iranian context. Imam Mohammed Fadlallah's preaching— *marji' at-taqlid*—professed that women could attain the highest level of jurisprudential training and interpret religious tenets despite the absence of such a norm in Shi'a jurisprudence (Deeb 2009, 251).

22. Interview with Faruq Rizq at *al-Mabarrat* headquarters, al-Ghobeiry, Beirut, October 18, 2012.

23. Interview with a local resident and shop owner, Haret Hreik, February 2, 2012.

24. The provider-recipient relationship in Dahiye is based on a social contract built on preexisting moral and social relationships between the two parties. During

Lebanon's civil war, Fadlallah spoke about the necessity of creating a human state—*dawlat al-insan*—to provide resources for people to help themselves and one another.

25. Interview with Faruq Rizq at *al-Mabarrat* headquarters, al-Ghobeiry, Beirut, October 18, 2012.

26. Interview with *al-Hadi* Association (branch of *al-Mabarrat*), tariq al-matar (Airport Road), Beirut, October 29, 2012.

27. Ouzai, Dahiye, December 4, 2012.

28. Tyre, October 8, 2012.

29. Interview with *al-Hadi* Association (branch of *al-Mabarrat*), tariq al-matar, Beirut, October 29, 2012.

30. Haret Hreik, January 18, 2012.

31. Interview with Mohammed Bassam, Tyre, October 8, 2012.

32. The quick return of war-stricken people to their homes was criticized, as decent living conditions could not be restored in such a short time. For instance, sulfur levels were much higher than before the reconstruction process (Makkouk 2008, 72).

33. Mossaitbe, December 13, 2011.

34. Interview with Amel director and founder Kamel Mohanna, Mossaitbe, Beirut, October 24, 2011.

35. Leader of the Education Committee of Bourj al-Barajneh, Municipality Bulletin 2013.

36. October 19, 2011.

37. Abu Faʻur and the predominantly March 14 government were accused by the Syrian ambassador in Lebanon of helping terrorists (referring to the Syrian opposition and many of the refugees), *Daily Star*, February 1, 2014.

38. The FPM was aligned with the March 8 coalition led by Hezbollah.

39. In response, Abu Faʻur ruled out such a decision, *NowLebanon*, September 27, 2013.

40. Between 2011 and 2014, Syrians were allowed to stay in Lebanon for up to one year with an ID card as long as it was renewed every six months; from 2012, it could be renewed from inside Lebanon. Furthermore, some professions previously reserved for the Lebanese became accessible to Syrians (Ministry of Labor 1/19 2013, Amendments of Articles 8 and 9 of the Resolution 17561 related to organizing the work of foreigners).

41. Discourse held at the Carnegie Middle East Center Conference, downtown Beirut, June 25, 2013.

42. According to research published by Development Initiatives in 2012, private funding grew from 17 percent in 2006 to 32 percent in 2010 (and totaled US $5.8 billion that year) as a share of the total humanitarian response. Development Initiatives found that, in 2010, 56 percent of NGO income came from private donors, but only 8 percent of UN humanitarian agency budgets were funded by private money.

43. The erstwhile president of the Lebanese Republic, Michel Suleiman, once declared that the UNHCR was dealing with the absence of the government on refugee issues in the Beqaa Valley (official interview, October 2012).

44. Tripoli, January 10, 2013. The organization, Our Akkar (in English), dedicated part of its budget to the development of technical skills of employable Lebanese separately from the funds dedicated to Syrian emergency relief.

45. In Akkar, the erstwhile government of Najib Miqati was often viewed as aligned with the Asad regime. Tammam Salam, seen as a more neutral political figure, succeeded Najib Miqati in February 2014.

46. Discourse held by Chedid at the Wilson Center, United States, October 29, 2013.

47. Interview with Kamel Mohanna, Mossaitbe, Beirut, October 24, 2011.

48. Interview with Patricia Nabti, founder of the International Association for Volunteer Services in Lebanon, Mar Mkhayel an-Nahr, Beirut, February 21, 2012.

49. Nowadays, UNIFIL is composed of six hundred local military staff and twelve thousand internationals from thirty countries.

50. *Al-Jarih* for the war wounded; *ash-Shahid* for the families of war victims; *al-Imdad* for local development and social welfare; *al-Qard al-Hasan* for provision of microcredit to local families; and *al-Ha'iya as-Sahiya al-Islamiyya* for health assistance and protection.

51. The Lebanese government obtained pledges of more than US $4 billion from international donors during Paris I in 2001 and Paris II in 2002. As mentioned, local people in Dahiye often recall these conferences as hypocritical symbols of international generosity.

52. The government was officially managing nearly 10 percent of all Lebanese health clinics and five out of one hundred sixty hospitals (Cammett and Issar 2010, 391).

53. Interview with Patricia Nabti, Beirut, February 21, 2012.

54. Conversation with Mona Harb, AUB, Beirut, January 31, 2012.

55. Conversation in ash-Shiyyah with ʿAli, February 3, 2012.

56. Interview with Francesco Bicciato, UNDP, downtown Beirut, October 25, 2011. However, such political moves did not exclude indirect financial contributions which ended up financing the reconstruction of Dahiye's infrastructures.

57. Qobaiyat, December 14, 2012.

58. Beirut, November 3, 2012.

59. Beirut, February 3, 2012.

60. Halba, December 30, 2012.

61. The UNHCR usually covers 85 percent of health expenses (excluding chronic diseases) when refugees are hospitalized.

62. Interview with the leader of the Beirut branch, November 21, 2012.

63. Wadi Khaled, January 29, 2013. The WFP initially provided beneficiaries with food vouchers redeemable at local shops. In 2012 and 2013, after the Jordanian experience, WFP decided to adopt the banking system (e-food ration cards), through which refugees are more autonomous over choosing their purchases.

64. October 10, 2013.

65. The delivery of larger amounts of food was announced in an official UNHCR meeting in January 2013 in al-Jnah, Beirut, which I personally attended.

66. These included NGOs Acción contra el Hambre in South Lebanon, Terre des Hommes in the North, and World Vision in the Beqaa Valley. Interview with an NGO practitioner from Acción contra el Hambre, Beirut, January 7, 2013.

67. Even though I was given gifts out of religious and/or cultural obligation during home visits, to me, these gestures were likely to have included the excess of some of the things people owned.

68. Bebnin, November 5, 2012.

69. Al-Bahsa, November 5, 2012.

70. Bebnin, November 5, 2012.

71. Bebnin, November 7, 2012.

72. Tripoli, February 1, 2013.

73. Qobaiyat, November 13, 2012.

74. In Akkar, children became orphans less by wars and more by disease affecting poorer parents unable to access proper healthcare.

75. *Dar al-Fatwa* was founded in Beirut and opened a branch in Halba in 2007. Other Islamic NGOs in the region boast a longer life.

76. Interview with Ahmed, a photographer living in Halba, November 24, 2012.

77. Conversation, October 21, 2012.

78. Interview with the director of the Coalition of Islamic relief organizations, called *I'tilaf*, Tripoli, February 3, 2013. More information can be found here: http://www.nna-leb.gov.lb/ar/show-news/17676/تقرير-تلاف-جمعيات-غاثة-النازحين-السورين-اعدادهم .فاقت-التوقعات-ونعمل-ضمن-الامكانات-المتاحة-

79. Interview with the Kuwaiti Education Association, Tripoli, January 14, 2013.

80. Interview with *Dar al-Fatwa*, Halba, November 21, 2012.

81. Interview with Taiba Association, Halba, January 7, 2013. Interview with *Dar al-Fatwa*, Halba, November 13, 2012.

82. December 24, 2012.

3 / Politicizing Aid and Moralizing Politics

Old Formulas, New Scenarios

Over the last few decades, governments have increasingly relied on their humanitarian affairs departments to manage domestic and international emergencies. Historically, political parties and the wealthy personalities aligned with them have also undertaken humanitarian relief programs in areas marked by crisis. The tendency of political actors to directly engage in aid is global, and Lebanon is no exception. Building on Ilana Feldman's argument that the way in which displaced people live *with* politics and *in* politics informs the politics of humanitarianism itself (Feldman 2018, 4), I suggest a twofold understanding of the politicization of aid in the Lebanese context. First, humanitarian policies and practices are instrumentalized and reattuned in local, regional, and global politics; second, the moralization, humanization, and neutralization that both humanitarian and political actors purport to put in practice through public campaigns are used to uphold international accountability, receive international funding, and subsist as aid interlocutors and mediators. In this vein, I show not only the ways in which aid is highly politicized in today's Lebanon—as it is worldwide—but also how the global political order has induced all actors to moralize their politics. These changes have offered to political and humanitarian actors a new ground to discard and belittle their rivals.

Humanitarianism becomes not only a space where assistance contributes to making and unmaking political imaginaries and actual polities, but also where refugees and locals use their expected political identities to access the assistance regime, continually readapt to the social environment, and develop self-protection strategies (e.g., Bouris 2007; Cammett 2011; Feldman 2012a; Fiddian-Qasmiyeh 2014). Against this backdrop, political neutrality does not always emerge in the same guise as we learned it in the framework of the ICRC.

Yet it remains a fundamental register that assistance providers need (more or less willingly) to relate to within the broader humanitarian arena.

Aid, therefore, is employed either as a way to humanize politics or as a political strategy—an issue largely researched by scholars (Prendergast 1996; Belloni 2005; Hoffman and Weiss 2017). On the one hand, the humanization of politics implies a public discourse on morality that aims to discard political rivals' accountability on moral grounds. On the other hand, aid used as a political strategy is either concealed, as with INGOs and UN agencies that claim neutrality and impartiality as cornerstones of their thinking and action, or explicit, as with what I call aspiring pan-politicization by Hezbollah in Dahiye and the political realism of Gulf NGOs in Akkar.

My analysis will develop as twofold. First, I researched the pan-politicization of Hezbollah in the July War, in which aid provision was dualistically framed in the region as either pro- or anti-Israel. In this case, pan-politicization, involving empathy with the ruling power, was not an ontological fact but rather the party's aspiration. Second, in the wake of the arrival of Syrian refugees, Gulf-funded NGOs in Akkar actively advocated for the removal of the Asad regime in neighboring Syria. Even though this overt political rhetoric seems to suggest a similar form of pan-politicization, my fieldwork with these NGOs showed different shades of humanitarian neutrality—heralded as the foundational principle of assistance by apolitical Dunantist humanitarianism (Henry Dunant having founded the neutrality-centered Swiss Red Cross)—that contrast with mainstream understandings. These different shades of neutrality powerfully demonstrated how political and humanitarian rights sometimes overlap and are sometimes separate. Indeed, while a large segment of Dunantist aid providers see humanitarianism as urgently alleviating human suffering and saving lives, humanitarian action remains deeply entangled in international, regional, and local politics. Discursive representations of humanitarianism powerfully decontextualize displacement and unbridle it from the politics that gave rise to it in the first place. Humanitarian depoliticization strategies have framed refugeehood as a biological rather than a political status in the Global North's discourse, whereas regional humanitarianism (e.g., in Gulf countries operating in Arab majority regions) offers articulated forms of political humanitarianism that challenge monolithic understandings of humanitarian neutrality.

POLITICS AND MORAL CAMPAIGNS

Political stability in Lebanon has cyclically been kept hostage under the guise of the Pax Syriana. After the withdrawal of the Syrian army from Lebanon, the Damascus-Beirut Treaty of May 2006 aimed to normalize the relationship between the two countries.[1] The treaty was contested in the Syrian government-owned editorial *Tishreen* (May 17, 2006), which affirmed that it had unjustly forgotten Syria's sacrifices and martyrs for the sake of Lebanon. Two months later, Israeli attacks seemed to prove to Lebanon that the country would not be safe without Syrian tutelage. In this context, where crisis seems to chronically lurk around the corner, the Lebanese state significantly defined its own service provision as "relief" (Fawaz 2005). Scholars have widely studied how INGOs and foreign government institutions form a sort of hypergovernance (Bhatt 2007) that can behave like a parastate, implementing governance through relief, education, health, and development. Such hypergovernance is not the exception but the rule in states historically stricken by conflict, blurring the lines between normal service and emergency relief provision, a complex nexus that I define as "develop-manitarian" (see chap. 6). Catastrophization has become a new form of governmentality (Azoulay and Ophir 2012) and ceased to be merely nongovernmental (Ophir 2010, 77).

In a context affected by political crises, the idea of the "political" is constantly negatively fetishized, with state actors and nongovernmental organizations endeavoring to build and preserve their humanitarian reputations on impartiality and neutrality (Carpi 2019). In Lebanon, the political is relegated to a collective imaginary characterized by reified immorality, but politics touted as morality remains a token of accountability. In the domestic aid arena, the Lebanese government competes with local political parties and NGOs that provide relief in zones of displacement. The rivalry is no longer between the political and the moral—around which several humanitarian actors purport to propose the ideal balance—but rather between moralities campaigned differently. In other words, the political merges into the moral. The humanitarian space becomes inhabited by diverse actors trying to delegitimize the moral authority of their counterparts to enlarge their own constituencies (Cammett 2011). This moral rivalry is pursued through compensation schemes: in Dahiye, postwar policies have aimed to prevent group mobilization in the areas destroyed by the Israeli Air Force, and in Akkar, schemes have been activated to meet the needs of residents under the "local community development" banner of INGOs and UN agencies in the response to displacement from Syria. Both compensation policies have been promoted with the language of morality while controlling evolving civil societies.

The politicization of aid (*musa'adat musaiyysa*) is continuously discussed in all realms of service provision as a sign of disaffection, social distance, and despair. Notably, the people excluded from either local or international assistance on the basis of their identity politics are, at times, those considered uncategorizable within demographic areas where a different political, national, or religious identity predominates. The lack of *wasta*—a network of useful connections—is identified as the main cause of exclusion. Disaffection is tangible in in times of relative stability as well as in times of war, drawing a line of continuity between flawed welfare regimes and discriminatory identity politics.

In many of Akkar's villages and in the Dahiye slum of Hay al-Gharbe, chronic needs, caused and perpetuated mostly by state neglect and a lack of sufficient aid structures, are not apparently connected to emergencies. Instead, the two humanitarian experiences show how recurring states of emergency, resulting from a cycle of internal displacement, are produced by warfare, regional refugeehoods (primarily Syrians, Iraqis, Sudanese, and Palestinians), and large-scale blasts, such as the one at the Beirut port on August 4, 2020. These events have compelled local systems of governance to deal with the international humanitarian organizations that rushed to provide relief during crisis and that, in part, decided to stay on the ground for a longer term. External intervention forces local systems of care to reshape welfare schemes and mobilize social and economic resources more rapidly (Calhoun 2004) to meet the growing needs of local residents and refugee newcomers.

Both refugees and locals tend to label the mismanagement of resources as corruption (*fasad*), with no distinction between cases (Gupta and Sharma 2006, 225). Politics, indeed, has become synonymous with "bad politics," emerging from a disenchanted common imaginary of a cumbersome hurdle rather than a catalyzer of change in Lebanon. Among the conversations that helped me understand such holistic disaffection was one with 'Ala, a young Syrian refugee:[2] "When I came here, I used to trust them [the humanitarians]. I thought they'd have been human. Instead, I had to beg to get my medicines paid for. These guys tell you they are here because they are good. They're as corrupt as the people who manage to get something from them [Lebanese politicians]"

Aid is not only associated with bad politics that create a humanitarian labor economy while leaving the root causes of human displacement unaddressed; it also generates cycles of expectations and social frictions. For instance, local Akkaris often refer to South Lebanon as more resourceful and generously financed by the international community: "The South is more beautiful because all of the money coming from outside goes there," argued a Halba resident.[3] Likewise, when I visited the Nahr al-Bared camp in winter 2011, several shelters were still destroyed and the wreckage visible because "no one pays our bills, unlike Lebanese Shiites [financed by Iran]."[4] Ahmed, a Lebanese resident in al-Ghobeiry, conveyed the image of Iranian airplanes overloaded with paper money that came one week after the end of the July War:[5] "Hezbollah's offices were full of cash to be distributed to people . . . It was amazing to see that. But this is Lebanon, not Iran; they should go back to where they came from."[6]

The words of Bassam, a native resident of Haret Hreik, confirmed how aid provision creates political, cultural, and countercultural imaginaries: "It is the state that rebuilt my building, not Hezbollah. In the July War, we mostly have to be grateful to the United Nations, I reckon. Their involvement in rebuilding Dahiye made me feel part of a *normal* international community."[7] The generalized sense of disaffection toward service and aid provision often made my job of ascertaining where people were effectively assisted (and to what extent) more difficult.

ASPIRING PAN-POLITICIZATION IN DAHIYE

While there were specific topographies of aid provision during the July 2006 War, the Lebanese, refugees, and foreigners I spoke to generally said that "everyone was everywhere," pointing to a chaotic situation. However, it became clear that local municipalities played a large role in aid provision and reconstruction during the July War in Dahiye.

Dahiye's municipalities are more than a de facto state. As the leader of a Dahiye-based Italian NGO affirmed: "Regardless of their official nature, Dahiye's municipalities represent Hezbollah's party, certainly not state institutions."[8] Most of the foreign practitioners I interviewed in Dahiye complained about having to gain municipal approval for every initiative, hampering freedom of action, while crediting the party for its vigilance and capacity to centralize administrative power.[9] The idea of Hezbollah having tight control over areas of intervention is also a common belief among local NGO practitioners. Noura, who assisted the internally displaced in 2006, defined the presence of the party's armed militia in the suburbs as military occupation: "If the majority of Shi'a were in the refugee camps, Hezbollah would be there too. These guys treat Shi'a as their hostages [*rahina*]."[10]

Dahiye's municipalities "upgraded their services after the July War through their cooperation with international donors that also funded the local welfare system," explained a social worker at the Haret Hreik municipal health center, which first started cooperating with the United Nations Development Program (UNDP) in 2007.[11] A project manager in the Bourj al-Barajneh municipality explained that the municipality started collaborating with the UN Development Fund for Women (UNIFEM) and UNICEF only after summer 2006, a collaboration that further internationalized local service provision.[12] Spain, France, and Italy set up decentralized cooperation partnerships with Lebanese municipalities for development projects and service delivery (Harb and Atallah

2015, 209). According to municipal staff, such internationalization allowed for financial and technical reinforcement of the welfare system in postwar Dahiye, whereby the "radicalization of development" (Duffield 2014) was implemented at a local level, reinventing aid and development as strategic tools of social reconstruction.

All of the INGOs stated that municipalities in Dahiye were their only real reference point and exclusive way to access local people. A UNDP officer called NGOs antigovernmental rather than nongovernmental, mentioning their minimal effort to rehabilitate and revitalize the state. He then stressed the importance of collaborating with decentralized forms of power:

> Hezbollah doesn't require our political alignment with them but rather our detachment from domestic politics and the mere transfer of our technical skills. This is an excellent way of maintaining a balance for both parts. The party has been pragmatic; they need our technical knowledge for developing a sustainable model in the interest of their citizens. We can teach them all of this, but they are obsessed with constructing buildings. In exchange for this new cooperation with Hezbollah, UNDP gained the reputation of being democratic, flexible, and cooperative. We all gained from this collaboration, although we, as the UNDP, have basically been reduced to the role of donors.[13]

Even though pan-politicization was the aspiration of the main rulers of the Beirut southern suburbs, the political orientation of each Dahiye municipality differed and influenced local decisions on reconstruction and cooperation efforts after the July War. For instance, the municipality of al-Ghobeiry, considered a "Hezbollah stronghold" in the international political discourse, apparently refused to cooperate with some large NGOs, such as Caritas, as it did not lack the funding or skills to pursue its own aims.[14] Unlike the Hezbollah-run municipalities of Haret Hreik and al-Ghobeiry, the Christian majority municipalities of Mreije and Hadath remained opposed to Hezbollah's services in Dahiye, committed to remembering the golden age when residents were predominantly Christian. During my fieldwork, the municipality of Hadath conducted campaigns recalling the Phoenician name and identity of the district to distinguish it from the "Arabs" (Hadath Municipality Publication 2012, author's translation). Similarly, Bou Akar mentions an informal June 2010 edict forbidding the Christians of Hadath from selling land or properties to non-Christians (2018, 55–56). Hadath also withdrew from the ART-Gold project led by the UNDP—meant to enhance health and social integration in the southern suburbs and enforce economic development through local authorities—with the election of a new mayor and an emerging need to show consistency with the new agenda.[15] In contrast, the municipality of Mreije seemed more pliable and compromising toward Hezbollah's administration, remaining a partner in the ART-Gold project that had inaugurated the first relationship between the UNDP and Hezbollah in Dahiye. However, to mark his political orientation against Hezbollah, the mayor of Mreije adopted pro-state rhetoric by saying that the Lebanese state had become much more efficient in the suburbs after the July War.[16]

Such pan-politicization—in which one aligns either with or against Hezbollah without envisioning the possibility of "alter-politics" that are able to build and transform beyond oppositional politics (Hage 2015)—can also be viewed as a cultural factor that connects aid providers and recipients to their territory. Local culture has been historically characterized by residents' engagement in social work and relief provision for the war-stricken, which further translates into personal attachment to Dahiye. A social worker in the municipality of ash-Shiyyah, for instance, repeatedly emphasized that she was born and bred in the neighborhood and that it was the spirit of territorial belonging that had encouraged her to start again "from a piece of wood to rebuild a table" destroyed in 2006.[17] Similarly, Mohammed, a builder I met when passing the Saiyyda Zeinab Mosque under construction in Dahiye, said: "I am building this pray space for *my* people, although I'm not sure how long this will last."[18]

My understanding of Dahiye's social response to crises and crisis management was that people, through the mere empiricism of unaddressed dire conditions, challenged Hezbollah's aspiring pan-politicization and the solipsism of international humanitarianism. But how did these actors view one another? Some US scholars, especially those who supported Israel during the longstanding Israeli-Arab conflict, depicted Islamic NGOs as political tools meant to buy people's consent (e.g., Ajami 1986). Hadi, from *Jihad al-Binaa*, explained how the politicization of international humanitarian assistance was viewed in Hezbollah's environment: "Humanitarian assistance is a strategy to exercise foreign politics; the actual goal is to mold Third World minds and, in Lebanon, spy on Hezbollah's affairs. That is why Hillary Clinton is promoting the foundation of seven hundred NGOs to assist the displaced of the July War. This way, they keep you under their control [*tahta yidon*]."[19]

Political actors viewed each other as using humanitarianism to strengthen, weaken, or challenge political rivals. A MoSA project manager working in ash-Shiyyah stressed the inherently political character of aid, recounting how "during the July War everyone was there and wanted their logo to be shown as a brand. And at that time, there were definitely more international brands than usual."[20] Humanitarianism became an opportunity for political parties and actors to gain symbolic capital as caregivers and welfare actors. On this note, during the 2006 conflict, Nayla Mouawad overtly stated: "I ask the US government to intercede to permit the establishment of humanitarian corridors, which would show the Lebanese people that the Seniora government is engaged and effective."[21]

Likewise, the way in which INGOs have operated in Lebanon throughout the years demonstrates the proximity of the humanitarian system to the private sector, fostering the idea of philanthropic entrepreneurship. For instance, Johan Verkammen, the Belgian ambassador to Lebanon, in the framework of the UNDP-funded ART-Gold project, discussed emergency as a new space for "Belgian people's goodwill" to develop a humanitarian market in West Beqaa (UNDP 2010). The pragmatism of humanitarianism underlies the contradiction of finding USAID—funded by the US government in support of Israel's war aims (Valbjorn and Bank 2012)—among the main aid providers in Dahiye after the July War, or Israel offering aid to Lebanon after the blast on August 4, 2020, to reconstruct Beirut's port and several of Beirut's suburbs.

HAY AL-GHARBE AND THE VIOLENCE OF ABSENCE

"In Lebanon, all social welfare
is an expression of identity politics."
(Jawad 2009, 88)

After ten months of research in Dahiye, I happened on an area I had never heard of and that, I realized, some Dahiye's residents did not know about. I first thought the area was a continuation of the Shatila refugee camp, dramatically known along with the Sabra gathering (in Arabic, *tajammu'*) because of the September 1982 massacre of Palestinian residents by the Lebanese Phalangists, allied with the Israeli Defense Forces at that time. The area was the illegal settlement of Hay al-Gharbe, which I could not find on maps of Dahiye's official geography even though the area is under al-Ghobeiry's municipal administration. Spaces less politically marked do not often benefit from either state or humanitarian services, while local providers warrant assistance to their constituencies or aim to enlarge them. International humanitarianism behaves similarly to the state, leaving some areas abandoned due to specific political interests. Nonetheless, the slum, called a gathering, plunged into a complex history of urban encampment (Knudsen 2016), attracted diverse demographic groups, including several from the Dom community, a population with an originally nomadic lifestyle whose native language is Domari, and migrant workers from Asia and Africa who settled there because of cheap rent and cost of living. Dahiye's dwellers consider Hay al-Gharbe the same way some Lebanese and foreigners consider Dahiye overall, namely, a no-go area.[22] The emergence of this slum is linked with increasing urban wealth in the rest of Dahiye after 2006.

The area underwent territorial exclusion, which led to forms of urban violence that do not directly threaten foreign countries. This resulted in a scarcity of humanitarian services.

To reverse the Israeli military urbicide in 2006, the *Waad* reconstruction project prioritized repairing heavily damaged housing and strengthening social welfare provision in the zones of Dahiye directly affected by war. As war damage in Hay al-Gharbe was insubstantial, the slum was not included in the renewal plan despite its longstanding needs (see fig. 3.1). The slum reminded me of Biehl's zone of abandonment (2005), where people are simply doomed to die in total invisibility and political unimportance. The only available clinic inside the settlement at the time of my visit was that of the *Tahaddi* NGO (meaning "challenge" in Arabic).[23] Health conditions are dire, with most of the ill suffering from diabetes, scabies, skin diseases, and insect and rat bites (Das and Davidson 2011, 281–85). In Hay al-Gharbe, living conditions are believed to be more difficult than in the Palestinian Shatila camp, where people can still benefit from the UNRWA services. The critical accounts that denounce the conditions of chronic poverty suggest that intervention cannot be limited to emergencies but must address the root of the poverty, which is political rather than social. Fassin, in this regard, calls for an examination of "the workings of justice in charitable practices" (2011, 473). Meaningfully, the education level of the district's youth is low and, at the time of my fieldwork, only *Tahaddi* provided the service in the settlement. Few people from the district have steady jobs. Most of them are occasionally employed as drivers, waiters, construction workers, chicken slaughterers, *narguileh* sellers, musicians at weddings and ceremonies, resellers of objects collected in the streets, or fruit and vegetable market sellers.

It is estimated that in Hay al-Gharbe, around 15 percent of the population are Lebanese, 55 percent are foreigners, and 30 percent are of mixed origin (Das and Davidson 2011, 270). There are inhabitants from the Dom community[24] (called *Nawar*),[25] Palestinians unable to find a place in the camps, older migrant workers (predominantly Egyptians, Sri Lankans, and Syrians), and a small percentage of poorer Lebanese. In other words, like Karantina (an eastern Beirut district), Hay al-Gharbe hosts the poorest and most socially isolated from all communities in Lebanon. As the residents of the district suggested, mutual mistrust is spread between these diverse groups.

Many residents are squatters who remain vulnerable to government decisions to reclaim land.[26] Hay al-Gharbe's inhabitants—more than ten thousand, mainly children and women (Das and Davidson 2011, 271)—have not crossed any international border to merit the status of refugees and access international aid.[27] But they are not even politically interesting enough to the international

Fig. 3.1 Hay al-Gharbe's landscape. January 10, 2012. Photo credits: Author.

community to become beneficiaries of aid. The residents of Hay al-Gharbe expressed the idea of being warehoused (*metkawtrin*), forgotten, and marginalized. Despite the presence of drug dealers and night prostitution, there are no state policemen or security of any sort in the district, indicating an actual state of abandonment.[28] Residents have been threatened with violence in the past and, more recently, by urban redevelopment plans. During the civil war, residents temporarily moved to the Camille Shamoun Stadium when "spaciocidal" (Hanafi 2012) fighting in nearby Palestinian camps made the area dangerous. In July 2006, they fled the slum again when the Israeli Air Force bombed the surroundings. Some of the displaced families later returned to the slum as they could not rebuild their lives anywhere else. Government pressure and the risk of eviction or property destruction remind the inhabitants of the existential paradox of not having any other place to go and of the chronic "urbanized warfare" (Fregonese 2020, 141) they live in.[29]

Hay al-Gharbe's history is somehow ironic as, according to Das and Davidson (2011, 273), the slum distinguished itself from the Shatila camp to be spared from continuous attacks during the civil war. The lack of homogenous sectarian identity or strong political affiliation enabled immunity from direct military attacks for the slum's residents, and the area consequently received neither media coverage nor services and aid. While vulnerability can only be assessed across community histories and regions, ethnic, religious, and political affiliation still conditions access to aid, irremediably tying humanitarianism to discriminatory identity politics (Feldman 2012a). The postwar neglect of disadvantaged areas has retraced lines of exclusion in spaces where war, unlike in what is considered central Dahiye, was merely a reminder for local longstanding forms of loss, general neglect, and misery.

A worker from the *Beit Atfal as-Sumud* of Shatila first took me to Sana's home in Hay al-Gharbe.[30] Sana is from North Lebanon and lives in a humid basement with her thirteen-year-old son; her mother-in-law pays the rent. Her husband, a violent man who spent all their money, abandoned them a few years ago. Sana cannot ask local Shiite organizations to take care of her son because they require official permission from the father if he is still alive, and the whereabouts of Sana's husband are unknown.[31] Her gender-marked lack of rights prevents her from accessing the assistance she is entitled to as a community member in a Shiite-majority suburb. As Chambers (2002) argues, de facto rights count more than normative citizenship in a context where the legal framework of citizenship fails to guarantee and protect legal subjects. My encounters with the inhabitants of the area made me reflect on the relationship between citizenship and humanitarianism in areas where all seems unchanged inside and outside of an emergency.[32] Iman, who is Palestinian, said she was not used to receiving visits like mine from the outside. Her poverty is evident—she lives in a crumbling building with electricity only available five hours a day. Everyday life means staying at home because of a sense of insecurity in an area, which Mohammed, Iman's Lebanese husband, called a *manta'a cocktail* (a mixed area). Iman's family's decision to remain mostly indoors is an inevitable choice of self-seclusion, and they rely on a trustworthy neighbor to shop for them. Local mistrust is deeply rooted and marks relational and family history. Mohammed and Iman's parents and siblings all died after looking for shelter in the Camille Shamoun Stadium during the Israeli attacks in 1982. They showed me pictures of the nine martyrs. Fatma, Iman and Mohammed's daughter, took her name from her aunt, who died as poisoned with alleged milk by her neighbors during the civil war. From their perspective, this invisibility has helped them preserve their dignity and increase their sense of safety. Social retreat for self-protection eventually results in invisibility to humanitarian and welfare service provision. Invisibility prevents blatant social rejection and acts as a reminder of being unwanted in historically marginalized suburbs. Fatma told me how she motivates her self-seclusion: "I don't have shoes that match; I'm ashamed of going out of the house like this."[33] She explained how morally distasteful it is to meet with friends who boast about their possessions to mark their higher status. "When I go out, I suffer much more. I prefer staying here with my parents: it gives me much more honor than hanging out with those girls." Fatma had to give up her hope of becoming a hairdresser because professional school was too expensive. A few years later, I learned from Iman that Fatma had allegedly committed suicide at home in 2014; the case was not investigated, reminding me of the preposterous solipsism of international development in areas where people have neither rights to basic services nor access to justice.

Ahmed, Iman's eight-year-old son, was able to attend school in Shatila thanks to his mother's Palestinian origins, as the UNRWA school fee was cheaper than that of other schools. Iman has been chronically sick for seventeen years and only receives financial help from *Beit Atfal as-Sumud*, which assists Palestinians in the neighborhood. In her critical words, "Hezbollah enriched only a few families. We weren't the protagonists of the July War. The war left us with no jobs and a higher cost of living, but we did not get any compensation."[34]

Mohammed, Iman's unemployed husband, explained how his disenfranchised life as a Lebanese was entangled with the Palestinians in Lebanon:[35]

> I'm a Lebanese citizen in Lebanon, and I can get no aid. Luckily, Iman is Palestinian, and we get some help from the UNRWA from time to time. You know, Israel, in a sense, unified Palestinians and the Lebanese. But when Israel left, we started fighting each other. We began to call each other *ghuraba'*, the strangers, although we share the same misery. I wanted to redeem my family from that misery, and I joined Fatah ad-Dahiye during the war of camps in 1985. I heard lots of promises at that time: "If you become a fighter, you and your family will get anything you need in return." I haven't seen any improvement, any help so far. I'm sick of big lies that parade as revolutions and resistance. My life is much worse now than in the years of the civil war.[36]

For Iman's family, during the civil war, access to services financed by the Palestinian Liberation Organization (PLO) was problematic.[37] The only accessible aid provision for Iman's family today comes from the UNRWA, inducing Mohammed to identify with Palestinian social membership. Mohammed said he had felt betrayed by Lebanese conationals when he was fired from the Sabra vegetable markets three years before:

> I passed Lebanese citizenship to my wife and children, but this did not change much for us. Israelis spared us their missiles. With Hezbollah, it works this way: "No physical damage caused by Israel? No help for you." To get services

in Hay al-Gharbe, no matter if you are a citizen or not, you need to pledge loyalty to local parties. Before the elections, candidates promise to provide affordable generators, sort out the problem with garbage dumps, and provide good quality water. If you don't want to pay for drinking water, you literally need to enslave yourself to political parties. Do you see my daughter's *hijab*? She doesn't wear it because she chose it or because my wife and I want that. She's wearing it because she started losing her hair due to the salty water in the shower.

As a Palestinian married to a Lebanese man, Iman is also deemed less vulnerable than other Palestinians in the eyes of UNRWA practitioners in the area. Neither long-term nor short-term humanitarianism is available for Iman's family, which has been weakened by chronic poverty, multiple displacements during the civil war, and discriminatory state policies. In this regard, I discussed the capacity building approach—*bina' al-qadarat*—with the project manager of the UN-Habitat Safe Cities project, meant to empower families not addressed by postwar reconstruction plans.[38] Safe Cities included the slums of Beirut where political affiliation is hybrid or lacking, as in Hay al-Gharbe (where only the flags at the entrance of the settlement point to the presence of Harakat Amal, which was never mentioned as an effective local service provider).[39] Hay al-Gharbe presents itself as the spectrum of the political, denouncing the selective care of Hezbollah's government. The indoor life of some inhabitants relegates the unwanted of Dahiye to invisible spaces, allowing governors to get away with deprivation. If the July War restratified Lebanese society, the lack of direct emergency aid during the conflict, aid that normally gives birth to a series of long-term projects, further disenfranchised the inhabitants of this area.

The reality of Hay al-Gharbe also reveals how Dahiye's spotted poverty is shaped by politics and identity. International humanitarianism does not intervene in places where there are no political interests and no political identities to plug into such interests. Most humanitarian agencies ignore this space as much as the Lebanese state and local municipalities. The major reason for external intervention during and after wartime is the declaration of a state of emergency. The nature of this declaration and the speed at which it happens measure the political value of a space, which is why war breaks out in the first place. Areas are spared by attackers or become victim to attacks for reasons related to transnational balances and geopolitical configurations. A technical advisor from the Italian Cooperation meaningfully pointed out that aid in Lebanon primarily springs up in areas of political interest and where money circulates better (see the case of sub-Saharan Africa in Polman 2011): "Let's face it—there are no real needs in the areas where we intervene. Places like Baalbek or Dahiye don't need more than other areas. It's about politics."[40] Against this backdrop, some scholars (e.g., Hannig 2018) tend to trace a less politically oriented trajectory of foreign aid (especially UN interventions) after the international interference into the Pakistan 1971 crisis, while, in those years, Sahel's famine was of lesser global interest. The case of Hay al-Gharbe challenges such historiographic tendencies. Indeed, both Lebanese institutions and humanitarian agencies often proved to neglect spaces not considered "humanizable" insofar as they reside outside of their political agenda. In other words, political plans imply the preservation of such spaces to keep the poor in place (Simone 2008, 186). The Lebanese living in Hay al-Gharbe, such as Mohammed, are not classified as suitable for aid in Lebanon's taxonomy of needs and remain cut out of both discriminatory state policies and the politics of inclusion Hezbollah has fostered, especially since 2006. The lack of ethnic, political, and confessional labels suitable for aid and of a strong *wasta* with the governors generate a life of neglect. In the larger context of Dahiye, the success of postwar reconstruction has been selective. Hay al-Gharbe confirms the continuity between war-caused urban destruction and reconstruction as an unequal reversal of that process. That continuity becomes disrupted when an urban area lacks political attention due to a less defined social identity within the broader Lebanese demography. While compensation strategies, to a great extent, have dodged mass resentment against Hezbollah, Hay al-Gharbe remains a powerful comedown of internationally acclaimed postwar reconstruction.

THE DEPOLITICIZATION OF SYRIAN REFUGEES

Many of the refugees from Syrian opposition areas I met in Akkar in 2011 believed that their adaptation to the host environment and their positionality as aid beneficiaries required them, to different extents, to undertake a process of depoliticization. Those actively supporting the protests in Syria, including refugee women and teenagers, highlighted their loss of mobilization and political rehabilitation. They often voiced frustration at being seen as mere recipients who accept any kind of basic help. More specifically, depoliticization was commonly seen as a project aimed to counter their rehabilitation into active political life. These refugees wanted organizations to provide support and advocacy beyond medical relief and social assistance. They expected the international community to help renormalize their lives through international solidarity and political action. In this politico-emotional environment, I found myself wanting to understand the extent to which humanitarian programs were actually depoliticizing people. However, the empirical tangibility of depoliticization is not easy to assess. I reflected on how depoliticization was the way in which some refugees understood themselves as displaced subjects with complex attitudes toward assistance regimes—and understood the more or less implicit ethical expectations of aid providers toward their recipients.

Many refugees showed steadfastness in upholding the political dimension of their being. In Wadi Khaled and Halba, four people admitted they were selling their food vouchers to financially support the Free Syrian Army (FSA) fighting next to Tel al-Kalakh.[41] Haytham, an engineer from the Aleppo region, sold food vouchers given to him by the WFP to donate to a medical association in southern Turkey that fabricated artificial legs for ex-combatants. Wael, a refugee from Bab 'Amr (Homs), pointed out the need for external spaces for Syrians, such as discussion areas:

> Three friends and I have started gathering once a week to exchange news about our villages in Syria and our ideas about the future of our country. Nearly all NGOs want to give us food and mattresses. It's easier for them. Many people wouldn't survive without all of that, but they cannot reduce their support to that. We need more help with rent and medicines: for a package of bread, I pay just 2,000 Lebanese lira. It's not a priority for many of us. They just pretend to listen to our requests. They see that we take whatever they give us, and they think they're addressing our greatest needs. Of course, we take if they give! Maybe we should start refusing aid so that our real needs emerge. We need a safe space to meet each other, not only shelter.

The municipality of Halba rejected their request to host public meetings. Likewise, the Jezzine municipality in the south of the country denied Syrian refugees the right to organize public gatherings (as reported by ALEF 2013). Most Lebanese residents concerned about local stability supported the decision, as they feared the Syrian presence in their villages and towns would turn into a markedly political one. Similarly, Lydia, an INGO practitioner in Qobaiyat, commented that, most of the time, Western donors refrained from funding projects that helped people known to be connected to armed groups in Syria: "I think this measure is hypocritical as everything right now is connected to weapons. Some people who are based in such areas risk starvation because of this choice, which is still political. You cannot really distinguish the kind of beneficiaries you have in front of you. So sometimes, they just don't finance the whole project."[42]

The ways in which some Syrian refugees referred to what I would define as the humanitarian project of depoliticization reminded me of Baruch Kimmerling's "politicide," namely, the elimination of (Palestinian) political will (2002). Humanitarian neutrality was often supported by residents and organizations that feared for Lebanon's relative stability (Carpi 2019). Thus, humanitarian action was perceived by refugees as an ineffective alternative to military intervention in Syria, large-scale advocacy, and political pressure on the Syrian regime. Moreover, the gloomy past of Syrian migrant workers in Lebanon and their discrimination and exploitation within Lebanese society (Chalcraft 2006, 2009) merged Akkar's domestic politics with refugee politics. In a nutshell, aid does not merely alleviate suffering and hardship—it also generates human expectations. Most of the expectations I came across, similar to Gabiam (2016), were not only about unconditional relief provision but also, more importantly, about political action to eradicate root problems in Syria. Locals and refugees tended to view aid provision as an instrument of politicking and voiced their anguish about being in an environment where politicization was already shaping and controlling social groups. Indeed, following a dense history of local community services (see chap. 2), Lebanese society became compartmentalized and anchored in demographically homogenized urban spaces ruled by decentralized powers. In this context, humanitarianism became a normalized care policy of nation-states (Fassin 2007, 508), similarly employing strategies of inclusion and exclusion and playing a complicit role in reassessing and cementing societal cleavages.

On the one hand, Hezbollah's politics of inclusion and empowerment (Roy 2009) has increased the agentive role of political membership in the southern suburbs. In pan-politicization, the stance of the party and those aligned with it are clear-cut and provide the rationale behind postwar assistance and support. On the other hand, a vast segment of INGOs employ compassion as an etiological factor behind aid intervention and embrace political neutrality as an official discourse, as I experienced in Akkar. The practices of such INGOs have resulted in a solipsistic presence on the ground, with no unmediated connections to or demands for refugee representation, resulting in their politicide.

THE POLITICS OF VICTIMHOOD

While the Syrian refugees who fled into Lebanon understood themselves as victims of repression, destruction, and fear, several believed that humanitarian providers thought of them as passive, traumatized victims rather than politically resistant subjects. Unlikely to become active citizens, many Syrian refugees in the north of Lebanon adapted to their new social environment, as I noticed over the years, while others resisted being framed as humanitarian victims. When Halba denied refugees an allocated space to gather, the municipality also symbolically denied refugees the possibility of socializing and historicizing their memory (Zenker and Kumoll 2010; Moghnie 2021). Between 2011 and 2013, refugees in the North often voiced frustration about aid providers seeing them simply as suffering bodies with a "cumulative experience that is represented and lived as a sedimented condition" (Humphrey 2002, 114). Humanitarian work throughout the twentieth and twenty-first centuries has not aimed to dismantle such a sedimented condition. As an INGO practitioner commented when I made him aware of the refugees' frustration vis-à-vis humanitarian neutrality policies: "I'm here just to let them survive, as it should be."[43] Humanitarian work was seen by many practitioners as a call for compassion, not for political action. Thus, it is often deployed to "depoliticize historical processes and portray people as passive and pathetic individual victims, rather than as members of a collective with its political claims" (Weizman 2011, 113). Refugees expressed frustration with being provided with survival relief while the international community did not act to uproot the conflict's causes in Syria and, hypocritically, tried to hamper resettlement procedures outside of the region.

Much to the dismay of the neutrality hardliners among humanitarian actors, Akkar, by becoming a shelter for Syrians, became a sociopolitical and linguistic laboratory for local claims, using humanitarianism as international leverage to gain rights to basic infrastructure. Ghassan, a Lebanese in Halba, put it in a few meaningful words: "We've long fought for our rights as worse-off citizens and hard laborers in Lebanon, but after the arrival of Syrian refugees, I've noticed my neighbors are even more conscious of what they need and way more willing to speak up to get it. We never managed to draw international attention to our everyday hardships before."[44] If the politics of humanitarianism cedes ground to the politics of the displaced (Weizman 2011, 61), the latter, in turn, paves the way for local claims.

My friend Amal started performing like an apolitical subject, encouraged by an environment that valued refugees' disengagement from politics. When I first met her in late 2011, she made strong political comments in the presence of locals. By 2013, Amal no longer wanted to broach political discussions. She had previously spoken out against the regime and supported the Free Syrian Army (FSA), which her husband fought for until he lost a hand. A few months later, when we visited her Lebanese landlady, Amal limited herself to stating that "the regime was difficult" (sa'b), and she hid the fact that her husband had previously fought for the FSA.[45]

Amal's husband bought an old TV from a Lebanese family to remain connected to the events in Syria and maintain his "symbolic capital" as a victim (Bourdieu 1986); he also wanted to be aware of the situation so he could discuss it in what Slyomovics calls the "power to narrate" (2009, 277). Notably, ownership of a TV used to make a difference in the everyday life of refugees, maintaining a strong link with the events in Syria. Powerful in this regard are Walid's words: "I don't feel like a human being either. I eat. I drink. I sleep. What life is it? I cannot even afford a TV to know what is going on in my hometown."[46] Attempting to regain political capital, refugees mentioned several times in conversation the categorical refusal of aid as the ultimate way to eradicate the causes of outraged violence. Refusal of aid would symbolize autoreconstruction, self-determination, and the rehabilitation of their political life, redeeming themselves from mere survival, which, instead, constituted the teleology of a large part of the humanitarian apparatus. In this framework, aid was interpreted as encouraging passivity and inviting refugees to embrace a politics of victimhood. Yet, for many, aid remained a main source of livelihood they could not give up.

In the context of resilience against promoted neutrality, refugees from Syria defined themselves as survivors of historical inequalities and injustice while expressing frustration—and, at times, even anger—toward aid providers who dealt with them as people coming out of a war where nothing could be understood, and no stance could be taken. The deeper confessional division of the country replaced what life in Syria was like before the large-scale conflict. Hozeifa contended:

> They think I need to heal my mind as a Syrian that lived this war because my country is divided by nature. I didn't use to hate anyone before all of this. I'm from a Sunni family living in Afamia, and we regularly used to have lunch with an Alawite family based in 'Ayn al-Krom, a village a few kilometers away from ours. Since the war started, the regime placed its tanks in these villages to fire rockets at the Sunnis. Since then, my family and our friends from 'Ayn al-Krom have not been able to look into each other's eyes. Here, they treat me as a sectarian person who cannot mingle with Alawites.[47]

During the latest stage of my fieldwork, some of my Syrian interlocutors turned into "complex political victims" (Bouris 2007, 99), mirroring the victimization strategies of aid providers to guarantee their access to international assistance. Initially, many had refused to be seen as refugees (laji'un) and victims (dahaiya), terms with a passive and depoliticizing connotation. They often self-identified as displaced (nazihun), suggesting they would soon return to Syria, or revolutionaries (thuwar), which, like the term "survivor," refers to political agency (Feldman 2004, 179) and the historical nature of their recent forced migration. Likewise, the terms "revolution" (thawra) and "oppression" (zolm and qama') were used infrequently by Amal in the presence of her neighbors, her Lebanese landlady, and even other refugees, replaced by the more generic *ahdath* or "events"—also employed in Lebanon to refer to the civil war—preventing the listener from identifying a specific political stance.

SIDE EFFECTS: THE MORALIZATION OF LOCAL AUTHORITIES

Access to local resources in Akkar is normally granted by *makhatir* and other local power holders, for example, a government representative—*mandub*—or a commissioner in charge of managing local affairs—*mas'ul* (responsible).[48] Since resourceful INGOs generally have a more ambitious outreach than local aid providers, during 2012 and 2013, it was common practice for local *makhatir* to provide a list of beneficiaries to INGOs and UN agencies. People included or excluded from aid provision believed that such intermediaries strengthened the network of connections between local authorities. In this context, INGOs pointed out their need to comply with local customs and regulations to deliver safe and quick aid to the needy. The role of the intermediary *mukhtar* often became an entry point for INGOs and, as some international humanitarian practitioners highlighted, was sometimes made redundant, since outreach often went beyond the beneficiary groups connected to the local gatekeepers.

In my experience with Syrian refugees, locals, and aid providers, those who ruled Akkar became moralized by virtue of their collaboration with international humanitarian organizations. In other words, this cooperation humanized local power holders who, sometimes, were unpopular among local villagers. Local inhabitants often questioned the political legitimacy of power holders, who found moral ground via an internationally recognized humanitarian role. Entrenched local clientelism and cronyism were realities from which some of the villagers and Syrian refugees wanted to liberate themselves. As a Syrian man in Bebnin contended,[49] "foreign aid providers wink at our longstanding local leaders who are interested in monitoring and monopolizing the aid distribution process. What's the result? Beneficiaries are still selected according to corrupt criteria." A UNICEF practitioner I interviewed in Qobaiyat (Akkar) expressed a similar idea: "The local authority provided me with a list of families entitled to get financial support for schooling material. After the distribution, many needy people came to me complaining that they hadn't even heard about this help."[50]

Some INGOs viewed cooperation with local leaders—and the tendency of foreign aid actors to bypass cooperation with the Lebanese state—as an inescapable need, reminding me that their goal was not to change Akkar's society or dismantle enduring pseudotribal social structures. In this sense, local hurdles were depicted as a structural sin (Bhaskar 2000) inherent in targeted locations. They were utilized to justify relationships with local power holders while giving up the ethics of consequentialism (Anderson 1999), which typically shifts humanitarian action from duties to consequences. For example, a local humanitarian practitioner working for an INGO based in Halba affirmed: "At the end of the day, what can we as humanitarians be criticized for? We haven't made Lebanese history, and we cannot just patch up the fragments of a part of society that has not yet modernized itself."[51] These words are significant: the humanitarian world sees no alternative to feeding into internal power cleavages while at times advocating for their elimination (Belloni 2005). Aid, in this framework, becomes a further resource within the local network of political nepotism.

This attitude, widely identifiable in the humanitarian realms I encountered during fieldwork, fed the mainstream humanitarian belief that in the so-called Global South, the land of interventions, INGOs and UN agencies bring political neutrality and modernization. In this sense, I developed the idea that some people perceived humanitarianism as a modern alternative to a corrupt state. Nonetheless, after the arrival of several humanitarian agencies, Akkaris and refugees did not deal only with the internationalization of fragmented local powers—who became gatekeepers, interlocutors, or intermediaries of international humanitarianism. To a smaller extent, they also dealt with the "domestication of external actors" (Bruszt and Holzhacker 2009, 115), who acquired new roles in the internal social fabric despite their frequent lack of knowledge of the local cultures, history, and language.

I felt the bewilderment of Lebanese villagers at the multimanagement of the region. On the one hand, some locals said they aspired to administrative modernization in contexts marginalized by the Lebanese state, affirming that they expected modernization as a reward for offering their territories to foreign humanitarian actors. A Lebanese resident of Qobaiyat contended: "This place became so crowded after the Syrians arrived. But we have to admit that we now have more hours of electricity per day and more products on the market. I expect the West to improve and modernize this place since it's 'using' it." On the other hand, these humanitarian actors largely relied on preexisting feudal structures, as they had to comply with local regulations to access people in need.[52]

A Syrian refugee from Homs who moved to Wadi Khaled affirmed: "I don't trust these new organizations that come here saying they will make things better. I argued with the *mukhtar* face-to-face as I was not provided with enough: I have five kids to feed! He used to listen to my requests up to a few months ago . . . but now he feels empowered and blessed by the West because aid providers come with no knowledge, and they need his help. I know they will all do business capitalizing on Syrian suffering."[53]

For their part, UN and INGO practitioners often expressed annoyance at having to comply with the rules of the local *makhatir* or of anyone responsible (*mas'ul*) for distributing services and resources. However, compliance with local rulers who have full decisional power is required for all providers, not just foreigners.[54] In this respect, some INGO practitioners in Akkar supported the centralization of power, stressing that administrative decentralization was confusing and often the reason for humanitarian failure in Lebanon. Local *makhatir* were not seen as an emanation of central power but rather as a sign of malfunctioning administrative fragmentation. An INGO practitioner complained that her organization needed to wait for the *mukhtar*'s approval even to address a small request, and she was aware that this happens in several villages. She put these thoughts in the following incisive account: "The high turnover of staff in my organization doesn't facilitate our independence from local power holders, as many would expect. I asked them what kind of projects they rolled out in the past and what was the biggest loss in the July War. No answer. They have no clue about the past. We need to centralize our humanitarian operations to counter such a tendency."[55]

The moralization of local authorities does not imply an intentional process started by international aid providers who, to some extent, instrumentalized local leaders, considering that local leaders also found ways to capitalize on the international humanitarian presence; nor do I refer to how locals started to see their local leaders. The moralization of local authorities instead involved the de facto external legitimization of local power holders throughout the Akkar region, becoming a complementary arm of transnational humanitarian governance (Duffield 2014) loaded with moral capital.

DIFFERENT SHADES OF NEUTRALITY

As emerged, the different forms of humanitarian assistance in northern Lebanon are not characterized by apolitical-political binaries, where international intervention is vested with universal humanitarian expertise while vernacular acts of assistance are loaded with political contention and religious bias. The apolitical, Dunantist approach to humanitarianism, widespread in the global North, maintains that actors must conceal their political aims and intentions and present themselves with no contextual interests (De Chaine 2002, 363). However, these traditional humanitarian principles of impartiality and neutrality are based on international customary laws rather than domestic legal systems (Blondel 1991). It has often been assumed that it is impossible for religious and/or local aid providers to uphold the humanitarian principles of impartiality and neutrality, responding to people's needs and not taking sides in conflicts so that decisions can be made independently (Mačák 2015, 161). Rather than questioning whether it is empirically possible to maintain neutrality and impartiality in aid provision driven by human-made crisis, I think of neutrality as a rhetorical device and attempt made by NGOs to enhance the *perception* of neutrality (Cutts 1998, 7). In this vein, what can neutrality achieve at a microsocietal level in aid provider-recipient relationships? With Akkar being populated by disparate aid providers, especially during the first half of the 2010s, I learned how different humanitarian models are based on nuanced understandings and practices of neutrality. Taking the freedom of not engaging with the related debates in the International Relations, the peculiarity of what I call the "political realism" embraced by Gulf-funded NGOs in Lebanon unravels different shades of neutrality, far from being a mere vessel of western humanitarianism.

In this context, it becomes particularly relevant to look at the policies of secular (local and international) NGOs, specifically the Amel Association, the UNHCR, the NRC, and the DRC, as well as the policies of Gulf-funded NGOs overtly inspired by Islamic values without being officially registered as FBOs—for example, the Kuwaiti Association, the Qatari Initiative, and the Saudi Taiba, as they were commonly named by local inhabitants. During my fieldwork, all of these NGOs were predominantly providing in-kind assistance, such as food, shelter, medical assistance, and education in North Lebanon. Although Gulf countries pursued a diversified politics of aid in the region, in my research, they can still be discussed under a single category in relation to their neutrality discourse and practices. The principle of neutrality not only played a different role across various implementation models of humanitarian action, but each stakeholder also conceived of it differently. Departing from Darling's definition of depoliticization (2014, 74)—a set of tendencies and alliances that produce and maintain particular perceptual orientations—apolitical Dunantist humanitarianism in the northern Lebanese context sought depoliticization as an actual condition for beneficiaries, which, from the perspective of INGO practitioners, better guaranteed people's survival and their recovery after war and displacement.

In contrast, Gulf NGOs adopted neutrality to produce a specific process of politicization by means considered internationally accountable. Where INGO neutrality rhetoric was assumed to secure access to local beneficiaries by gaining the trust of local authorities and building self-legitimacy, there was a common belief that Gulf NGOs used neutrality to cloak political competition with a moral aura. Scholars have discussed how NGOs inspired by Islamic and other religious values were often believed to have an inherently problematic relationship with neutrality (Ferris 2011, 618). My aim here is not to delegitimize types of humanitarian action by ascribing them to political motivations. Instead, I am concerned that these diverse humanitarian discourses of neutrality have not yet resulted in a common ground of communication and deeper mutual knowledge between local, international, secular, religious NGOs, and those that do not fully identify with any of these broad descriptors.

When viewing Lebanon as a chessboard where identity politics defines geographic and demographic spaces, specific factors bias the conditionality of aid provision and the implementation of neutrality and impartiality agendas. These factors include providers' geographical location, the political origin of funding sources, the channeling and allocation of funding, and the political orientation of humanitarian staff. Local and international NGOs throughout Lebanon adopt diverse strategies to uphold standards of neutrality while resorting to different understandings and configurations. Despite the ideological variety of NGOs' manifestos, most of the INGOs whose representatives I interviewed in Akkar sought to uphold neutrality standards by refusing to address beneficiaries somehow involved with the political parties at war; they were in search of the "ideal refugee" (Fiddian-Qasmiyeh 2014) who would epitomize the expectations of donors and aid providers. Defined as "prophetic humanitarianism" (Duffield 2014, 76–82), the neutrality ideology underpins emergency-driven action and the alleviation of human suffering, while not altering the status quo.

Some larger local NGOs have branches in different political spaces. For example, the Amel Association used to have a branch in 'Arsal (Beqaa Valley), where one of the informal bases of the FSA was said to be located; it also has a large branch in Haret Hreik, which, as discussed, is considered Hezbollah's stronghold. During interviews,[56] Amel representatives often referred to such a political diversity in their territories of intervention to promote their accomplished strategies of political neutrality.

Financial independence constitutes one of the main avenues for obtaining operational neutrality. An NGO worker from the Qatari Initiative operating in Wadi Khaled argued that "unlike other NGOs, Qatar does not need to get money from anyone else. This allows the government and our NGO to make their own choices."[57] In summary, neutrality can be defined as an enhanced moral status gained by being funded by either NGOs or Islamic charities rather than foreign governments, which are too openly political. The Lebanese leader of a Tripoli-based Kuwaiti Association highlighted its financial independence from Kuwaiti politics, "as funding comes from NGOs that are located in Kuwait City rather than the Kuwaiti government."[58] In this respect, some Western organizations adopted a similar behavioral politics, refusing to finance projects where certain political actors were involved. For instance, the NRC confirmed it did not accept funds from the United States because of political sensitivity, whereas it did accept funds from other foreign governments, in particular the

European Community Humanitarian Office (ECHO), which works for aid and civil protection. ECHO is believed to have greater financial independence as it does not depend on UN funding.[59]

INGOs in Akkar pursued operational neutrality by avoiding cash-in-hand policies and providing payments to homeowners to host refugees for a limited amount of time.[60] Contrary to the politics of neutrality that implied cash restrictions for beneficiaries, a politics that also included some Gulf donors, the Saudi Taiba, previously located in Halba, overtly embraced political and pragmatic realism by giving cash directly to refugees.[61] Cash-in-hand was considered a quick, albeit temporary, path to self-reliance and has only recently been recognized as a dignity tool worldwide (Lehmann and Masterson 2014; Harvey and Bailey 2015, 2). Cash was adopted in the first instance by the Saudi NGO in Akkar but is now increasingly promoted within the broader framework of international aid providers in Lebanon, such as Save the Children, a member of the Cash Learning Partnership (CaLP), and the Lebanon Cash Consortium (LCC).

A further avenue pursued by international aid providers to obtain operational neutrality was hiring staff who supposedly held different political opinions and orientations. Indeed, the majority of INGO representatives I spoke to stated that a small number of their staff supported the Syrian regime. However, they specified that all NGO practitioners were expected and even requested not to share their political opinions in the workplace in compliance with the deontological code of apolitical humanitarianism. Against this backdrop, Syrian aid beneficiaries, and especially refugees excluded from humanitarian services, viewed neutrality not as a key behavioral value but as hypocritical.[62] Despite NGOs embodying multifarious approaches to neutrality, refugees developed their own understanding of humanitarian politics, from which their political views and reactions emerged. For instance, most refugees from a political opposition background viewed NGO neutrality discourses as a tacit strategy to uphold the legitimacy of the Asad regime, not remotely intent on eradicating the source of the conflict and generalized violence. This idea resonated in the words of Walid, a Syrian refugee from Aleppo: "They [an international NGO] said their role is not taking sides when I asked for medication. I have a maimed hand, as you can see . . . I was fighting with the FSA. That's why they don't want to help me. It's because they still want Bashar [al-Asad] to be my president."[63]

Distress, increased fear, and anxiety among refugees were often the responses to such neutral "organizational culture" (Barnett 2005, 728). Ahmed, a Syrian refugee who relocated to the rural hamlet of Bellanet al-Hisa, told me: "We don't want food and shelter to survive in Lebanon; we want you to help us to stop all this."[64] These thoughts undermine the cornerstones of minimalist humanitarian neutrality (Weiss 2006), which never sides with war-stricken victims but still purports to "heal" them and, despite a more recent historical turn toward "political humanitarianism" aimed at improving societies (Duffield 2014), still predominates in the contemporary philosophy of hegemonic humanitarian aid provision.

POLITICAL REALISM

Muslim NGOs have reportedly been neutralizing language and practices in recent years, probably as a result of international pressure to adopt less overtly religious approaches to humanitarian endeavors (Wigger 2005). In the context of Syrian displacement, most INGOs still resort to operational neutrality as a way of cultivating international accountability, yet the representatives of NGOs funded by Gulf countries have openly declared that they started programs to support Syrian political opponents fleeing into Lebanon, taking a maximalist stance and showing proximity to the victims (Weiss 2006). More specifically, the Saudi NGO Taiba and the Kuwaiti Association claimed they were the first to establish systematic assistance programs for refugees (from April 2011) from Syria. The Gulf humanitarian scene presents itself as more diverse than what mainstream geopolitical accounts seem to suggest. Indeed, while the INGOs and UN agencies I knew in Akkar tended to refer to Gulf humanitarianism as an ideological and operational monolith, Qatar and Saudi Arabia are at odds with each other in regional politics, creating a layered regional aid scene. Nevertheless, both fund the Coalition of Islamic relief organizations (*I'tilaf*), which coordinates the majority of local Islamic NGOs in Lebanon (Schmelter 2019, 6). This form of humanitarianism relies on realistic ways of operating—namely, recognizing one's own role in crises and elevating political realism to a moral standard. Mobilizing public morality in official rhetoric can counter or support the political agendas of other aid actors. For example, the July War became an opportunity for foreign governments and NGOs to gain international and regional accountability by supporting the reconstruction efforts of the Hezbollah-led March 8 coalition across Lebanon, a coalition that has long supported the Syrian regime's presence in Lebanon (1976–2005) and the Syrian regime during the conflict (2011–present). Similarly, aid providers known to be close to the March 14 coalition, led by Saad Hariri's *al-Mustaqbal* Party, are now believed to be the political entity most heavily involved in the provision of aid to Syrians because of their political aim to topple Asad's regime. According to March 14-oriented NGOs, the realism of assistance provision as a political act in situations of conflict and displacement is not only unavoidable but also morally desirable.

In this hybrid scenario that is neither apolitical nor political *strictu sensu*, aid is adopted as a quick strategy to show or discard the impartial humaneness of political parties, confessional groups, or NGOs. Providers who embrace political realism, like the Gulf NGOs, do not generally disguise their political agenda, but in interviews, local staff hastened to point out that they do not merely intervene in line with political interests. Gulf-promoted humanitarianism drops neutrality as a moral standard and embraces political morals, revealing different shades of neutrality. International humanitarian agencies in the Global North, such as the UNHCR, DRC, and Save the Children, generally aspire to global accountability through impartiality and neutrality, while Gulf-funded NGOs overtly share their political aims and ensure that their beneficiaries and other aid actors do not perceive their practices as neutral. However, Gulf-funded NGOs parade their intentions behind assistance as unconditionally humane. For example, while the Qatari Initiative states that its work in the Syrian crisis is comparable to the assistance it provided in the July War, it still acknowledges that its aid allocation normally reflects Qatar's foreign policy: "Hezbollah's victory in the July War and an eventually successful regime change in Syria represent two opposing regional scenarios. Qatar intervened in both cases. Qatar implements its humanitarian practices regardless of political circumstances. However, it's normal that aid provision seeks to further the foreign policy of any state, and, at the time of the July War, Qatar needed to play a greater role in regional politics to establish itself. At present, in the capacity of an established political actor, it would rather pursue goals that better suit its own domestic politics."[65]

In summary, advocates of political realism (as I define them) in Akkar's villages consider humanitarianism as a distinct and valuable form of politics, according to which the very ideology of political neutrality is unethical and impeachable. Although they can still be defined as "solidarists" (Weiss 2006), aligning with political victims and implementing political projects through assistance to refugees, Gulf-funded NGOs cannot be classified simplistically under the banner of political, "new humanitarianism" (Prendergast 1996, 42). In fact, these NGOs resort to more complex neutrality discourses; recipients should not perceive that they are dealing with a neutral actor for such humanitarian practices to be deemed successful, but these NGOs still resort to the rhetoric of impartial humaneness and neutrality to moralize their politics and negotiate their place within an arena of international aid culturally dominated by Western actors. Gulf-funded NGOs reject operational neutrality in managing their relationships with beneficiaries while operating outside of UN coordination and of other international partnerships.

It is evident that moral demands increasingly populate international and domestic political space. While the beneficiary is expected to represent the ideal polity (see Harrell-Bond 1999; Fiddian-Qasmiyeh 2014) of the provider in all cases, they become an *a priori* deserving member of humanity in apolitical Dunantist humanitarianism. In political realism, the beneficiary is recognized as human only when adhering to specific political partisanship. As a matter of fact, however, refugees were never asked about their political stance in order to access such services, as the identity politics they were vectors of mattered most. On the one hand, Dunantist humanitarianism deprives victims of any political dimension and expects them to be apolitical. On the other hand, political realism expects victims to have the social and political motivations that best correspond to their primary purpose. Both tendencies, while showing an apparent polarization of humanitarian action, try to preserve the sociopolitical order that suits the desire to survive as successful humanitarian actors.

Humanitarian and political actors in Akkar adopt diverse strategies to bring humanity into politics and politics into humanitarianism. While apolitical humanitarianism has traditionally been opposed to political humanitarianism, the Lebanese scenario of humanitarian provision appears more hybrid and muddled than this binary model. Gulf-funded NGOs adopt hybrid strategies of neutrality to seemingly comply with Western standards of modern humanitarianism while simultaneously embracing political realism. In terms of neutrality, the idea of "being human" is used as a method of accountability by all humanitarian actors, while secular—and mostly Western—actors, disconcertingly, define the very paradigms of humanitarian neutrality.

While contemporary humanitarian accounts show that apolitical humanitarianism is the norm for a large segment of INGOs in Lebanon and worldwide, Gulf-funded NGOs pursue political advocacy through aid provision. The latter explicitly aims to support the cause embodied by displaced Syrians while seeking to rhetorically humanize their political agendas.

Reflecting such diversities into the domestic scenario, NGOs with proximity to the two major political orientations in Lebanon—identified above as the March 8 and March 14 coalitions, in place since 2005—increasingly promote their moral intentions of serving humanity through aid provision. These predominant attempts to humanize politics enable humanitarian and political actors to enhance their accountability in international and regional politics. Nevertheless, such attempts remain ineffective before the widespread domestic disaffection of political and religious institutions in Lebanon at a grassroots level. If neutrality is universally proven to endure as a strong rhetoric with which to campaign for humaneness and morality, it has so far failed as a device in crisis management, as it is unable to enhance coordination, accountability, and effectiveness on the ground. Furthermore, it has brought no change to political failures that underlie Lebanon's protracted emergencies.

Since the start of forced displacement from Syria in 2011, both the Dunantist and overtly partisan NGOization of Akkar have contributed to the political polarization of the country through which the Syrian crisis has been understood. On the one hand, the neutral language developed by international actors, while supposedly introducing good governance without the aim of changing societies, ends up preserving mistrusted political elites in Lebanon. On the other hand, partisan language inherently fosters and supports the cause of beneficiary groups that, in turn, must reflect the aid provider's political expectations and desires by preserving their presumed identity habitus (e.g., Syrian refugees with a Sunni Muslim background from opposition majority areas become the perfect recipient of Gulf aid). Some future research focusing on Gulf-funded NGOs in Akkar might unravel further shades and understandings of neutrality, especially at a time when some Gulf states revised their relationships with the key conflict actors in Syria.

Operational neutrality is often believed to positively contribute to peace negotiations or the avoidance of conflict but, as my time in Akkar demonstrated, it has exacerbated people's mistrust of most providers. Thus far, neutrality seems to be failing as a diplomatic instrument intended to expedite peace through aid provision in Lebanon's crises. Instead, it is employed in moral campaigns as another political token of conflict and competition between international, regional, and local actors. The widespread politicization of aid and humanization of politics I have outlined here depicts Lebanon's political scene as an arena of multiple power circuits that enact political competition and competition over their own ethical reputation.

NOTES

1. The treaty was stipulated between the anti-Syrian government group led by Michel Kilo and the Syrian Muslim Brotherhood.

2. Al-'Abdeh, January 12, 2013.

3. November 18, 2011.

4. Conversation with a camp dweller, Nahr al-Bared, December 3, 2011.

5. In our conversation, scholar Prof. Mona Fawaz mentioned US $100 million cash being distributed within seventy-two hours of the cessation of hostilities.

6. December 4, 2011.

7. Interview with Lebanese resident, Fourn ash-Shebbak, Beirut, February 1, 2012.

8. Conversation, ash-Shiyyah, February 15, 2013.

9. Interview with a UNICEF practitioner, Beirut, February 2, 2012, and with the technical advisor of UNPD ART-Gold, Beirut, October 25, 2011. While many practitioners complained about the impossibility of operating independently from the municipalities' consent in Dahiye, some UN staff affirmed their willingness to comply with this necessity.

10. Interview, Sin el-Fil, Beirut, November 30, 2011.

11. Interview, Haret Hreik, November 29, 2011.

12. October 6, 2012.

13. Downtown Beirut, November 24, 2011.

14. Interview with a Caritas-Liban social worker, Ashrafiyye, Beirut, October 24, 2011.

15. Interview with a project manager from Oxfam-Italia working in the area, Beirut, October 18, 2011.

16. Interview, Mreije, November 14, 2012.

17. Interview, October 28, 2011.

18. The Mosque of Saiyyda Zeinab was constructed in the style of its namesake mosque in Damascus on the street from Bi'r al-'Abed to Haret Hreik in Dahiye (from donations of the Islamic Association *Jami'at al-Baqiyat as-Salihat*). It was inaugurated in March 2012, while I was in Dahiye.

19. February 2, 2012.

20. Interview with Naziha Dakroub, manager of the Social Development Center, Office of the Ministry of Social Affairs, Ash-Shiyyah, October 30, 2011.

21. Wikileaks cable, July 21, 2006. Nayla Mouawad was the Lebanese minister of social affairs at the time of *harb tammuz*. The mentioned Fouad Seniora was prime minister of the Lebanese Republic from 2005 to 2009, before Najib Miqati's first mandate.

22. Hay al-Gharbe, Sabra, and Shatila were initially called rackets or criminal trade. The old name of these slums is specified in the *Vocabulary of the Flash Language* by James Hardy Vaux, written in 1812 (Davis 2006, 21).

23. *Tahaddi* is led by Syrian Swiss Catherine Mortada. The association is affiliated to Terre des Hommes-Liban, created in 1976 during the civil war to provide emergency assistance to injured children (Karam 2006, 63). Interview, Hay al-Gharbe, November 2, 2012.

24. In the wealthy eastern suburbs of Beirut, it is common for Dom children and residents of Hay al-Gharbe to speak Arabic and tell people they are from Aleppo (Syria) to raise compassion and collect alms. Dom children are likely to be asked to beg for money in the street (Das and Davidson 2011, 276–77).

25. *Nawar* is a derogatory term for Doms, indicating selfishness and dirtiness. Many Dom parents do not teach the Domari language to their children to protect them from prejudice (Das and Davidson 2011, 286).

26. Squatting is the result of the eviction of Lebanese Muslims and Palestinians from eastern Dahiye, predominantly by Harakat Amal, ex-president of the Lebanese Republic Amin Gemayel (1982–88), and the continuous struggle between Hezbollah and Amal in the last phase of the Lebanese Civil War.

27. Twenty percent of local men are said to be in jail. The average age of Hay al-Gharbe's population is young (Das and Davidson 2011, 271).

28. Interview, January 30, 2013.

29. For example, in May 2011, clashes took place between the Internal Security Forces (ISF) and inhabitants. The ISF demolished recently built shops and suffocated people with tear gas and gunfire. A bulldozer destroyed personal belongings (Das and Davidson 2011, 274).

30. December 12, 2012. *Beit Atfal as-Sumoud* (The House of the Children of the Resistance, also called the National Institute of Social Care and Vocational Training) was founded after the Tel az-Za'tar's bombing carried out by Syrian President Hafez al-Asad in August 1976. It was opened to provide assistance and accommodation for orphaned children.

31. In Hay al-Gharbe, I met five families whose Lebanese breadwinner was dead, sick, old, or could not easily find a job. Palestinian wives were able to empower their family or, at least, guarantee their survival. In fact, being Palestinian was a token of entitlement to the services of *Beit Atfal as-Sumud* such as education, cultural activities, and health.

32. January 29, 2013.

33. Hay al-Gharbe, January 29, 2013.

34. Hay al-Gharbe, February 15, 2013.

35. Hay al-Gharbe, February 15, 2013.

36. Mohammed fought in the Beqaa Valley and the South until 1991.

37. The PLO was forced out of Lebanon in 1982. Palestinians in Lebanon are not allowed to create associations (Ministerial Decree No. 17561 of July 10, 1962); they must include Lebanese staff and be registered in the country. After the PLO's withdrawal, services for Palestinians were only replaced by the Palestinian Red Crescent Society and the UNRWA.

38. Interview, 'Adlieh, Beirut, September 27, 2012.

39. This project aimed to address the underlife and urban violence in the neglected areas of the Lebanese capital and elsewhere (e.g., the lack of street lighting system encouraging nighttime violence).

40. January 2, 2013.

41. November and December 2012.

42. January 20, 2013.

43. Qobaiyat, February 4, 2013.

44. Halba, February 5, 2013.

45. January 2013.

46. Al-Bahsa, January 28, 2013.

47. Al-'Abdeh, January 29, 2013.

48. Local state officials represent the de facto organization of power, but they are also powerbrokers who intercede between villagers and international and local organizations.

49. September 23, 2012.

50. February 7, 2013.

51. Interview, September 26, 2012.

52. January 13, 2013. She used the terms civilize (*hadara*) and modernize (*tahdith*).

53. January 12, 2013.

54. This happens throughout Lebanon. For instance, the Imam Sadr Foundation, as a local FBO, stated that it needed to negotiate its presence and the suitability of its projects with local authorities in the areas of intervention (interview with Mohammed Bassam, Tyre, October 8, 2012).

55. January 25, 2013.

56. January 3, 2013.

57. Tripoli, December 18, 2020.

58. Tripoli, January 14, 2020.

59. NRC also receives funds from the UNHCR, which is, in turn, financed by Australia, Japan, the Gulf, the United States, and the European Union. Interview with the program support manager in Lebanon, Beirut, November 21, 2012.

60. Interview with representatives from the DRC and UNHCR, Qobaiyat, Akkar, February 2013.

61. December 14, 2012.

62. Interviews with Syrian refugee men living in Bellanet al-Hisa and Halba, March 2013.

63. Al-'Abdeh, December 24, 2012.

64. January 8, 2013.

65. Tripoli, December 18, 2012.

4 / Ethnocracies of Care and Order

Scholars have shown how modern humanitarianism, a phenomenon that intertwines historically with late colonialism (Barnett 2005), marks and constructs racial and national identities and contributes to group making in societies targeted by humanitarian projects. The tendency of humanitarian logistics to meet needs and provide services on the basis of nationality is common in Lebanon. Throughout the years, I have observed how Lebanese, Palestinian, Iraqi, and Syrian displaced people have responded to nationality-based logistic. To explain how the ethnicization of needs and services plays out in the humanitarian experience, I make a sociological effort to think of the refugees I met beyond their individual stories. Interrupting individualized narratives helps to capture how social groups understand themselves within Lebanon and their transnational relations, how groups relate to each other, and what groups' collective experience with assistance is. A focus on groups rather than individuals does not remove people's singular experiences but instead sheds light on the societal translation of such experiences into recurrent group-oriented patterns. New waves of conflict-caused forced migrations can nuance, radically change, or merge into such social responses to crisis.

Over the past few years, I have examined the societal consequences of established ethnocratic systems of aid provision to vulnerable local citizens residing in Dahiye, along with older Sudanese and Iraqi refugee groups that inhabit the suburbs and Syrian refugees who relocated to Akkar after 2011. Humanitarian agencies approach demographically mixed areas on the basis of national differences, using and replicating the idea of ethnicities as a political marker of national belonging and identity (Smith 1981). In this case, identity boundaries are marked between the Lebanese, Syrians, Palestinians, Sudanese, and Iraqis.

Ethnopolitics have been employed previously to explain the political sectarian scenario in Lebanon (Hanf 1993; Khalaf 2002; Salamey and Tabar 2008); humanitarian agencies approach different demographic and religious groups as divided ethnicities due to their particular political histories in a multiplicity of cultural, confessional, and linguistic elements. While I distance myself from adhering to nationality-driven conceptions of ethnicity, I find the term "ethnicization," in its causative form, particularly reflective of how humanitarianism operates practically on the ground. This approach includes tackling (predominantly Arab) neighboring demographic groups as though they are different ethnicities innately at odds with each other and in need of reconciliation, disregarding continuities and dissimilarities across social classes and political backgrounds. Local geographies are also understood through nationality criteria because some refugee groups tend to live in the same areas, especially the Iraqis and Sudanese. Syrian urban refugees, however, establish a different demography in cities due to their larger numbers. Unlike Haqqi Bahram's analysis of Syrian Kurdish refugees' politics of belonging and "intra-ethnic" displacement (2020), I encountered very few non-Arab refugees and internally displaced people in my research sites. As a result, I have been motivated to reflect on whether humanitarian practices create and manage "ethnic communities" to build social cohesion and stability within the receiving society and, most importantly for global actors, to preserve a convenient social and political order. By using ethnicization as a lens, I examine how Iraqi and Sudanese refugees understood themselves vis-à-vis relief management during the July War and in response to the local and international political climate. Despite their experiences all being particular, the overall pattern of ethnicization defines, to me, how the Iraqis and Sudanese became even more distinct social groups in Lebanon after the July War; they were separated from local society but also from one another. I observed a similar process among Syrian refugees and Lebanese residents in Akkar. In the aftermath of the July War, as well as after the arrival of refugees from Syria, most humanitarian organizations—whose services ranged from making shelters to organizing play activities for the displaced—addressed social groups separately, believing that humanitarian programming should play it safe and reflect the local relational histories between groups to avoid generating friction. However, after the first draft of the Lebanon Crisis Response Plan (LCRP) in late 2014 (Boustani et al. 2016), humanitarian programming began addressing all social groups together by promoting what, in this context, where ethnicity becomes a thing, may be named interethnic projects—to reflect how humanitarian logistics work in making and unmaking identity. Especially since 2014, humanitarianism has embraced a new ethnicization of care, presuming that tensions and violence predominantly occur inside nationally hybrid regions and, in doing so, cementing the idea that peace as a regime becomes possible only in compliance with an ethnicized order. A few years after the arrival of refugees from Syria into Lebanon, humanitarian programming was redesigned for inclusion and for social groups to mingle with each other as though there was no previous intergroup relational history. The partial dismantling of the ethnicization of needs and services has practically been replaced by a new ethnocracy of care—so to speak, a system still based on ethnicized belonging—that boasts nationally inclusive programs.

Importantly, the interrelation between humanitarianism and ethnocracy in Lebanon is not an exceptional case. Key international humanitarian actors historically supported national/ethnic/religious homogeneities. One of many examples is the 1979 Orderly Departure Program (ODP) established by UNHCR during the Cold War. The Socialist Republic of Vietnam, with the shared interest of the United States, wanted to expel the Sino-Vietnamese to not alter their ethnic make-up. Similarly, the neighboring countries enforced a ban on boat people when the latter had mostly become of Chinese and Hoa origins in the late 1970s (Kumin 2008, 106).

ETHNICIZATION OF NEEDS AND SERVICES

Ethnocracy—from ancient Greek, the power of an ethnic group (broadly meant, as abovementioned) over others, or a regime primarily based on ethnic identity—is not a phenomenon that only applies to Lebanon. It is rather identifiable in places—like urban Israel—where "ethnoterritorial logics" (Yiftachel and Yacobi 2003) dominate life and space, essentializing group identities. The normative definition of forced migration sees refugee groups, such as the Sudanese and Iraqis living in Dahiye, as a "political form of migration" (Hein 1993, 43–44). In contrast, migrant workers from African and Southeast Asian countries who live in the southern suburbs for cheaper accommodation are aprioristically seen as an economic form of migration. During my years of research in Lebanon, I realized how peculiar but similar these forms of migration are, as they are both forcible and politically grounded. Focusing on official forms of conflict-produced humanitarianism, I engaged exclusively with those who had fled political crises in their home countries, who risked persecution, and who had not primarily migrated in exclusive search of labor. Conflict-produced refugees live at the mercy of how conflicts evolve in their country of origin; their presence in receiving societies has been experienced as a threat to domestic stability, a trigger of tension and international insecurity within the regional neighborhood, especially since the Cold War (Loescher 1992). Nonetheless, the social and political management of migration does not take into account the forced nature of migrations deemed to be officially unforced.

Refugee groups are managed, controlled, and assisted in different spaces further compartmentalized by welfare and humanitarian regimes. The logistics of how different refugee groups are assisted end up strengthening an ethnic-oriented modality of aid provision (with "ethnic" misconceived as innately conflictual). Of the numerous programs I encountered in Dahiye, I chose to focus on the Amel Association in Haret Hreik, which provides training courses specifically for Iraqi and Sudanese refugees, and on the NRC, which works on projects with Palestinian refugees in camps. Their length of time working with protracted refugees in Lebanon means their humanitarian aid provision has become normal and, therefore, must cater to people's basic needs or to be combined with local welfare provision. At first glance, the replacement of a normal welfare regime with humanitarian care might not seem troublesome, especially in contexts where the same welfare provision is neither effective nor accountable. However, with the outbreak of new emergencies, the politics of crisis-making reproduces itself through the amnesia of the past and the tyranny of the present: resources are inevitably taken from welfare and diverted to urgent action implying relief provision (Calhoun 2008).

IRAQI REFUGEES AND THE JULY WAR

Iraqis have migrated to Lebanon from the 1990s, when large segments of the Shi'a population fled Saddam Hussein's persecution. Additionally, Christian Iraqis believed they would be more protected in an Arab state founded on a French Christian basis (Sassoon 2009, 92). Before 2003, there were only ten thousand Iraqis in Lebanon (Human Rights Watch 2007, 12). According to the Lebanese Ministry of Internal Affairs, until a decade ago, there were around one hundred thousand Iraqi refugees; other organizations, such as the International Organization for Migration (IOM), suggest there were around fifty thousand (Schininà 2008).[1] Until today, there are still no official statistics. Many refugees who entered Lebanon with a one-month tourist visa or were smuggled through Syria were not registered with the UNHCR. With unemployment, lack of safety, threats to life, unaffordable education and healthcare, illegal work, and exploitation, Iraqi refugees end up living in self-seclusion or detention. They are often invisible in the public space and do not benefit from any protection regime.[2] Most of the Iraqi refugees I met highlighted that community belonging did not matter in everyday life in Iraq before 2003; however, in Lebanon, they resettled in areas that reflected their religious affiliation. Once resettled, although they did not abandon hopes of moving to a different country, they found access to local resources and welfare by residing among ingroup members and in Christian- or Shiite-majority areas of Beirut's southern suburbs.

Iraqi refugees arrived in Lebanon in great numbers right before the July War. In February 2006, the bombing of the al-'Askari Mosque in Samarra resulted in people fleeing the wave of retaliation that killed thousands of civilians in Iraq. The bombing was presumably an Al-Qaeda plot, but it was never claimed by any group. In my interviews with Iraqis, Beirut's UNHCR offices emerged as their first point of call to request refugee status, obtain a guaranteed airplane ticket to resettle in a third country, and find protection from arrest in Lebanon. It is significant that not a single UNHCR staff member—either in Beirut or in Tripoli, where I conducted my interviews with UNHCR—could provide any policy history regarding the arrival of Iraqi refugees from 2003, probably due to the high turnover of staff in UN agencies.[3] The best source of information turned out to be the locals.

In the media, the protracted predicament of Iraqi refugees was eclipsed to a large extent by the arrival of Syrian refugees. Lebanon represents an incubator where refugees, since "punctuated" forms of humanitarian assistance appear and disappear (Feldman 2018), are uncomfortable reminders of aging emergencies. During the Iraqi refugee crisis, the European Union (EU) donated €11 million for refugee aid in the region but abdicated their responsibility to assist in the resettlement of refugees.[4]

The Iraqi refugees I met at the Caritas Center in the Dahiye district of Laylaki in autumn 2011 affirmed that some NGOs had supported Lebanon's governmental repatriation policy on Iraqi refugees, while pretending that people were repatriating voluntarily. Three refugees recounted that many of their conationals hoped to reenter Lebanon illegally. At that time, both the International Organization of Migration (IOM) and the Iraqi Embassy were in charge of repatriating people, creating an alternative to prolonged arbitrary detention in Lebanon (Trad and Frangieh 2007) without addressing the causes of mass displacement.

Fear and insecurity due to marginalized and illegal conditions were predominant, particularly in the narratives of Iraqi refugee women, generally more socially isolated than men. Rajaa, Samira, and 'Alia, three refugee women from southern Iraq, mentioned their sense of isolation and how it had worsened after the July War. Samira told me: "I live in chronic fear. I experienced lots of threats because I don't have documents. The Lebanese did not even leave me alone with my despair during the July War. I've decided to no longer open the door to anyone."[5] For some of the Iraqi refugees, the July War generated mutual mistrust and friction between social groups, increasing their sense of fear and loneliness.

Zeinab, a refugee woman from Basra, told me: "I used to have a Lebanese friend, but after the war, she started caring about her own business and collecting as much stuff as she could; she doesn't want to speak to me anymore. Everyone became more suspicious here, although most of us Iraqis are Shiites like them [the Lebanese Dahiye residents affected by war]."[6]

The July War set a precedent of uncertainty in Iraqi refugees' lives in Lebanon. Threats, detention, fear of deportation, and physical violence rendered this war a further miserable episode in uncomfortable normality. Yet, Iraqi refugees resisted adversity and hardship, resorting to self-harm protests such as hunger strikes and beating their heads against a wall (Houri 2010).

The self-seclusion and sense of insecurity that Iraqi refugees are doomed to live with are, to some extent, similar to the experience of Hay al-Gharbe's dwellers. Such living conditions do not create opportunities for social groups to encounter each other and find mutual support with outgroup members. In this context, humanitarian action does not trigger the "otherization" of outgroup members but rather builds on preexisting compartmentalized spaces and reinforces boundaries. Nour, a female refugee from Baghdad, recounted that siding with one of her neighbors in a dispute resulted in her being threatened by other Lebanese residents.[7] Munira complained that Lebanese neighbors would throw their garbage on her balcony and, whenever she complained, would threaten to call General Security (al-amn al-'amm) and have her arrested.[8] Hanan, another female refugee from Baghdad who I met at Caritas, had to move from the Christian majority district of 'Ayn ar-Remmaneh to the Shiite-majority district of ash-Shiyyah because a man kept following her when she walked her children to school: "This person blackmailed me to have sex with him, as he knows I'm undocumented. I didn't want to give up my honor, and one day, Lebanese General Security came to my door and asked for documents. We had to move out, and my husband was hit by my suitor a few days later."[9]

Years after their arrival, Iraqi refugees' primary need is still material support—food, housing, and services—but NGOs now aim to make them employable through training courses in subjects such as information technology (IT), mathematics, and English. Food was provided when they first arrived, but it was years before they were eligible to access professional training to become employable. Over this timespan, their material circumstances, in most cases, have remained unchanged. Refugees must adapt to new practices and eligibility requirements to access international assistance (Feldman 2012a, 2018). This blinking presence of humanitarianism may have deleterious effects on individual and collective lives; eligibility to access assistance is employed as an "on-off switch" to introduce or end vulnerabilities and stability

(Feldman 2012a, 392). Just like processes of identification and belonging, humanitarian definitions do not involve singular events (Feldman 2012a, 392), and as such, the ethnicization of needs and services triggers new "experiences of gain and loss" (Feldman 2012a, 392).

Over a decade ago, Pupavac (2005) highlighted how humanitarian practices shape the subjectivities, expectations, and perceptions of beneficiaries rather than transforming the material conditions of people in need. She illustrated how humanitarian therapeutic practices in ex-Yugoslavia were meant to shape crisis-stricken subjects through mental care while preserving their poverty and deprivation. In the absence of material transformation, humanitarian assistance reforms people's perceptions of good and bad services, priorities, and secondary needs. In other words, adaptation emerges as a process tacitly requested from aspiring aid beneficiaries, not through responsive humanitarian practices.

Pupavac identified this tendency, which explains why aid beneficiaries' expectations of relief become political expectations (Fiddian-Qasmiyeh 2014; Gabiam 2016; Feldman 2018) and why they see humanitarian assistance as a conservative force, incapable of adapting. Mustafa, an Iraqi refugee who arrived in Lebanon in early 2006, first received a mattress and then food items every week until the July War broke out. Mustafa's neighborhood, ash-Shiyyah, was less affected by war than other Dahiye suburbs, such as Haret Hreik. Therefore, he did not receive compensation to repair the walls of his apartment. In his words: "I sheltered in the room of an association that was dealing only with Iraqis [. . .]. Some services for Iraqis stopped after the war, as the displaced people in Lebanon were in greater need than us. How is a war that leaves cracks in my walls not also *my* war? I was no longer eligible for aid after the war, but my life hasn't changed much compared to before."[10]

Mustafa was treated as a protracted refugee rather than an internally displaced, war-stricken individual. Among Iraqi refugees, aid inadequacy recurrently entails different types of failure. For instance, Khaled from Baghdad explained that refugees can only obtain aid through bribery and connections, making refugees particularly vulnerable during a war. He described aid as "locked up within a luck cycle," where individual chance determines if one will survive or not:

> Most of us are unemployed because we lack documents. Our life cannot
> evolve in any direction as long as we remain in Lebanon. As an Iraqi, I was
> told to go to Caritas or the UN during the July War, but they said they needed
> to prioritize families, as they don't have many resources to offer. It's been two
> years since I got married, but nothing has changed for me. You get the same

answer from all of them. I've been here for ages, and I'm still begging for food and rent. And what do they provide, if they ever do? Courses of English for free! How can I become employable if I can't even access food?[11]

Qais, from Baghdad, arrived in Lebanon in 2004. He expressed a sense of powerlessness and skepticism: "There's no safe hand that can bring aid to the people. Corruption soaks every single thing in the Middle East, and foreigners are out there, greedy for new emergencies. We are nothing."[12] Similarly, Munira from Basra expressed her emotional detachment from the July War, defining herself as a guest. She saw herself as a person not entitled to broach politically sensitive subjects in a country that is not hers, motivating her lack of access to the same resources as the locals. As a widow whose husband was killed in the 2003 American invasion of Iraq, she was also concerned about her lack of prospects: "In the July War, as Iraqis, we were only allowed to get aid from particular organizations. We didn't have to mix with the other displaced, and we were separated from what was allocated to them. May God punish me if I'm lying! They always need to remind us that we're only Iraqis, and as such there won't be much room for us here . . . Being optimistic or pessimistic is not possible. For Iraqis in Lebanon, the future simply does not exist."[13]

Her words seemed to annihilate any temporal perspective, caught between the impossibility of integration in Lebanon and the unfeasibility of returning to Iraq. Refugees are deprived of the right to temporality, the right to exit the purgatory of displacement and think about future plans (Dunn 2017, 213). While refugees have often been described as struggling to find a future outside of or beyond humanitarianism (Feldman 2018, 230), Munira suggested that a future is not conceivable even within humanitarianism. Longstanding refugees did not list integration among their daily priorities; their key argument was the inadequacy of service provision vis-à-vis their basic needs. Such inadequacy was associated with their predicament of not being treated humanely, even in humanitarian spaces. All of them expressed desire to leave Lebanon, and they referred to some Iraqi diaspora as privileged because, through *wasta*, they had managed to emigrate to a country in the global North. Samah, from Baghdad, affirmed that Canada would have been "the last stop" for her misery. She spoke fondly of the days of the American invasion of Iraq, imagining that Western countries were her last hope for personal protection: "In Iraq when the Americans left, the problems started again. Do you know what we lacked in Iraq at that time and what we lacked here during the July War? Protection."[14]

Iraqi refugees viewed aid as synonymous to the chronic wait they had already been doomed to since before the July War. Advancing claims beyond aid and resenting the NGOs' request to certify her aid eligibility, Munira affirmed: "Aid was not enough in the July War and should not become enough. We just want to leave Lebanon. Here, what is worse is that you need to go to the NGOs yourself and beg for anything you need. They [NGOs and foreign governments] want lots of answers and papers as evidence of your disgrace, but then they prioritize new disgraces."[15]

According to the Iraqi refugees I interviewed in the Caritas Center, aid arrived eight to ten days after the Israeli attacks began in summer 2006. Caritas was one of the main organizations taking care of Iraqis during that war. The Iraqi refugees explained that they were all warehoused in detached shelters where they shared space with other Iraqis.[16] I met Raad from Basra in the Haret Hreik Amel Center. Having lived in Dahiye since 2006, Raad talked to me about his sense of alienation from the Lebanese context, although he shared misery and aid with his Lebanese neighbors during the war:

> The July War was not *our* war. That's why we, Iraqis, obtained much less than the Lebanese Shiites. You ask me about the July War, but it's really not changed a lot for us. Luckily, at that time, I didn't have a job so at least I didn't lose it [...]. We were all sheltered in a place where there were no Lebanese, only us. The Lebanese probably had a better place to shelter. Organizations had already decided what to give us without asking: "Iraqis want this and that." But we took all of what they gave. Do you see any other option?[17]

Other Iraqis recounted to me that Caritas-Liban provided a space within the Shiyyah municipality for them to shelter. In our conversations, Iraqi refugees frequently spoke about being assigned to a type of intragroup shelter. Rather than remembering it as a moment of ingroup collectivity for Iraqis in Lebanon, they referred to it as a political strategy of detachment from the surrounding society. This memory seemed to me to actively ethnicize their predicament way beyond the suffering caused by war per se. Iraqi refugees ended up otherizing the July War as "the war of the Lebanese" even though Dahiye's Iraqi inhabitants were also hit by the Israeli Air Force; those who were employed lost their jobs and access to basic goods. Moreover, Iraqis expressed frustration at not even being the targets of the war and, as a result, becoming victims of overlapping levels of neglect: they were neither recipients of special assistance after the war nor priority refugees, but rather the subjects of aging, forgotten emergencies.

Their chronic predicament has consigned refugees to live in areas "with no future, no money, no evolution, no hope," in Raad's words. This lack of prospects combines with the moral frustration of deserving minimum humanitarian rights, if not political rights (echoing Feldman 2018). I met Rajaa, from Basra, at the Caritas Center, and she reiterated that Iraqis "deserved those services more than the displaced Lebanese [in 2006]. All NGOs pretend they're assisting us for free, but with our blood and our petrol, we already paid for all of this one thousand times."[18] Rajaa's viewpoint powerfully highlights that humanitarianism is not merely perceived by displaced people as compassion from the white humanitarian: it is received as the minimum political obligation of the international community (Gabiam 2016, 158; Feldman 2018, 142–43). Such an obligation is, however, understood by refugees as a political responsibility rather than a moral duty (see chap. 5).

By delivering services and aid to different groups while keeping provisions separate, humanitarian programs are unable to capture articulated and blended forms of social membership; they can even create social cleavage or friction. In the framework of the UNDP's 2013–2022 Lebanese Host Communities Support Program, a geography of vulnerability rather than ethnic or religious politics emerged. As seen, humanitarian practice during war shelters people from the same nationalities in the same spaces while creating distance from other groups. Ethnocratic practices presume the endemic homogeneity of such groups and define social membership along nationality lines. A new ethnicization of care can grow out of such agendas, rather than assistance provision abandoning ethnicization. In fact, international humanitarian providers tend to presume that stability and well-being are particularly endangered in areas where different groups share the same space, and recent programs often focus on these hybrid areas. War creates the precarious existence of refugee groups; it can result in dire living conditions across different social groups. And it is at this point that humanitarian practice can either further separate groups or result in being redundant, undermining the collective potential of war-caused suffering, rather than generating social and emotional proximity.

SUDANESE REFUGEES AND WHITE HUMANITARIANISM

The number of Sudanese refugees in Lebanon to have escaped the fighting in South Sudan and Darfur is estimated at around six thousand. Their conditions are comparable to those of Iraqi refugees, although their group is smaller in number.[19] Sudanese refugees used to reach Lebanon through Syria, taking advantage of the open visa policy for Arab citizens and the historically porous Lebanese-Syrian border (Chalcraft 2006). Like the Iraqis, the Sudanese resettled in areas where other ingroup members lived. While Christians fleeing Darfur lived in the Christian majority districts surrounding Beirut and the few affordable Christian districts of the Lebanese capital (Dorai and Clochard 2007, 8), such as ash-Shiyyah, Sunni Sudanese resettled throughout Lebanon.

Like other refugee groups, the Sudanese regularly face slurs in the street. This has fueled the tension between the two countries and made migration management a longstanding soft power instrument (Dunn 2017, 100).[20] However, the resentment of the Sudanese is not only toward the Lebanese but also the Iraqis, with whom they believe they have been forced to compete over resources. The Sudanese normally work in gas stations and the sanitary sector and are considered potential rival laborers for the Syrians and Lebanese. Hadi, a refugee from South Sudan, whispered to avoid being overheard by the migration center's workers: "We face a lot of racism. When we walk down the street, we are constantly cursed and insulted. For Iraqi refugees, things are better because they pretty much look like the Lebanese. The Sudanese have darker skin color, and we are targets of more insults. There are areas in which people even throw eggs and tomatoes at us [. . .]. You ask about my memories of the July War, but after then, nothing has really changed for us."[21]

The Sudanese emphasize their distance not only from the internally displaced people of the July War but also from other refugee groups in Lebanon. They think NGOs are unable to eradicate human marginalization. Khaldoun went to the Haret Hreik Amel Center to take computer classes and explained that, to him, the UN's failures are caused by its incapacity to develop human relationships with the refugees: "If you just want to speak to one of them, you need to make an appointment. If you simply want to get documents and stay in the country as any human being, you need to bribe someone. Who's going to help us? There are always thousands of people raising their hands—they want the media to see their hands raised. They don't want to see our eyes, which beg for their help: when you knock on their door, no one will answer."[22]

Khaldoun's idea of humanitarian assistance indicates an experience of loss, revealing how conflict contributed not only to his disenfranchisement but also to his life in the monotonous violence of the humanitarian present, leaving him no prospects. Like Hadi, Ibrahim, who arrived in Lebanon in 2003 from Darfur, raised the issue of racial discrimination, mentioning how humanitarian policies and practices often keep racism in place by not approaching the Sudanese as a particularly vulnerable category among Arab refugees. The implications of racism and racialization in aid are unfortunately underresearched (Turner 2020). Main humanitarian discourses and critiques approach intersectionality around gender and age-based factors. The act of not associating humanitarianism with whiteness cannot, of course, go unheeded; under the banner of cultural universality lies a strong white identity that has historically shaped the humanitarian discourse. Some Sudanese refugees voiced that they were treated as mistrusted Black people not only because of their forced migrant status but also because they represented "easily racializable" refugees versus other groups in Lebanon. Ibrahim expressed his feelings of powerlessness at the palpable distrust with which NGOs approached him, reminding me of refugees being considered insincere and unreliable by journalists, policymakers, and administrators (Malkki 1995, 385):

> I have kids here. They're insulted because they're chocolate-color skinned. Whatever we're given is like blowing air in a ball that has a flaw in the fabric ... You let me speak for long; it means that you believe me, unlike the UN. I would like you to go to the UN now and report my case, as they have also contributed to our oppression. Most of them are Europeans with white skin. Are they not supposed to know better than all of us what is a human being, and how one should be protected and taken care of?[23]

First Palestinians, then Iraqis and Sudanese, and now Syrians reside in Lebanon as illegal migrants; their rights have been fully eroded as subjects of aging emergencies, and they are employed as menial laborers in the local economy, doomed to a life of uncertainty and frustration over continual readaptation. Humanitarianism provides an in-between space of "meaning-making and meaning-breaking" (Khosravi 2007, 330) where people socially, politically, and morally respond to humanitarian presence and absence.

The Caritas and Amel Migrant Centers take care of specific groups of Iraqi and Sudanese refugees by providing different sets of services based on national group. Similarly, Save the Children-Sweden affirms that it diversifies and tailors programs for different groups using different modalities and addressing different needs accordingly.[24] As a Save the Children project manager contended, "The aid provision based on nationality criteria should be dismantled, as it promotes confessionalism and racism. A national system that takes into account every special case would be the ideal."[25] In areas like the Bourj al-Barajneh refugee camp, inside its namesake Dahiye suburb, Palestinians are aprioristically excluded from services that do not specifically address them.[26] By exceptionalizing Palestinian refugeehood, the UNRWA, by definition, operates in a way that may also "ethnicize" these refugee groups in Lebanon's social realm when they try to access services.

While the local narrative of community support during the July War acknowledges unprecedented cross-community relief provision, Dahiye's war-stricken refugee groups find themselves in partitioned spaces where needs are assessed and international aid provided predominantly on a nationality basis. This has led to the active ethnicization of the experience of war and subsequent predicaments. However, the ethnicization of needs and services rarely starts from scratch in humanitarian programs; instead, services are inscribed within preexisting compartmentalized spaces, especially in the areas populated by different refugee groups. This ensures the maintenance of humanitarian order and, importantly, local social order.

LOCAL HOSPITALITY AS AN ETHNICIZATION FORCE

Over the last decade, critical studies on governments as well as citizen, migrant, and refugee groups that provide hospitality to people fleeing war and violence have flourished (e.g., Rosello 2002; Shryock 2004, 2008; Brun 2010; Pitt-Rivers 2012; Rozakou 2012; Thorleifsson 2016; Fiddian-Qasmiyeh and Qasmiyeh 2017). Concepts such as "hospitality" (Derrida 2000), where hospitality coexists with hostility, and "gift" (Mauss 1969), where the act of giving is a cultural obligation expected to be repaid, have been extensively used in the international scholarship to deconstruct the ontology of hospitality. Likewise, hospitality has become the main discursive framework for capturing the ways in which Lebanese residents live side-by-side with Syrian refugees in humanitarian spaces. The hegemonic hospitality discourse dismantles the longstanding relational history between these populations as well as the presociology of the Syrian presence in places like northern Lebanon, where mixed marriages used to be the norm. NGO reports and international media have increasingly focused on locals from Lebanon, Turkey, and Jordan who hosted "refugee guests" and who, subsequently, were given international legitimacy as "hosts" whatever their attitude toward the refugees' arrival. As a result, hospitality is a fundamental factor in actively ethnicizing relationships between locals and refugees and in building antagonistic descriptions of social facts revolving around Lebanese versus Syrians. Moreover, it is sensible to use hospitality in a social context because, when we talk about hosts, we ethically acknowledge one group or one category of people against another; to some extent, we predetermine social roles. Hospitality in the Syrian neighborhood complied with the local government's use of forced migration as a soft power instrument to shape state-to-state relations and gain international benefits, with the 2016 EU-Turkey agreement being the most blatant case.[27] International media coverage bestowed morality on regional hosts and their material (in)capacity to host and welcome refugees. This was particularly paradoxical in a country where there is an increasingly desperate fight for economic survival and where people have been chronically neglected since the French mandate (1920).

Previously, with Pınar Şenoğuz (Carpi and Şenoğuz 2018), I examined refugees' situation in Lebanon and Turkey, where political commentaries used hospitality to ethically compare host countries (e.g., most welcoming versus least welcoming states). Discussing hospitality at the state level is different from discussing it at the grassroots level. Forgetting the separate nature of these two levels paves the way for dangerous interchangeability between micro- and macropolitical levels. However, the governmental, humanitarian, and everyday workings of hospitality overlap to some extent, exercising an assertive politics of sovereignty over refugees and delivering the idea of hospitable nation-states. The politics of crisis-making acts at this intersection. As long as we remain within the terminological repertory of "hospitality" and "host states," refugees do not become an integral part of the local social fabric. The hospitality discourse, addressing neighboring societies that once formed the same political entity, can be a powerful force for societal fragmentation, undermining the relationships that some Syrian nationals had been developing with locals in countries such as Lebanon and Turkey before the war in Syria. The hospitality discourse can also be viewed as an ethnicization force that builds historically mindless, slapdash imaginaries of Syrians versus Lebanese. This divisive climate is reinforced by the official acknowledgment of crisis that emerges through global political discourse, as well as the emplacement of international humanitarian actors in the region. The promotion of the host state's political virtue actively serves to divide citizens from refugees who, in many cases, are older migrants in Akkar now faced with new legal, social, and economic hardships. The hospitality discourse actively overshadows the exploitative nature that local-refugee relationships acquire once locals unconditionally become hosts and neighbors become refugees and, therefore, guests. In the Akkar context, humanitarian discourse strategically merged into hospitality discourse, neglecting the longstanding presence of Syrian laborers in Lebanon and the difficult political relationship between locals and the Syrian army after twenty-nine years of occupation (1976–2005). Hospitality and, more specifically, the humanitarian enabling of local hospitality eventually produced a localized form of Lebanese nationhood vis-à-vis the new Syrian Other. Unlike the research conducted by Aubin-Boltanski and Vignal (2020, 72) in the Beqaa Valley—where locals call Syrian nationals displaced (*nazihin*) or workers (*'ummal*) in compliance with the official governmental language—in Akkar, local people speak of Syrian nationals as refugees (*laji'in*) or simply, Syrians (*suriyyn*). The collective act of producing outsiders by "refugeeing" the entire Syrian presence in the region enabled the Lebanese Akkaris to preserve social order. However, refugeeing Syrians was, to me, a sign of political proximity to the new refugees and of opposition to the Syrian government, which, in the first instance, had produced refugees by persecuting and endangering its own citizens inside Syria. The absence of a well-bonded Syrian community in Lebanon, "melting like sugar in tea" (Chalcraft 2009), facilitated the task of othering the refugees. This gradual process of otherizing Syrians in Lebanon was an effective local way of marking the territory as belonging to locals, that is, to manage and control "the home." In a geopolitical scenario where a state of emergency is officially acknowledged, safeguarding the home comes into play as an in-crisis strategy of local self-determination. Local Akkaris reinvented their relationship with the preexisting Syrian nationals in response to the announced crisis and the physical emplacement of the crisis-making machine.

The otherization of Syrians resulted in local people developing new social meanings of the physical border between the two countries. I call this phenomenon "neo-borderization" (Carpi 2020a), where cultural and social affinities and even common kinship ties become marginal factors in the Syrian-versus-Lebanese antithetical pattern and in the Lebanese givers-Syrian takers antihistorical imaginary (Carpi 2013). In other words, the ethnicization of the Syrian-Lebanese relationship has given rise to new borderscapes (Lebuhn 2013) of inclusion and exclusion in Akkar, according to which Lebanese people undercut the past presence of Syrians by highlighting the precarious character of Syrian labor before the crisis. The presence of borderscapes emphasizes the continuous burden of managing crises—typically constructed by humanitarians as watershed events—and of rapid and unregulated population growth. The local act of attributing new meanings of social fragmentation to the border is a reminder of Akkar's past political and economic relationships with its neighbor, a strategic invitation to recognize local needs and support the local workforce while making the Other's presence temporary. International humanitarian agencies accepted this invitation only after addressing refugees exclusively and once they realized that local order was easily compromised if vulnerable local groups were not assisted along with refugees. The desperate fight for economic survival in Akkar only became evident when humanitarianism had already contributed to making war and displacement experiences of human division.

Except for mixed families hosting Syrian relatives who had escaped the war, hospitality, in the majority of cases, relied on financial returns through rent paid in cash by humanitarian organizations to Lebanese landlords. Other refugees, unable to access housing refurbished and provided by agencies, paid a sum of US $50 to $100 to Lebanese landlords for a tent or piece of land. Especially during 2012 and 2013, news reports tended to disguise these money circles, which renewed classic patron-client relationships in Akkar, to depict the Lebanese government as hospitable though under strain. While some Lebanese housekeepers received cash from humanitarian organizations to accommodate Syrian refugees on a temporary annual basis, several Lebanese families initially argued they hosted refugees in the name of blood ties, old friendships, and personal favors. For instance, a Lebanese family in al-'Abdeh said they were hosting a Syrian family of five as a personal favor for their family doctor, with whom they had a longstanding friendship. Throughout 2012, when there was a small number of INGOs in the region, I realized that some local families were financially supported by networks of people between Lebanon and Syria who made the effort to support the livelihoods of the community or family members in Lebanon.

Most INGO practitioners I interviewed from UNHCR, Concern Worldwide, and DRC believed that a humanitarian crisis of such a scale and duration could not be managed through cultural values of moral responsibility and hospitality. For some, providing financial support to local families so they could host refugees was a real need; for others, the policy incentivized local people to take advantage of humanitarian assistance, which did not sort the crisis out but rather made refugee accommodation temporary and living conditions even more vulnerable when year-long agreements between local families and NGOs ended. Sarah, who worked for an INGO in Qobaiyat, contended: "I don't think it has been a good move to pay families to host Syrians. We made them dependent on people who are not independent themselves, and it's only a year-long arrangement. What are they going to do next? What have we changed by doing so?"[28]

In other words, the culture of hospitality was marketized through official humanitarian policy, paradoxically making the crisis sustainable. In early 2013, both INGOs and regional NGOs, such as those funded by the Gulf, embraced this policy by either sending direct payments to Lebanese landlords or providing a living allowance to Lebanese host families and working on house repairs to better accommodate the refugees.

Some residents ended up renting out small private pieces of land to make ends meet in a region where patron-client relationships still determine the individual's economic status. Zena, from al-Bahsa, was the owner of the land where Amal's tent is located. She owned a small villa next to this piece of land. In our conversations, she often emphasized her deteriorating financial position. She had to withdraw her children from private school, as it had become unaffordable: "For a long time, we've had this piece of land in front of the house, and now we rent it. What else can we do with neither employment nor a way of expatriating?"[29] Some Akkar residents pretended to be refugees to pursue legitimate desires of migration; seventeen of them purchased fake Syrian passports so they could be shipped to the Australian coast, but they eventually drowned, local media reported.[30] This tragic episode demonstrates the most violent and bitterly ironic face of identity politics, when vulnerable hosts pretend to be refugees to guarantee their economic survival and justify their migration via the support of the international assistance regime. After this episode, Akkar's roads were blocked as a sign of protest and solidarity. In the aftermath of the accident, when I was already back in Australia writing up my doctoral dissertation,

Hamed, a local Akkari, during a call, mentioned his desire to redeem his own people from chronic poverty and deprivation.[31]

COMPENSATORY HUMANITARIANISM: A CHANGING HABITAT

The type of NGOs supporting local families to host Syrian refugees was a determinant in assessing the reputation of those host families. For example, Naziha, a Lebanese resident from Bebnin, said about her neighbor: "I don't trust them. I know they take money from a Saudi association to host a Syrian family. They've become corrupt like their funders."[32] Another local family was seen as opportunistic for changing their political views to profit from humanitarian funding. "Those who host refugees are not doing it for humane reasons. They want to enrich themselves taking money from countries that should not be here," commented Lama, a Lebanese resident from Halba, about her neighbor being financed by a Kuwaiti organization to host two Syrian refugee families.[33]

'Ali, a coffee-shop owner in Halba married to a Syrian woman from Homs, built an extension onto his house to rent to Syrians because his income had recently decreased from the economic crisis: "The assistance provided to Syrians exemplifies the chaos [fawda] of this region. Under the Asad regime, it has always been bad, but this is a country of benefits—balad al-manfaiy'at. Don't listen to people telling you that things are now worse. If they do, it means they were collaborators in the years of the Syrian occupation [...]. Now, I need this chaos to pay for my bread."[34]

Financed hospitality for refugees became an opportunity for economic development or survival for local families. Simultaneously, people from elsewhere in Lebanon tend to believe that this Lebanese region's people are rude, uneducated peasants bearing an inherently negative identity. With the humanitarian incentivization of local hospitality, Akkar's people dragged behind them a negative identity of being bad hosts in everyday narratives circulating in Beirut and other areas of the North, as I could personally observe. They, the people with boorish manners, were likely accused of taking advantage of Syrian displacement to increase housing prices, exploit the cheap workforce, and unfold racism against the Syrians as revenge for historical Syrian oppression.

Osama's family in Bebnin hosted a Syrian family from Duma throughout 2012 without receiving any money from NGOs.[35] They were well connected to the local mukhtar, who interceded and requested that an INGO select them to receive financial support. Osama's neighbors had also accommodated a Syrian family without asking them to pay rent, but when they saw that Osama's family received financial support, they decided not to continue offering their hospitality. According to Osama, his neighbors' financial situation had not changed, but they expected an INGO to finance them when they saw that Osama was receiving help. This anecdote demonstrates how humanitarian policy marketized a cultural value like hospitality, commodifying cultural identity (Comaroff and Comaroff 2009). In other words, hospitality became the vector of macroethical judgments; locals were seen as either greedy or bountiful, although greediness and grievance can go together and, at times, greediness is a symptom of grievance.

With the official political discourse revolving around Syrian refugees as an existential problem for Lebanon at a domestic and international level, the fact that refugee guests had overstayed their welcome was, from an international humanitarian perspective, compensated by the services and aid provided to local communities. It was also compensated by increased revenues for politically influential and wealthy oligarchic segments of Akkar, which, as in other refugee destinations (Anderson 1999), temporarily benefit from increased local consumerism from the large presence of refugees and aid actors.[36]

By early 2013, INGO practitioners affirmed that the relationship between the local population and Syrian refugees had deteriorated tangibly. Similarly, scholars identify a "clear social separation nowadays between Syrians and Lebanese" (Mouawad 2023, 184) in border areas such as Wadi Khaled. The local feeling of being burdened with a now long-term displacement was associated with the belief that refugee newcomers constituted the main source of economic, political, and security risk. As stated by Walid, a resident of Halba: "There used to be empathy—ta'atuwf—with the Syrians, but now it has disappeared. You can feel the tension now. I'm not surprised: after hosting them, we even get robbed by them."[37] ALEF (2013), a Lebanese NGO, reported that people in Kab Elias (Beqaa Valley) named the unofficial camps where Syrians were resettling musta'amarat—as Palestinians usually called Israeli settlements—expressing high levels of unacceptance.

Some locals who referred to the act of sharing space and resources with the Syrians in terms of hospitality (diyafa) used religious belonging as a means of expressing emotional distance from the Syrian crisis—for instance, portraying hospitality offered to refugees as "a Muslim thing." Noha, a Christian Lebanese resident, suggested that Syrian refugees tended to relocate to the Muslim villages around Qobayat because the Christian majority villages' authorities rejected them.[38] With this statement, Noha referred to her own confessional community to detach herself from the arrivals of refugees and the regional management of these arrivals. Nawal, a Lebanese woman from Halba, also disclosed the need to separate her life from the presence of Syrian refugees, but she contradictorily conveyed emotional proximity to and identification with the Syrian predicament: "I would never host them. I no longer want to hurt my mind."[39]

International humanitarianism intervened while disregarding local capacities to cope and maintain stability and ignoring the common experiences that united local, refugee, and migrant residents of the Akkar region. Instead, humanitarian agencies capitalized on what used to divide the inhabitants and, in the early stages, built their programs on that basis. Aid was initially provided according to presumed societal divisions, such as Syrians not having to deal with the Lebanese—as though they had never met before—rather than focusing on longstanding connecting factors. In this framework, local initiatives such as Refugees=Partners working across Lebanese and Syrian demographics, against stereotypes and the violation of the Syrian refugees' rights in Lebanon, were sidelined (Fiddian-Qasmiyeh 2019).

The Syrian refugee experience in Akkar reminded the development and aid sectors of how dire local needs are and that, as a matter of fact, there are no *either* local *or* refugee needs. There are, instead, human needs wedged between the amnesiac workings of the politics of crisis-making, forgetful about the past, and the tyranny of a historically underinformed present. Preexisting local needs could not be merely associated with refugee crises, and such local claims needed to be addressed singularly. Today's inclusive humanitarian programs are still based on models borne of emergencies in settings where so-called local hosts were also deemed vulnerable. In 2017, local practitioners and Lebanese people who attended income-generating activities explained to me that such inclusive practices are often set according to the refugees' conditions. Long-term humanitarianism no longer seems to be about war and people forcibly on the move, as it spans large timeframes. Emerging compensatory humanitarianism puts programs in place for all; the programs sometimes do not succeed, however, in attracting local attention. Overall, the Syrian refugee experience in Lebanon provided the opportunity to formulate and address local rights and needs, going far beyond inclusive assistance programs implemented because of refugee arrivals. In this historically neglected area that no compensatory policy could ever pay back, hospitality became the epistemic construction of an environment where locals waited to see their needs acknowledged and satisfied. Nada, from Wadi Khaled, showed me her new heater on a cold evening in December 2012, but she was not happy that she had finally been given one for the first time in her life: "I received it because I'm hosting a Syrian family. I mean, that's still hard to accept." Thus, the Syrian refugee presence became the *sine qua non* condition for some Lebanese to become de facto citizens and beneficiaries of assistance. Likewise, Dima, from Halba, bitterly recalled that there was no welfare provision in the region before the arrival of Syrians: "There was no help in place before then. Did we need the Syrians to deserve electricity and paved roads?"[40] Indeed, compensatory humanitarianism cannot heal old wounds. Few were the residents emphasizing the benefits ensuing Syrian displacement in Akkar. Othman, a Lebanese from Wadi Khaled, affirmed: "After the arrival of Syrian refugees, we've witnessed the opening of public schools with Lebanese curricula in Wadi Khaled and a local clinic. That's amazing to witness this after fifty years."[41]

HOMEMAKING PRACTICES AND LEBANESE RETURNEES

In parallel with the climax of compensatory humanitarianism and the formalization of the Syrian refugee crisis, the media portrayed Lebanon as a vexed host state, triggering microsocial responses to the crisis in Akkar's society. On the one hand, from the orthodox perspective of long-term displacement, refugeehood historically evokes the global need to label receiving societies as hosts who receive public acknowledgment for their protracted hospitality. On the other hand, the Halba experience shows that the formal humanitarian response to the crisis encouraged Lebanese residents to reconfigure previous Syrian migrants as refugees in a bid to reclaim their homes. While some Syrian migrant workers ran shops in Akkar before 2011, in the wake of the official response to the crisis—institutionally enacted only with the first LCRP in late 2014 and becoming visible with the emplacement of an unprecedented number of INGOs—they became homogenously portrayed as refugee guests whose presence had to be temporary. This was especially relevant for Lebanese residents returning from abroad, having worked for different periods in places such as South America or other Arab countries. Owning and managing shops and discouraging Syrians from accessing public spaces were collective practices of homemaking that allowed the Akkari hosts to reinvent their relationship with the Syrians.

Halba's residents opened shops selling a combination of hardware, tires, carpentry, and garden tools. The shops containing hardware and tools (locally known as *mahallet khardawet w adawet zira'iyye*) were seen as a guarantee of local ownership: "There's no Syrian refugee or migrant that ever opened such shops in the area. They normally work in this sector as occasional assistants. In the beginning, during the war, there were only two or three shops like this," affirmed Hadi, a Lebanese resident. "It eventually became the largest business in Halba."[42] Many shops were owned by Lebanese who had lived in Tripoli and decided to go back to Akkar during the Lebanese Civil War as there was "less political trouble" in the villages if they wanted to open a shop.[43] Many shop owners had personal stories of past mobility and economic migration, especially during the 1980s, when, as some locals recall, Syrian nationals worked in hardware shops in greater numbers. Waleed migrated to Baghdad to work as a waiter for one year before he decided to return to Lebanon and inherit his father's shop, which is still located close to Halba's roundabout. Likewise, Hadi migrated to Venezuela, where he ran a clothing shop for eleven years. In 1986, he decided to come back to Lebanon to give his children access to the same education he had received, and he opened a hardware and agricultural tool shop.

A temporal dimension now divides Syrian nationals, who previously managed these hardware shops, and Akkari returnees. From a local perspective, Syrians have always been entitled to provide temporary labor in Akkar as they used to do in the capacity of migrant workers before the Syrian conflict. Throughout the twentieth century, indeed, Syrians mostly provided seasonal work with neither the intention nor the social comfort to create a proper Syrian community in Lebanon by bringing their families with them. The concept of circular mobility describes such migration and inhabitation patterns. Aubin-Boltanski and Vignal (2020, 67) found a continuum between preconflict mobility patterns and the current situation of refuge. The return of Lebanese migrants and their exclusive entitlement to own hardware shops contrast with Syrian nationals' inability to cultivate a sense of personal stability in Lebanon, leading refugees to experience a sense of "permanent temporariness" (Yiftachel 2009). Local refusal to have Syrian nationals in the same jobs as Lebanese not only highlights the typical rejection of sharing life and welfare with the refugees, which happens everywhere, but also points to a struggle over the Other's temporal horizons. This tension between refugees and locals, along with the increasingly long-term perspective of the humanitarian system (traditionally thought of as providing temporary and short-term action), gives rise to a double clash of temporalities in which permanent Syrian nationals in Akkar are considered threats. While refugees seek to expand their temporal perspectives (lacking other options), residents struggle over their exclusive right to return to, live, and proliferate in Halba with no temporal restrictions. Among the so-called host communities, the role of returnees in this practice of homemaking has gone unheeded. The expectation for Lebanese returnees to work in Halba's hardware shops is locally experienced as a collective act aimed at morally and economically monopolizing a commercial activity. It also illustrates the interface between human experiences of migration—in this specific case, between Lebanon, Venezuela, and Iraq—and historical trajectories of socioeconomic practices (Carpi 2020c). Hardware shops in Halba mark an assertive, collective form of homemaking to which refugees are not entitled. In other words, owning and managing a hardware shop becomes the local signifier of national legitimacy to claim "home" and implement comfortable patterns of social order. Such practices of homemaking and order-making are the local response to the officialization of crisis. The resulting existential divide between Lebanese residents and Syrian refugees in respective ability and inability to develop long-term perspectives in Halba—echoing the lack of temporal perspectives for Iraqis and Sudanese in Dahiye—plays a role in negotiating territorial permanence. As Brun (2016, 402) incisively writes, "this emptying of the future [of refugees]—or the rendering of an abstract future—shows that the emergency imagery decontextualizes and 'de-situates' the lives of people experiencing a crisis." In this way, the historical sociology of the Syrian presence in North Lebanon was swept away by the in-stitutionalization of the so-called Syrian refugee crisis, shifting the global focus from political terror to individual trauma (Humphrey 2002) and giving rise to the denormalization and pathologization of the Syrian presence in Akkar.

AN ETHNOCENTRIC TAXONOMY OF NEEDS

In March 2016, Amal called me; she was alarmed at being unable to withdraw money from a local ATM in Halba with her e-food ration card. Had she been deregistered from the UNHCR records as a Syrian in Lebanon? I spoke to my humanitarian contacts in Beirut to access her UNHCR dossier. Although I was unsuccessful, she soon found out through the local UNHCR contact that she and her family were believed to have returned to Syria. From 2011, the eligibility of Syrian refugees to access international assistance has not been a one-time process: registration and deregistration are recurrent, revealing the punctu-ated nature of international humanitarianism (Feldman 2018). This "politics of policing categories" (Feldman 2012a, 394) presumes that beneficiaries must fit into specific categories to qualify for services and goods. It convinces people that their needs have to be presented and performed as ethnicizable, namely, as pertinent to their community and distinct from other social groups, and that protection and assistance can be ensured only by normative identity—the identity they are accepted with in the assistance regime (Feldman 2012a, 394).

Even though it is a common belief that FBOs perform an ethnicization of needs and services by feeding religious identity, all the FBOs I came across in Lebanon over the years would, on paper, provide services to anyone. In practice, they were predominantly accessed by ingroup members.[44] Likewise, particular segments of the Syrian refugee population, such as the Alawite com-munity I came into contact with, were often reluctant to access INGO, UN, and FBO support, even though some of them had also fled Syria for fear of persecution and everyday violence. This group of Syrians was considered privi-leged for having the same confessional background as Syrian President Bashar al-Asad and, outside of Syria, was the object of great mistrust from other Syrian groups. Furthermore, many Alawite refugees tended to mistrust both FBOs and secular NGOs.

To be accepted within local groups and access welfare services as religious community members instead of international assistance as refugees, an Alawite family I knew in a Kesrawan village (Mount Lebanon) converted to Christianity. The refugee response to such an ethnocratic taxonomy of needs often generated performative attitudes meant to comply with the expectations placed on the beneficiary's identity. Erica Bouris (2007) highlights the role of refugee performance when refugees instrumentalize their identity stories to decide how to emerge in academic and NGO narratives. Similarly, Elizabeth Dunn (2017) refers to "professional refugees" as those who produce the answers that aid agencies want to hear. I came across such interrelations between performance and vulnerability in both Dahiye and Akkar; I remained interested in how humanitarian governance triggers and even encourages such standardized attitudes and responses. Today I challenge my own past interest in how refugee performance plays out because, as an ethnographer, my full, spontaneous self in all of my field encounters is per se an unconscious presumption.

As further evidence of the tottering identity politics of humanitarianism, Lebanon's UNRWA counted twenty-nine thousand refugees from Syria at the end of December 2019. These included Palestinian camp dwellers, especially from the *mukhaiyyam* Yarmouk, destroyed by clashes between the militias opposing and supporting the Asad regime. As services for Palestinians are normally covered by UNRWA's mandate, some NGOs initially denied aid to these refugees. According to INGO practitioners, however, since 2013, organizations that usually did not work with the Palestinians—for example, the DRC—have gradually adapted their policies to become more flexible and blur the lines of refugee categories. Some INGOs temporarily adopted exceptional measures to address *ad hoc* cases of Palestinians from Syria, but the Syrian refugee-led organizations I interviewed in 2018 in Tripoli and Beirut when I was conducting fieldwork for Elena Fiddian-Qasmiyeh's "Southern Responses to Displacement" project,[45] such as *Lamset Ward* and the *Tamas* network, affirmed that they have kept their eligibility criteria flexible throughout the history of Syrian refugeehood in Lebanon. Against this backdrop, Hala, a Palestinian from Syria's Yarmouk camp who relocated to al-ʿAbdeh in Akkar, stated that her applications for help were rejected by some INGOs and the UNHCR after she crossed the Lebanese border. She became a second-degree refugee: "I've always lived like any other Syrian citizen in Baramke [Damascus neighborhood], and now I'm treated as though my identity was not worth a single cent. I was bombed like all other Syrian citizens. I also lost my job and my beloved because of the conflict. How many times in my life do I have to become a refugee?"[46]

"Overlapping refugeedoms" (Fiddian-Qasmiyeh 2011), such as Palestinians from Syria, challenge the humanitarian logic of assigning a single victim identity to the displaced. Ingroup frictions often occur as a result of taxonomic governance, since all refugees carry a diversified burden and suffer from different extents of social abandonment as a consequence of war and conditions of deprivation. According to refugees in Akkar, practitioners ignored such experiential diversity. The trauma of category change (Feldman 2012a) generated many ingroup frictions and was activated by abrupt changes in aid distribution and the selection of beneficiaries. For example, the WFP, after guaranteeing the unconditional provision of food to earlier Syrian refugees fleeing to Lebanon, opted to cut their expenses by shortening their beneficiary list.[47] The value of vouchers for buying food in local shops, owing to budget shortfalls, varied from 46,000 LL per month to 35,000 LL, in addition to the WFP excluding some previous beneficiaries from future assistance.[48] Such a policy change caused much resentment among the refugees and raised suspicion about the way they had been selected. I heard caustic comments from Syrians about Palestinians from Syria and about other Syrians. Most refugees pointed to *wasta* as the only possible way of preserving eligibility and access to assistance and wanted freedom from category change paranoia. Once, when I visited Amina's tented settlement in al-Bahsa, she was crying. That year, her family had not been given diesel (*mazut*) for the winter. Amina despaired over her loss of recognition (Feldman 2012a), a recognition that, as a Syrian, had initially allowed her to be a first-degree refugee. She said the UNHCR promoted inequality: "The UN told me they changed their policy. We've been here for three years, and now they need to prioritize the newcomers. Have they addressed our dire conditions? Have we been helped to change any of this? Are we doomed to die from cold this year? Even the Palestinians got diesel; I saw a Palestinian woman who was my neighbor in Homs, and she was carrying diesel. I asked her if the UN had given it to her, and she nodded and sneered at me. I'm sick of being humiliated."[49]

Most humanitarian professionals I interviewed in Akkar rejected the argument that their programs ethnicize needs and fuel social friction. Instead, local tensions were explained as preexisting structural problems, reminding me of Ferguson's work in Lesotho (1994), where locals' ignorance or lack of domestic infrastructure was advanced as the only reason. In interviews, practitioners working for either INGOs or local NGOs were particularly insightful in articulating local deficiencies as the cause of project failures. For instance, a Lebanese professional working for the Qatari Foundation in Tripoli mentioned the increasing number of programs addressing both Lebanese and Syrians: "The social integration between the two populations has always been there, despite regional politics. There's no need for specific projects to reduce mutual resentment. Western humanitarian agencies use the narrative of Syrian-Lebanese tensions to clean up their image after having caused so much damage."[50]

Although I mostly interviewed foreign practitioners in Akkar, I realized that the ethnicization of needs was not their prerogative. A practitioner from a Lebanese NGO explicitly affirmed that nationality-based aid provision was inevitable for logistical reasons and to comply with foreign donors' agendas: "We have a different agenda for Iraqi refugees, Syrians, and Palestinians. We deal with all of them separately as it's just easier to do things this way."[51] The social response to this identity-loaded logistic impinges on mutual perceptions and relationships. As Ahmed, a Palestinian from Syria's Yarmouk camp, contended: "I can get only assistance from the UNRWA. If I had not been Palestinian, I'd have had hundreds of NGOs I could rely on. They're very careful not to confuse a Palestinian with a Syrian."[52] Thus, displaced people must survive within preestablished spaces where their rank in the taxonomical aid pyramid either ensures or denies support. As a further example, NRC practitioners said they divided their budget between education programs for Palestinian camp dwellers and Syrians joining the Back to School program, which opened classes for Syrian children in Lebanese public schools in Baalbek and Zahle (Beqaa Valley).[53] When Palestinians from Syria arrived, they were automatically included in the programs for Palestinians, according to a NRC practitioner.[54] This decision neglected their possible identification with Syrians rather than with Palestinians from Lebanon. In a similar vein, Khaled, a refugee from Sudan I met in al-'Abdeh, clearly expressed his feeling of being part of a moral taxonomy of basic needs, which neither took into account the temporality of refugeehood nor enacted a fair, time-cognizant system of support: "The Lebanese state doesn't even satisfy the needs of its own citizens. But there's a cruel hierarchy in Lebanon: the Lebanese come first, then the Palestinians, and finally the Iraqis and the Sudanese. None of this aid comes in for us, although we've been here for longer than others."[55]

Nationality is not primordial but rather a construction of the modern era (Calhoun 1993). The fictitious and vacuous character of ethnicity was acknowledged but accepted by practitioners, who stated that ethnicization of aid was an unavoidable reflection of Lebanese society, which they did not aim to change with their jobs. Arnauld, an INGO practitioner in Akkar, affirmed: "I worked with the Palestinians for a long time, and I can say that it's them that don't want to work with Lebanese organizations and INGOs."[56] Assessing the extent to which humanitarian programming either fueled the ethnicization of local needs and services or inscribed itself within preexisting cleavages remains a chicken-and-egg situation and highly dependent on specific contexts. I endeavor here to make sense of how displaced people responded to such programs and connected humanitarian logistics to the local workings of identity politics.

TOWARD A NEOETHNICIZATION OF CARE

Social networks in Akkar's villages were able to reveal a configuration of identity based on common practices and disentangled from ethnicity and religion. This occurred specifically in North Lebanon, where Syrian refugees worked as unskilled migrant laborers way before the 2011 uprising. A good example was the everyday practice of car sharing I became familiar with in al-Bahsa (western Akkar). Car sharing was a relatively common practice among Syrian and Lebanese residents from the Akkar region, as they were poorly served by public transportation. Many low-income Syrian and Lebanese families could not afford to have their own car. During my prolonged stays, I became aware of Syrian and Lebanese families that purchased secondhand cars and shared the costs of using and maintaining them, or even shared the purchase cost. Such collective practices contradict the predominant narrative of intergroup tension and are signs of longstanding mechanisms of self-sufficiency. Such mutual livelihood arrangements were aimed at supporting families beyond predefined national identity. Predefined group belonging, on which most international livelihood programs used to be based until recent years, cannot capture distinct tactics of survival, which, in this case, formed a wide network of mutual support and negotiation. In this framework, the practice-based approach is a powerful tool to unfold how social membership and economic status are not nationally defined, in line with the scholarly shift from the structural determinism of boundary making to the emphasis on human agency (Wimmer 2008). Although the search for and management of resources is generally more difficult for refugees (given that they have weaker connections and networks to build on than locals), economically vulnerable Syrian refugees and Lebanese citizens face the same costs of living and, in some cases, receive nearly the same salary. Manar is a Halba resident whose husband worked in a Beirut factory for US $450 per month, half of which was spent on his daily commute.[57] She used to assist Syrian refugee children with their homework in the afternoon free of charge, and the children's family paid her a monthly rent for the land where they built their tents, choosing her plot of land over others. This demonstrates the importance of developing a deeper understanding of how identities blur through shared practices. Eschewing the prescriptive language of culture-oriented values and norms allows for the grouping of people based on what they actually do rather than who they supposedly are and how they supposedly feel in the host environment. By transcending boundary categories and observing common or dissimilar socioeconomic practices, such practice-defined groups relate to larger contexts as collective groups (Warde 2014) instead of nationality-defined silos. This confronts the orthodox demographics of the humanitarian system. Examining practice and arrangement bundles and their historical development can tease out actual social memberships. Yet refugees still need to respond to standardized criteria of eligibility by waving identity flags to qualify for food, healthcare, education services, resettlement, or even the right to move. The practice-based approach creates room to define a more authentic epistemology of needs and assistance regimes.

In February and March 2017, I attended a training course on making chocolate financed by the EU and UNICEF for four weeks. Making chocolate has become a frequent success story in the Syrian refugee diaspora (especially in Canada), and the motto of this business success is known as "peace by chocolate."[58] The workshop took place in Halba twice a week over three months and was managed by the local NGO Akkar Network for Development (AND), which runs several livelihood programs in the region. According to the aid practitioners, chocolate making was not a proposal based on a market skills gap analysis, created instead according to the resources available.[59] Among nine trainees, there were six Syrian and three Lebanese women who suffered from very similar economic vulnerabilities. Their transport costs were covered to enable them to reach the AND branch. The humanitarian attempt to produce income-generating chocolate making was not primarily aimed at refugee self-reliance (Carpi 2020c). The purpose was explicitly to enhance citizen and refugee participation in local markets to foster social cohesion and avoid tension. Social mingling between the Lebanese and Syrian women in that specific context did not actually happen, as I continued meeting the trainees outside of the program. However, from what I personally experienced, this does not mean that social mingling never occurred between the Syrians and Lebanese in general, especially in the case of people from Bedouin origins who tend to minimize their belonging to a nation-state and focus on the continuities of Bedouin life across regional borders. In contrast, in my conversations with practitioners working on social cohesion, the lack of social mingling—especially among youths and children—during or in the aftermath of a program led donors to deem it a failure, as though local societies were exclusively functioning or not functioning because of humanitarian programming. The most important matter was that, despite the intergroup matrix, this humanitarian livelihood program was unable to capture the more articulated and blended forms of social membership that stem from common practices and mutual support, albeit within hierarchical and unequal economies. An ethnocentric approach, therefore, ignores practice-defined social memberships and treats social cohesion and stability as identity based. Having worked on the local mapping of livelihood programs in Akkar throughout 2016 and 2017, I noticed that none captured preexisting arrangements for economic survival, such as the car-sharing practice, approaching different national groups as separate entities that needed to meet and reconcile. The ethnocratic character of humanitarian programming leads to persistent neglect of preexisting intergroup practices—and it is not exclusive to humanitarian action in Lebanon or, more broadly, in the Middle East, as shown in Carpi et al. (2020) in discussions on the commonalities of refugee-led practices across Lebanon, India, and Greece. Throughout the program mapping, however, I realized that the number of INGOs that consistently implemented projects for different national groups was far larger than in previous years, therefore suggesting the idea of a neoethnicization of care.

In my conversations with INGO practitioners, the primary concern was social cohesion to enable local stability. Multigroup programs were discussed as though meant to engender first encounters between Lebanese, Palestinians, and Syrians—demographic groups that have long shared space and resources in the region and elsewhere. As much as the Middle East is often exceptionalized in media and academic accounts, humanitarian ethnocratic approaches are not confined to the region. For instance, an ICRC practitioner in Nepal commented that it was harder to hold community meetings in cities because they normally happen with multiple communities at once. This belief suggests that the "strategically managed creation of a neutral space" is needed, rather than acknowledging and building on the multigroup nature of such meetings in urban settings (British Red Cross 2012, 35). Today's tendency to include different national groups in a single humanitarian program is reflected in governmental, nongovernmental, and private sector collective efforts following the NWOW approach. This approach revolves around reinforcing, rather than replacing, preexisting contextual capacities and support networks. The number of programs designed for Syrians, Palestinians, and Lebanese altogether, as confirmed by a UNHCR protection officer, is now much larger than before 2016.[60]

Many intergroup projects, however, continue to be promoted in public rhetoric and formal campaigns rather than effectively practiced (Carpi and Diana 2019, 145). Between 2015 and 2016, Chiara Diana and I critically examined the intervention of the Canadian-founded NGO Right to Play (RtP) on local and refugee children in al-Qobbe, an economically disadvantaged neighborhood in North Lebanon's Tripoli. RtP has been working with Palestinian refugee children in Lebanon since 2006 and has investigated the impact of the Syrian war on refugee children and local communities since 2013. This INGO currently coordinates play and sports activities for Lebanese and Syrian children in the Tripoli governorate. RtP aims to encourage young people to mingle with their peers, be socially engaged, and refrain from joining armed groups or any other form of political violence. Our fieldwork suggested that play activities that originally involved children from different national backgrounds separately, which later became inclusive to foster cohesion and stability, contributed to shaping children's social subjectivity based on their nationalities rather than the political and social circumstances in which they live. Programs were later configured in terms of mixed nationality, as we observed in playgrounds, but today's play activities still very frequently develop as intergroup activities only at an ideal level (Carpi and Diana 2019, 145). In the Qobbe case study, the actual small number of intergroup activities did not mean that children from different national backgrounds were not playing together in everyday life; instead, they were rarely doing it within the formal framing of humanitarian programs. In other words, they were playing together in public areas *beyond* humanitarianism. Such social cohesion concerns emerge in the recrafting of programs aimed to be nationally inclusive as a strategy for alleviating tensions that are allegedly more likely to happen in nationally mixed settings. In this sense, with the current multigroup, interethnic approach, some needs and services are addressed through an area-based approach and, hence, are defined by geography rather than identity politics. The prioritization of social cohesion programs in demographically hybrid areas is, however, still based on preemptive security measures, revealing the enduring ethnicization of care.

NOTES

1. The number is far smaller than in Syria, where there were around one million refugees before the conflict broke out. In Jordan, there are currently seven hundred fifty thousand.

2. In November 2007, the HRW published a report declaring that five hundred eighty Iraqis were in detention. To explain the policy, a midlevel security official said to Nadim Houri (March 25, 2010), previous director of HRW: "We don't want them to get too comfortable."

3. Interview with Fouad, working for UNICEF, Beirut, February 2, 2012.

4. While the EU set a time limit of three years to guarantee protection, the UNHCR does not set any time limit, which increases uncertainty in people's lives (Trad and Frangieh 2007).

5. Interview, Laylaki, December 4, 2011.

6. February 5, 2012.

7. Interview, Laylaki, February 5, 2012.

8. Interview, Laylaki, February 5, 2012.

9. February 5, 2012.

10. December 10, 2011.

11. October 13, 2011.

12. Haret Hreik, October 13, 2011.

13. February 5, 2012.

14. Interview, Laylaki, February 5, 2012.

15. February 5, 2012.

16. Laylaki, December 4, 2011.

17. December 7, 2011.

18. Interview, Laylaki, December 4, 2011.

19. Two hundred sixty of them were jailed for entering Lebanon illegally, as reported by the *Daily Star* on October 9, 2009, and were sent back to their country on a Sudan Airways flight. The Sudanese refugee community expressed resentment toward Lebanese institutions and the UNHCR by organizing a hunger strike in June 2012, asking for fairer treatment.

20. For instance, Abdel Meneem went on hunger strike for sixteen days in 2010 to end racist policies and the arbitrary detention of people fearing political persecution in Sudan. In the same year, the Lebanese General Security attacked a group of Sudanese refugees during a cancer fundraising event in Ouzai, western Dahiye.

21. February 7, 2012.

22. February 7, 2012.

23. October 13, 2011.

24. Interview, November 23, 2011.

25. Interview, Hamra, Beirut, November 23, 2011.

26. Interview with 'Abdel Hadi 'Arab, member of the Municipality Council, November 24, 2012.

27. According to the March 2016 statement of cooperation (see https://www.consilium.europa.eu/en/press/press-releases/2016/03/18/eu-turkey-statement/), every person arriving irregularly (e.g., by boat without official permission or passage) to the Greek islands, including asylum-seekers, would be returned to Turkey. In exchange, EU member states would take one Syrian refugee from Turkey for every Syrian returned from the islands.

28. January 14, 2013.

29. Al-Bahsa, February 12, 2013.

30. Turkmen and Bedouins also pretended to be Syrians to obtain basic services.

31. October 2, 2013.

32. January 14, 2013.

33. January 14, 2013.

34. October 6, 2012.

35. January 14, 2013.

36. Aid providers usually need local drivers, housing for themselves, retailers selling goods to be distributed, and other working staff employable in their field (Anderson 1999).

37. Halba, October 5, 2012.

38. Interview, November 11, 2012.

39. November 11, 2012.

40. August 10, 2012.

41. Interview, December 28, 2012.

42. Interview with Hadi, Halba, March 6, 2017.

43. Interview with Hadi, Halba, March 6, 2017. The city of Tripoli was caught up in the fight, and the Tawhid brigade was used to threaten people in the city.

44. For example, in an interview, project manager Mohammed Bassam from the Imam Sadr Foundation confirmed that beneficiaries belonging to confessional groups other than Shiʻa were decreasing because people in community-oriented societies tend to ask for assistance within the community with which they feel affiliated (Tyre, October 12, 2012).

45. "Analysing South-South Humanitarianism to Displacement from Syria: Views from Lebanon, Jordan and Turkey" is led by Professor Elena Fiddian-Qasmiyeh and funded by the European Research Council under the European Union's Horizon 2020 Research and Innovation Program, with Grant Agreement No. 715582.

46. January 7, 2013.

47. The WFP stated that their policy changed because their eligibility criteria for assistance could not be established using predictable methods earlier. Therefore, the agency had initially opted for large, nationality-based distribution.

48. The UNHCR began to automatically deregister refugees who do not go to food distribution centers for three months in a row. In the first week of November 2013, thirteen thousand Syrians were deregistered in Lebanon for this reason.

49. December 14, 2012.

50. December 18, 2012.

51. Interview, Halba, October 17, 2012.

52. Al-ʻAbdeh, January 12, 2012.

53. Beirut, January 15, 2013.

54. Beirut, January 15, 2013.

55. January 4, 2013.

56. Qobaiyat, October 4, 2012.

57. Halba, February 27, 2017.

58. "Sweet Success: How the Haddads Went from Refugees to Employers in 1 Year," *CBC News*, January 7, 2017. "Peace by Chocolate" also became a movie set in a small town in Nova Scotia (Canada) where a family of refugees from Syria resettled and started their business.

59. Halba, February 24 and March 6, 2017. During my interview, representatives confirmed that the UNDP had set up a chocolate-making facility in Akkar, but large segments of locals and even aid workers themselves were not aware of the facility. Halba, February 28, 2017.

60. Interview, Qobaiyat, February 6, 2013.

5 / Humanitarian Distances and the "Southist" Need to Be There

This chapter tackles the moral hierarchies that humanitarianism engenders among the internally displaced and forced migrants in Dahiye and Akkar by providing, withdrawing, or denying assistance during and after crisis. By proposing the notion of "Southism," I build on the vast body of literature about the paternalistic and solipsistic attitude of international humanitarian actors, and I reflect on positionalities in this complex realm. I focus particularly on the relationships between local, regional, and international practitioners. Despite high diversity—also across INGOs and UN agencies, not exclusively between local and foreign actors—humanitarian actors, in the eyes of the displaced, often come to form a homogenous arm of governance unable to empathize or enact solidarity.

The politics of crisis-making, in fact, acts through a peculiar relational economy, where humanitarian actors develop moral and socioeconomic distance in a climate of generalized disaffection. Bringing to the fore Syrian refugees' and Dahiye displaced people's conceptualizations of the international community, I articulate how humanitarian distances are created and maintained, framing my discussions around i) material discrimination, ii) politics of blame, iii) humanitarian "tourism," and iv) epistemic failure.

This chapter explores North-South encounters and mutual imaginations within "humanitarian economies," a term I use to refer to an organized assistance provision that addresses people affected by war who rely on their own repertory of values and norms. I critically reflect on the tension that exists between the philanthropic spirit of the humanitarian system as implemented in the Global South (Butt 2002) and local and refugee responses to what I call "Southism." The Southist intent of the Northern humanitarian system to care for, rescue, upgrade, and assist the global South—which partially transcends physical geographies—combines personal affection, necessity, collective compassion, and professional aspirations. In this sense, the concept of Southism resonates with the "monumentalization of the margins" (Spivak 1999, 170) that crystallizes needs and areas of need in the South beyond the intentions of humanitarian workers. As such, Southism indicates a structural relationship instead of the mere act of assisting the South with a philanthropic spirit. Specifically, it preconceives the South as disempowered and incapable while cementing it as the key symbolic capital of Northern empowerment, accountability, and capability.

I am of course not the first researcher to advance considerations on the hegemonic culture of aid provision and the diverse responses of beneficiaries to such hegemony. Nevertheless, a close analysis of how North-South relationships and imaginations are reproduced in the specific context of these Lebanese settings opens further avenues of inquiry into and concerns about hard-to-die humanitarian hierarchies.

The humanitarian approaches to thinking about and assisting the needy discussed here concern disparate sides of the world. The global humanitarian lifestyle I explore is about social class, economic status, and the freedom to move inside vulnerable areas, opting for educational and professional migration. Taking the enduring coloniality of modern humanitarianism as a conceptual point of departure, my analysis strives for the contextual alternation of geography-free and geography-informed interpretations of Southism. While passports and nationalities still prove their efficaciousness in times of risk, my interpretation focuses on the identification of comfort zones that protect lifeworlds, ease, and privilege across passports. The hegemonic culture underpinning the NGOization of postcolonial settings (Ferguson 1994; Fisher 1997; Schuller 2012) is a discourse theory that, on the one hand, can be adopted regardless of the geographic context of its primary subjects and, on the other hand, can reveal the organizational and individual ethics of international and local practitioners in Southern settings defined by crisis. The geography-free approach articulates the "too-easy West-and-the-rest polarizations sometimes rampant in colonial and postcolonial discourse studies" that legitimize the (Northern and Southern) colonial attitude itself (Spivak 1999, 39). From a conceptual perspective, when talking about humanitarian Southism, there can be no "outside."

My analysis limits itself to the moral and material implications of Southism. After all, the feelings, intentions, and aspirations that often underlie the humanitarian career (Malkki 2015) mean that Southism cannot be addressed straightforwardly in the short term. More specifically, my notion of humanitarian Southism comes from an analytical framework that investigates humanitarian actors' tendency to believe that Lebanon, like other "fragile states" (Fayyad 2008), would collapse whenever a new emergency breaks out without their help. Within the framework of my field research in Dahiye and the villages of Akkar, it has been possible to analyze the behavioral patterns of international humanitarianism that, importantly, counts both local and international practitioners among its staff. Using the discursive strategy of Southism, I discuss the encounters and imaginations that characterize the Lebanese humanitarian economy. While encounters indicate material human processes that can be evidenced, imaginations refer to collective discourses and perceptions that imply rational thinking and theorization—but, for the sake of an accurate epistemology, need to be differentiated from encounters. Therefore, encounters and imaginations cut across the everyday realities of both displaced people and aid providers. First, I unfold actual North-South encounters by adopting two analytical categories: the epistemic failure of humanitarian workers who lack fine-grain knowledge of the targeted area, including local language, customs, and history; and, echoing Redfield (2012), the material discrimination within the humanitarian organization of labor, which bases pay scales, individual safety measures, and professional accountability on the nationality of staff members.

Second, I examine the mutual imaginations of beneficiaries and providers within the humanitarian economy using three themes. The first theme, humanitarian tourism, is locally generalized as the international approach par excellence to areas of contemporary Lebanon exposed to cyclical outbursts of violence. The second theme, humanitarianism's politics of blame, burdens local society with the structural sin (Bhaskar 2000) of preventing successful foreign interventions. In the third theme, the Southern moral and political expectations placed on the global North are translated into how Syrian refugees imagine the so-called international community and its actions. This chapter addresses articulated North-South dynamics that shape and are shaped by the humanitarian economy.

NORTH-SOUTH HUMANITARIAN ENCOUNTERS

The concept of Southism that I seek to advance embraces various segments of the international community and Lebanon's globalized middle class, which is increasingly employed in humanitarian organizations due to the governmental imperative of enhancing local employment in response to domestic and regional crises. In the wake of neoliberal job creation (Hanieh 2015, 133) and the increasing professionalization of humanitarian assistance provision, both local and international practitioners typically move from one organization to another frequently, changing tasks inside the same organization or moving to different regions within Lebanon or elsewhere. These factors render nationality an important variant, as it can problematize humanitarian recruitment policies and professional ethics. Through NGOization and the professionalization of philanthropy—as some scholars have already noticed (Mac Ginty and Hamieh 2010; Mercer and Green 2013)—local humanitarian practitioners develop a hegemonic culture vis-à-vis the needy. This becomes a culturally nuanced habitus of a hegemonic provision composed of a shared sense of epistemic superiority, where practitioners always presume to know more about domestic vulnerability and systematic solutions than what crisis-affected people themselves do. Hegemonic provision is also composed of moral self-legitimization, assisting and speaking for individuals who, allegedly, can only be assisted and given a voice (Arendt 1958; Agamben 1998; Pandolfi 2000a).

Moreover, in this framework, material privileges and epistemic authority tacitly grant professional accountability, knowledge, and prestige to international staff members (Anderson 1999). The latter's "resource-hungry lifestyle" (Spivak 1999, 6) has been defined as "socially light and materially heavy" (Redfield 2012, 360). International humanitarians are scarcely engaged with local history's legacies and relationships but demand a substantial economic and moral return because they are living uncomfortably, or because their lives may be endangered. Social and material gravity (Redfield 2012) are acquired, in different degrees, through nationality. I have kept these important considerations in mind while discussing the specificities of how epistemic failure and material discrimination play out in the field.

Epistemic Failure

Epistemic failure implies insufficient local knowledge, for example, of the language, customs, and history of the area of intervention. Scholars and practitioners have long noticed that, most of the time, epistemic accountability is exclusively attributed to international actors (Anderson 1999; Polman 2011; Redfield 2012; Mercer and Green 2013), while aid recipients simply allow the former to gain understanding but are allegedly unable to explain things themselves. During my research experience in Lebanon, humanitarian providers often suggested I should not trust the words of local beneficiaries if I wanted to conduct rigorous scientific research. This dynamic is reminiscent of the Arendtian binary of biographic and biological lives, according to which the world is divided into voiceless victims on the one hand and people who can witness, narrate, and better explain the lives of such victims on the other (Arendt 1958).

An international practitioner who worked in a war-affected zone of Beirut in the summer of 2006 stated: "Local NGOs in Lebanon are all family run and tribal-like, whereas we don't have clan ties with anyone, and, therefore, the internationals are the only ones who can become accountable to people without having to bargain something for something else."[1]

Nevertheless, my field research shows that NGO and UN workers were highly dissatisfied with the lack of institutional coordination and the consequent overlapping of projects, something I had experienced myself years before as an intern at UNDP-Cairo. Self-criticism was evident in their accounts, which conveyed how bad coordination actually was, largely due to limited knowledge of the context of intervention and the impossibility of acquiring knowledge while carrying out daily tasks (which already required working extra hours). The high turnover of staff also led to reliance on contextually inexperienced staff over time.

Likewise, my fieldwork indicated that most local and international practitioners are scarcely aware of previous projects conducted by their organizations, funding sources and policies, domestic and international regulations, and local customs. INGOs and UN agencies usually justify lack of contextual knowledge through requests for technical skills, universally applicable regardless of local specificities. This frequently observed lack of knowledge in international humanitarian environments is valued as a guarantee of moral detachment and impartiality during times of conflict (Prendergast 1996). In addition to technocratic recruitment criteria (Carpi 2022), one reason behind such epistemic failure is physical distance. An international practitioner working for an NGO in Qobaiyat (an Akkar village) contended that: "We all work in the same building: INGOs and UN agencies. I mean . . . it looks like an ivory tower. We're totally out of people's reach."[2] Especially compounds have by now become a "metaphor for contemporary humanitarian intervention" (Smirl 2015, 113). Even though humanitarian workers in Lebanon generally do not lead an in-compound life—as they do in Afghanistan, Nigeria, and South Sudan—humanitarian lifeworlds are still protected and preserved through softer forms of "physical bunkerization" (Duffield 2015, S85), which hampers the development of contextual knowledge.[3]

Material Discrimination

The second type of encounter is material discrimination that, in most INGOs and UN agencies, sets pay scales, individual safety measures, and capacities to move according to the nationality of humanitarian staff members.[4] This leads to the internal reproduction of hierarchical relationships within the humanitarian economy. Material discrimination builds on the specter of social class, as the latter is seldom brought into debates or questioned in international summits and NGO programming, and the relational history between wealthy foreign humanitarians and local classes most often remains a taboo topic. This taboo can hardly be challenged "through delusions based on the hope that some bourgeois apparatus might carry us to a better tomorrow" (Chit 2014, 116).

In the interviews I conducted in Dahiye and Akkar, regional humanitarian practitioners, mostly Lebanese locals or people from other Arab countries, often highlighted the disadvantageous pay scales they were doomed to receive, even when possessing more than one passport or being dual citizens of both a Northern and Southern country. According to them, some NGO policies institutionalize material discrimination by allocating payments to cover rent for international staff members only. Generally, neither regional nor local staff had their rent paid by their employer, and only a few of them stated that they benefited from a small housing allowance.

While NGOs tended to exclusively deploy local staff in the field for security reasons—a policy that sometimes exposed them to actual risk—local staff mobility remained limited and their privileged lifestyle unguaranteed. Unlike international practitioners, who could move from one organization to another in an environment where professional mobility was highly rewarded, for locals such a mobility was difficult. Another example of stunted local mobility was the possibility of evacuation in times of actual crisis or global risk; this was proved in September 2013 when the United States indicated they might intervene in Syria to topple the Asad regime. I personally recall that Beirut was emptied in two days. NGO branches across the country were shut down, and international staff were called to Beirut to be ready for evacuation if needed. In the meantime, local staff had to remain in their unsafe lifeworlds.

Geopolitical uncertainty marked an uncomfortable line between Northern and Southern subjects within the humanitarian economy. However, Dahiye's internally displaced people and refugees significantly expressed their resentment also toward those local professionals who, often with a Western educational background, were allowed easy access to international (resourceful) networks and represented the only "local good governance" (Mercer and Green 2013, 113) which foreign governments aspired to work with. This exacerbated the moral divide across local and refugee social classes. Furthermore, Lebanese regulations allowing the employment of only a small, fixed number of Lebanon's Palestinian refugees and Syrian nationals in the local staff of humanitarian organizations ended up "ethnicizing" the class divide.

HUMANITARIAN IMAGINATIONS

I adopt humanitarian Southism as a framework of analysis to explore the mutual imaginations that providers and humanitarian workers produce within the humanitarian economy. First, I disclose a form of local disaffection, which I call humanitarian tourism. Then, I examine the humanitarian politics of blame on local structures and mentality. Finally, I unfold the refugee discourse around the betrayal of the international community, which stands in contrast to the humanitarian-claimed "need to be there." While displaced people tended to understand this "need to be there" as the need of some Northern states to outsource unemployable citizens to crisis-affected areas to create a sustainable economy of international labor, the humanitarian actors I met in some Akkar villages stressed their idea of being necessary for the particular area. They considered their intervention to be legitimized by their supposedly neutral and impartial intervention. An international practitioner working in an Akkar village contended: "We *have to* be there, since local people, particularly if affiliated with other religious groups, won't do anything for other communities. There would simply be a huge void in the places in which we're currently intervening. Moreover, social services here are corrupt and weak. We cannot really change what, historically, has been the cancer of this region."[5]

This statement supports the conviction that if positions were not covered by an allegedly impartial Western practitioner, they would never be taken by local or, more broadly, regional humanitarians, who certainly would not want to challenge their system of values and beliefs by taking part in such a social endeavor. International practitioners specifically referred to the idea that a Christian Lebanese national would not feel safe or at ease working among Sunni Syrians who had relocated to the Sunni villages in Akkar in substantial numbers. Thus, most of the NGO and UN practitioners I interviewed spoke in terms of "Churchillian responsibility" (Spivak 2004), or the self-legitimated right to intervene as a moral duty toward the assisted rather than the right to work somewhere. Most did not see their job simply as a way to earn a living (and, quite frequently, earn it with additional privileges) but as a mission. I will now discuss the specificities of local imaginations around humanitarian tourism in Beirut's Dahiye, the politics of blame in the humanitarian system, and the discourse voicing the expectations of Syrian refugees toward the international community in Akkar's villages, which constitutes a particular politics of blame.

Humanitarian Tourism

In in-depth interviews and participant observations I conducted in Dahiye from 2011 to 2013, locally displaced people who benefited from humanitarian assistance at the time of the Israel-Lebanon war of July 2006 pointed, in hindsight, to the aid system's touristic approach by describing the international humanitarian as *'aber sabil*: a passerby. Likewise, local NGOs highlighted the humanitarian scandal that occurred when the UNDP and some staff from the ICRC left Lebanon because it was believed that Israel would destroy Hezbollah within three days.[6] Although foreign aid is perceived as ephemeral and opportunism-driven, its negative moral legacy turns into a "permanent topography of assistance" (Smirl 2015, 111). Beyond the distress caused by the war itself, this perception among the locals of humanitarian tourism increased the sense of uncertainty in Dahiye. Local NGOs claimed that they had to trade local knowledge for financial resources and greater public visibility (see Zakharia and Knox 2014), competing (and often overlapping) with other local actors to survive. The localization of the aid agenda, launched at the 2016 Istanbul World Humanitarian Summit, was supposed to catalyze preexisting social forces and structures. In the development discourse of INGOs, partnerships with local NGOs were described as exchanges of ideas, skills, and information, but the flow was predominantly unilateral, with local counterparts simply expected to adopt the UN language of development (Zakharia and Knox 2014). This unilateralism was perpetuated through enduring belief in agencies, such as the UNDP and Oxfam, whose staff often pointed out to me how their local counterparts would ignore the need for coordination without external assistance.[7] In turn, some local NGO practitioners I spoke to questioned the domestic impact of INGOs. As a project manager from the Imam Sadr Foundation argued: "Is the humanitarian aid coming from the UN, international, and local NGOs able to catalyze social change, dialogue, and democracy, or do they reinforce the existent relations of power? If the answer is no, the future is not promising."[8]

Dahiye's war-affected population especially grew to distrust and sometimes act with hostility toward the international community (*al-mujtama' ad-duwali*), which had allegedly rushed to rescue them in 2006 in the wake of the Israeli Air Force attacks. A press release in *al-Akhbar*, which I accessed in the archives of the Lebanese newspaper, reported that tons of emergency relief tools due to be supplied by the UNHCR, including mattresses and aid kits, were burned before they could be distributed as they had become spoiled because of inadequate protection while in storage.[9] This particular episode was compared to the smell of corruption (*raihat al-fasad*) in the Lebanese government's High Relief Commission and the utter unreliability of UN staff who, from a local perspective, did not actually care about people's safety.

The widespread local perception of dealing with opportunistic war tourists that I observed speaks to the historical framework of Beirut's southern peripheries. Dahiye has long had an image of urban wreckage and massive destruction, deprivation, and misery. The area suffers from external stereotyping and neglect (Deeb 2006; Harb 1995, 2006) and has frequently drawn the interest of outsiders during times of emergency and displacement. Social responsiveness to touristic international humanitarianism in 2006 seemed to encourage locals to show greater entitlement in claiming a particular territory as theirs during both war and peacetime. This action was meant to counter the international aid industry's temporary exploitation of war-affected areas. "Westerners are all tourists, even if they've spent thirty years in this country," said the leader of a prominent local NGO.[10] "Instead, we've been taking care of Lebanon since 1976, the beginning of the civil war."

Recalling the studies conducted on refugees mistrusting and being mistrusted (Daniel and Knudsen 1995, 2, in Dunn 2017, 147), the endemic mistrust toward international aid was expressed by a resident from ash-Shiyyah who told me: "Nothing dies if it comes from the inside. Corruption and exploitation increase because of the presence of foreigners here."[11] In response, international practitioners imagined society in Lebanon as an unchangeable and reified realm. Thinking about local immutability as existing independently from the effects of humanitarian work, international practitioners tended to portray local actors as inherently failing and weak.

Mistrust of international aid and a broader anti-Western imaginary came to a head during the July War after being encoded in the social ethics of the major Lebanese Shiite party, Hezbollah, which rules many of Dahiye's municipalities. The UN and the US government were often mentioned as the real criminals and "the people who have always lied,"[12] while *Al Jazeera* was denounced as a media coward that paid lip service to Western politics.[13] Indeed, United Nations Security Council (UNSC) Resolution 1701, which ended the July War, imposed an arms embargo on Lebanon, approaching the destroyed country as the aggressor. *Al-Akhbar* journalist Rajana Hammiye expressed contempt about the ephemerality of the UN's commitment to dealing with Dahiye's tragedy: "Their visit lasted just fifty minutes with the leaders of all municipalities."[14]

Because of the (locally defined) voyeuristic and touristic approach of international practitioners to the psychological grievances of war-stricken populations, local residents viewed Western-funded reconstruction with resentment and suspicion despite official rhetoric boasting an unprecedented level of North–South collaboration.[15] Local perceptions of the fleeting nature of international assistance stood in stark contrast to how locals faced misadventure with a spirit of positive normalcy. The war-stricken people's identification with and sense of belonging to their territory emphasized that Western interference was unwelcomed in some Dahiye districts, recalling how thin the line can be between perceived occupation and assistance, despite potential benefits.[16] The fact that Dahiye was the birthplace of many social workers upheld local pride in postwar reconstruction and humanitarian efforts. In this regard, a local social worker in postwar Dahiye stated: "The majority of the staff here have grown up in the neighborhood. I'm a child of this district myself [*ana bint al-manta'a*]. We know our beneficiaries personally; we recognize their faces in the street. That is something a foreign NGO can't do."[17]

Similarly, a government social worker observed: "Most of the people who sought shelter in this office during the July War were all acquaintances or already our beneficiaries."[18] The moral importance of being born and bred in the area was also highlighted by a member of the Choueifat Council in Dahiye: "In this municipality, we're all local members."[19] The same attitude of pride and local heroism in remaining and providing services for the community was expressed by the deputy mayor of al-Ghobeiry's municipality in Dahiye, who supported the common spirit of assistance and territorial belonging of all members of the Union of Dahiye's Municipalities (*Ittihad al-Baladiyyat fy'd-Dahiye al-Janubiyye*).[20] These accounts suggest how local dwellers perceived Western-led humanitarian aid as an ephemeral and opportunistic routine business.

The Politics of Blame

While researching Akkar's villages, it became apparent that INGOs frequently adopted a "politics of blame" rhetoric (Antze and Lambek 1996, XXII) to explain why projects were not succeeding: they blamed donors, local mentality and structures, or evil warlords. It seemed their focus was on protecting their organizational moral reputation instead of acknowledging their role in a system of inequality. Most of the international practitioners I interviewed believed their programs were not responsible for deepening divisions between emergency areas and chronically marginalized spaces. In this environment, where no one seemed to have the capacity to cause change, providers disengaged from the consequences of humanitarian assistance, self-legitimized by the very humanitarian reason of doing good unconditionally (Fassin 2013; Duffield 2014).

By adopting the politics of blame, humanitarian practitioners often reciprocated people's mistrust, gradually pushing the former to walk away from obligations such as extending outreach and properly tailoring projects to the local context. Humanitarian practitioners related several episodes in which their beneficiaries lied because of greed. For instance, a humanitarian practitioner living in an Akkar village affirmed: "Beneficiaries always say that nothing is provided to them or that we are corrupt. They don't understand when we simply lack the resources to implement a project properly [. . .]. Don't believe them when they tell you this; they'd go on and on to complain about everything on Earth. Some of them speak in the name of greed, not grievance."[21]

The corrupt central state and confessional structure of Lebanese society—where parliamentary seats and governmental roles are allocated on a sectarian basis—were usually used by international practitioners to justify the aid apparatus's shortcomings. Such a politics of blame was functionally adapted to the Akkar environment, where the distribution of aid to refugees from Syria antagonized the long-neglected Lebanese among whom they lived. This point harks back to the aid sector's "culture of justification" (Terry 2002, 229) when facing failure. Local and refugee groups' general and undistinguished mistrust toward the international humanitarian system proved how little effort humanitarian actors made in allowing aid recipients to get to know the nuanced heterogeneity of their programs. This highlights the effects of the overall sociology of humanitarian dominance, which protects and reproduces moral sovereignty over the assisted while cementing moral distance from them.

As mentioned earlier, practitioners' Southism certainly did not come without an element of self-criticism; indeed, the self-criticism of some practitioners deepened their skepticism about the humanitarian practice itself. Many practitioners in Akkar villages were skeptical about the projects they were working on, including practical changes, long-term sustainability, territorial development, and organizational approaches to the areas of intervention. Notwithstanding such self-criticism, which counters the epistemic failure explained above, humanitarian practitioners tended to make a rigorous distinction between their skepticism about the material results of their work and their good intentions, as though the latter could almost redeem them for having approached or assessed territories of intervention inappropriately. The humanitarian politics of blame I have illustrated so far, to a certain extent, points to the moral solipsism of humanitarian action in the everyday life of Akkar's villages while also suggesting the inequality of the "moral economy" of humanitarianism (Fassin 2005, 365).

Syrian Refugees and the International Community

Between 2011 and 2013 in Akkar villages, despite diverse forms of aid intervention, Syrian displacement became synonymous with international abandonment. This refugee discourse is a revealing form of geopolitical imagination in response to Southism. The continuation of the Syrian conflict was, at that stage, largely attributed to the inaction of international actors—in this case, international politicians—who, as the majority of the refugees I interviewed pointed out, had militarily intervened in Iraq and Libya.

Most Syrian refugees highlighted the tendency of aid providers to misinterpret the Syrian conflict and expressed concern that aid actors would soon turn into reconciliation actors who would misrepresent their cultural values and social system. This suggests that some of the refugees were already formulating their thinking on how postemergency reconciliation would deal with the Syrian political crisis. The humanitarian presence was locally perceived as a for-profit enterprise trying to attract as much funding as possible, with humanist values becoming market gains of reconstruction and relief projects (Potvin 2013, 8).

Until early 2013, the vast majority of refugees I met referred to the events in Syria as revolution (*thawra*), as most came from political opposition-majority areas. Hence, Syrian refugees vented their frustration with Western media depictions of the Syrian conflict as a civil war (*harb ahliyye*), when it was mainly militias that were fighting each other. Media narratives played a large role in the refugee discourse around the international community in Lebanon. A Syrian refugee originally from ar-Raqqa, based in Bebnin at the time of our interview, explained how the warring parties—the government, its allies, and the variegated opposition—were often incorrectly represented as having the same means.[22] Another Syrian refugee from Afamia voiced his rejection of the dominant global North narratives by stating that Syrians were not buying weapons to fight each other but rather to liberate the country.[23]

Humanitarian reports increasingly portrayed the conflict as religiously motivated, and some refugee aid recipients were resentful of how they were dealt with. From the refugees' perspective, in designing projects to address their needs, aid providers should have been able to "distinguish between the root and proximate causes of conflict" (Anderson 1999, 70). Mohammed, a Syrian refugee originally from the countryside of Deir ez-Zor, said he felt unrepresented when watching the news on TV, and he expressed a sense of being betrayed by the international community.[24] "Betrayal" is a term that I often heard in refugee campsites in reference to the part of the Syrian population that remained loyal to the regime, but also in reference to the international community, "with whom we'll also need to reconcile."[25] In this sense, "the international community's betrayal" (*khianet al-mujtama' ad-duwali*) in Akkar consisted of the decision to remain politically detached from the events in Syria while parading humanitarian support. Bodoor, a Syrian refugee woman from Homs, similarly argued: "The West and a part of Syrian society have betrayed [us]; that's the reason why we're still dying everywhere."[26]

The moral indictment that I recorded among refugees from Syria over the years was primarily directed against the international community, which, in their eyes, I represented in my capacity as an academic researcher. Because of the Western origin of humanitarian orthodox principles, the distance between aid intervention and the areas in which decisions are made and discussions take place reproduce North-South power relationships and imaginaries.

In the same vein, refugees thought that Islamophobia in the North influenced the international community to misrepresent the Syrian conflict. For instance, Sami, a Syrian refugee, said that the international community feared abstract forms of Islam and drew an arbitrary line between an extremist, "terrorist" Islam and a "moderate" Islam acceptable to the North: "The international community believes that we need to learn what humanity [*insaniye*] and reconciliation [*musalaha*] mean from the outside."[27] He expressed his frustration that the international community limited itself to providing aid, epitomizing its "modern conscience given an alibi" (Rieff 2002, 96). Humanitarian operations were viewed as a surrogate for the international community's political inaction; refugees suggested that such a moderate form of support was a way of compensating for not taking a clear stance in the Syrian conflict and not actively supporting the popular uprising. This assistant-like but apolitical form of Southism was locally rejected because of the international community's inaction.

THE SOUTHIST "NEED TO BE THERE"

In conclusion, there is a complex and changing interspace between locals and internationals, which, in discussing Southism, still marks the importance of passports and nationality. Foreign aid providers in Dahiye and Akkar often stressed their "need to be there," suggesting that locals are unable to do what international actors do because locals cannot replace international actors in areas where locals do not feel politically or religiously comfortable. An international practitioner in Qobaiyat (Akkar) described a Lebanon that, without international aid providers, would face even greater hardship, as the local is unable to act out of humanity: "Local people don't want to work in places that don't territorialize their own community and, as a result, wouldn't act in neutral ways when facing issues that should be dealt with in a merely 'humane' way."[28] However, the implicit rendering of "humane" synonymous with "neutral" and "apolitical," and the perspective of feeling politically impartial and materially necessary in the South, were not exclusive to internationals but also present in some segments of local society. The humanitarian practitioners interviewed believed that, without external "therapeutic intervention" (Pupavac 2004), endemic social changes would only engender higher levels of domestic violence and instability. From this perspective, the alleviation of daily grievances is only possible through international aid. Such a logical implication does not take into account that any external intervention, even if humanitarian, reduces territorial and historical self-esteem to a certain extent (Harb 2006) and triggers the inner feeling that suffering can only be alleviated from the outside.

The widespread belief that humanitarian neutrality is solidly tied up in the official legitimacy of international interventionism—and that international aid providers are most capable of upholding such neutrality—contributes to the North-South imaginary that locals are inherently weak and need to be managed and therapeuticized from the outside (Carpi 2022). Against this backdrop, many refugees I shared experiences with reconfigure humanitarian presence and action in terms of political solidarity (e.g., Rozakou 2012).

Running the double risk of diluting and unlearning the "Souths" in a stigmatized singular "North," scholars have generally identified a monolithic humanitarian common culture as a mere expression of the "international humanitarian" (Sen 1981). I have argued that Southism should be degeographicized as a more complex discourse instrument, since local actors increasingly adopt the role of trustworthy partners for foreign aid providers, temporarily blurring separation lines that reemerge with high significance in times of actual risk. International humanitarian actors, however, emphasize their increasing cooperation with locals to secure indigenous guidance and localize work.[29] Since 2016, there has been an institutionalized form of cooperation with local partners that, simplistically, tends to translate humanitarian effort into respect for local specificities and desires, as if such cooperation could ever guarantee overarching neutrality, transparency, and professional honesty. Local participation has not turned out to be a guarantee of subaltern knowledge (Spivak 1999). Hence, we need the flexible geography of Southism that disappears when irrelevant and reemerges when able to unfold the *ad hoc* performative roles of nationality. Southism powerfully generates the distances that the politics of crisis-making reproduces.

In the framework of the humanitarian economy, "Northern subjects" currently approach "Southern subjects" in two ways. The first involves realizing a concerted need to help that can ideally merge Northern and Southern standards and models of care. The second involves the implementation of this need through a gradual disengagement from responsibility and donorship (Slaughter and Crisp 2009). In this relational economy, the South projects onto the North its interpretation of humanitarian provision as an integral part of political solidarity and of solutions so far deemed insufficient or lacking in both the case of the July War and the Syrian political crisis. In this sense, the humanitarian economy is an interrelational realm where passports simultaneously hold partial and contextual relevance. I have tried to unfold this relevance to examine North-South encounters and imaginations and to problematize ethnicized, racialized, and political geographies. The discursive strategy of Southism can help capture humanitarian lifeworlds and their (actual and imagined) encounters with local and refugee thinking and behaviors.

Likewise, Southism explains how, in my teens, I started developing an interest myself in understanding war and in becoming "essential" for war-affected people. Southism can unpack how interconnected with coloniality, racialization, and inequalities such constructed "instincts" are in reality. When I was a child, images from the Second Gulf War (the 1990 Iraqi invasion of Kuwait) and from ex-Yugoslavia—to which, as an Italian, I had geographic proximity—used to populate my TV screen. Certainly, public narratives and visual cues played a major role in shaping my child psychology. State institutions, schools, and the media constructed me as a white child, growing up in a colonial power as a compassionate subject, apt to become a savior. If Southism cannot fully explain all of my wavering engagement with humanitarianism, it can hopefully reveal how there is no such a thing like a "natural instinct" to be a humanitarian.

NOTES

1. Interview with representative of an INGO, Beirut, November 9, 2011.
2. Interview, Qobaiyat, northern Lebanon, November 30, 2012.
3. In Lebanon, an example of permanently "bunkerized" reality is the one of UN staff living in Naqura (Lebanese southern border town marked by the so-called Blue Line), where the UNIFIL headquarters are located.
4. Some local NGOs have overtly declared that they set the same salary scales for international and local staff (Maxwell Hart, Mohanna, and Lefebvre 2020, 65).
5. Interview, Qobaiyat, northern Lebanon, December 9, 2012.
6. Interview, Mossaitbe, Beirut, October 11, 2011.
7. For some organizations, coordination is unlikely to happen: "Overlaps are kind of unavoidable when you work in a very small country." Enrico Azzone, CTM-Lecce, Beirut, October 25, 2011. In other cases, coordination is even seen as unadvisable: "We never coordinate with other NGOs, especially INGOs, because we don't want to adapt our projects to foreign aims, and we don't want to be conditioned from the outside." Interview with a representative from the Lebanese Red Cross, Spears, Beirut, February 1, 2012.
8. Tyre branch, October 8, 2011.
9. Tha'ir Ghandour, *al-Akhbar*, September 13, 2006.
10. Interview, Mossaitbe, Beirut, October 11, 2011.
11. Interview, Ash-Shiyyah, Beirut, February 3, 2012.

12. Conversation with a resident in Haret Hreik, Beirut, November 24, 2011.

13. It is worth noting that *Al Jazeera*, at the time of the July 2006 War, was clearly allied with Lebanon and not Israel. However, people in Dahiye referred to the channel's political attitude as in opposition to Hezbollah and the Axis of Resistance and in support of the Muslim Brotherhood.

14. The article is dated September 6, 2012, Arabic edition.

15. Hezbollah's members embraced the "increased cooperation with the West" rhetoric when referring to the presence of international providers. Interview with the deputy mayor of Haret Hreik, Beirut, October 20, 2011.

16. Scholar Didier Fassin explained this concept in a speech at the School of Social Sciences, Institute for Advanced Studies in Paris (April 26, 2012).

17. Interview, municipality of ash-Shiyyah, Beirut, October 28, 2011.

18. Interview with Naziha Dakroub, manager of the Social Development Center, Office of the Ministry of Social Affairs, Ash-Shiyyah, Beirut, October 30, 2011.

19. Interview, Choueifat, Beirut, November 27, 2012.

20. Interview, Al-Ghobeiry, Beirut, November 26, 2012.

21. Interview, Halba, northern Lebanon, November 28, 2012.

22. Interview, Bebnin, northern Lebanon, January 28, 2013.

23. Interview, Al-'Abdeh, northern Lebanon, September 29, 2012.

24. Interview, Halba, northern Lebanon, January 28, 2013.

25. Interview with a Syrian refugee in al-Bahsa, northern Lebanon, January 28, 2013.

26. Interview, Al-Bahsa, northern Lebanon, December 2, 2012.

27. Interview, Al-'Abdeh, northern Lebanon, January 28, 2013.

28. Interview, UNHCR, Qobaiyat, northern Lebanon, December 12, 2012.

29. Interview with an international practitioner in Fourn ash-Shebbak, Beirut, October 13, 2011.

6 / The Trojan Horses of Humanitarianism

What we have learned to call humanitarianism can at times undermine both "positive solidarity"—the collective pursuit of a common good—and "negative solidarity" (Hayden and Saunders 2019, 186), where individuals and groups become united and perceive themselves as a whole through common experiences of war, suffering, and oppression. Humanitarianism can separate individuals and groups that have the potential to share worlds with others and, from an Arendtian perspective, share political agency. It can also distance local citizens from each other, as in the case of reconstruction and compensation policies in postwar Dahiye. It can distance refugees from local internally displaced people even when the former, in the capacity of circular migrants, have historically inhabited common spaces and are not a new presence by any means. It can distance aid providers from aid recipients, overshadowing the circumstances in which the two roles overlap. As a moral force that makes aid deserved or undeserved, humanitarian management and the politics of crisis-making it produces can also distance refugees from one another along nationality lines. Indeed, Calhoun (2004) suggests that our ordinary imaginary around emergencies not only shapes the attention we pay to social life but also organizes dimensions of social life itself. If the politics of crisis-making significantly contributes to making and unmaking social, political, and moral economies, this book has endeavored to inform how that politics is subject to change, for identity is never set in stone and can be transformed into a way to access sustainable care.

In the entanglement of protracted "emergencies" on a ground where chronic predicament existed long before crisis, the lives of longstanding and recent refugees are enmeshed with those of locals, some of whom have repeatedly experienced displacement and hardship. By this token, group belonging and intergroup relationships are indeed not made by crisis per se, but rather by the officialization of such crisis: namely, the discursive and operational application of a crisis-defined approach to everyday life. While international humanitarian discourse has made crisis a self-evident explanation for material deprivation, human suffering, and political failure, crisis does not entail any self-evidence. A crisis-driven understanding of welfare remains today's greatest engine for international funding. In other words, rather than emergency itself, it is emergencization—the official declaration of crisis and the emplacement of international humanitarian actors—that reshuffles ingroup and outgroup relationships and identity work at an individual and a collective level. Notably, crisis, as an official discourse and framework of action, makes and unmakes the social membership of forced migrants and internally displaced people, giving rise to the unequal political, ethnicized, and moral economies I have explored. *The Politics of Crisis-Making* contributes to the academic—as much as social and political—responsibility to research forced migrations and humanitarianism *across* rather than merely *within* (or between) social groups. Even the ethnocratic approach, as seen, can carry dangerous presumptions concretely impinging on people's lives.

Today's routinized humanitarianism adopts the strategy of addressing local predicament and longstanding vulnerability, not only human displacement. This combination of intents and practices, defined by different temporal purposes, complicates the illusory solution of surrendering to the "tyranny of emergency" (Minear 2002, 52), where funds are destined for the latest crises. The tyranny of emergency inevitably takes to the tyranny of the present: an ahistorical present. Over humanitarian history, the tyranny of emergency has questioned "adhocratic" forms of humanitarianism (Dunn 2012)—ruling by improvisation—aimed at sorting out immediate needs while failing to provide long-term perspectives. Today's develop-manitarian approach, as I call it, is typical of contemporary aid interventions in Lebanon, and while illusorily presenting a long-term perspective, it merges into "crisis thinking" (Calhoun 2004) and "emergency imaginaries" (Calhoun 2008). In develop-manitarianism, short-term relief can both precede and follow long-term projects that manufacture activities to rehabilitate normal life, but it also encounters chronic poverty and predicament, as in many areas of Dahiye and Akkar. This wrestling of temporal perspectives and programs forestalls improvement in the lives of both refugees and locals. The crisis-making machine not only posits wars and other human disasters as unpredictable events that produce crisis but also posits the prediction of the political consequences of "crisis" as unachievable. Explaining social and political processes through the crisis repertoire enables the alleviation—rather than the ending—of poverty, suffering, and deprivation as the rule rather than the exception. In crisis thinking, the provision of foreign aid is an unquestionable need, assuming the political acknowledgment of crisis as the only condition that, making aid inevitable and unconditional (International Crisis Group 2020), enables Lebanon to survive and develop. In this geopolitical space of deep-seated conditionalities, little focus is placed on locally grown realities accountable to locals, on local knowledge, and its social legacies.

Hegemonic humanitarianism dominated by the agendas of foreign donors and implementing agencies is not only an arm of governance—the "left hand of empire" (Agier 2003)—but also an existential condition (Feldman 2018) where social groups coalesce, fall apart, or maintain distance from each other. A critique of crisis-making does not imply that human, infrastructural, and economic situations are not particularly critical moments that interrupt normal affairs. Nor does it deny that effective coping mechanisms and tactics of survival may be needed more than ever. Instead, it means that crisis becomes the only way of making human, economic, and political systems work—the only way of providing livelihoods and services and of being acknowledged in international decision-making. Crisis-making is a logic that rests on the violent perpetuation of the minimum "humanitarian reason" (Fassin 2011). Humanitarian programs have bound people's survival to postwar reconstruction efforts and official declarations of new emergencies. In this context, local development appears as the underresourced follow-up to humanitarian programs once postcrisis stability is established. Although humanitarian agencies increasingly invest in long-term assistance with the support of development actors or reprioritize their original development tasks, international donors tend to defund protracted displacement. Humanitarian interventions in Lebanon have encouraged people to think of improvement either as a result of war or a compensatory form of material consolation for war-caused suffering and destruction. In a climate of generalized disaffection toward the political, the emergence of the humanitarian to mobilize international resources and offer normal welfare is convenient, as it is considered the only possible avenue to create a relatively stable existence.

Publicly presented as an abnormality, emergencies are not exceptions in politics, and Lebanon's crisis history can relate to broader analogous processes. As Calhoun (2008) proposes, emergencies are mainly associated with the so-called South of the world, as though a smoothly functioning normal system of global processes ever existed in the North. The emergency imaginary generates a sense of ethical obligation to intervene in some areas of need rather than others; however, it also develops greater tolerance toward the makings of politics in a world where politics itself seems to be about managing emergencies and crises. As a result, there emerges a global tolerance for crisis-driven modalities of governance and development practices that survive and thrive on the "we do what we can" mantra.

Between Dahiye and Akkar, a Sisyphean cycle is evident, with historically marginalized areas becoming politicized because of the officialization of crisis and the physical emplacement of humanitarian actors. Whenever a new emergency is presented to us, long-term humanitarianism steps back to the short-term provision of first aid before returning to farsighted development and normal service provision in the aftermath of the crisis. The tyranny of emergency induces international and local humanitarian organizations to take resources from long-term interventions, causing the cyclic weakening of local welfare.

The crisis-making machine thrives on emergencization, rather than on emergency per se, insofar as ordinary affairs are believed to worsen if aid is withdrawn. Lebanon's history shows that humanitarianism cannot leave a better welfare system in place. Against this backdrop, the emergencization of Lebanese society, and the knowledge produced around such emergencization, should be challenged to enable the country to subsist and thrive regardless of crises. On the one hand, the paradoxical presence of permanent refugees in a Lebanon of transit constitutes the Trojan horse of economic and political insecurity (from which humanitarianism derives its legitimate emplacement). On the other hand, the international aid machine in Lebanon is the Trojan horse of the chronic emergencization of Lebanon's society and politics.

DEVELOPMENT-*ARIANISM*?

The current debate about the humanitarian-development nexus among refugee-recipient countries and donors raises important questions about the extent to which humanitarianism should alleviate suffering and attend to basic material needs or develop farsighted perspectives (Otto and Weingärtner 2013; Mosel and Levine 2014; Gabiam 2016). The lack of a clear-cut definition of this nexus has hampered collaboration between what are effectively two distinct sectors. The approach OCHA has been promoting since 2015 with the NWOW strategy recognizes that greater coordination and coherence between humanitarian and development actors is a priority. This strategy has not led to an effective localization of humanitarian practices, since local actors are still relegated to the role of field operators who can easily be put at risk due to unequal partnerships with INGOs (Fourn 2017; Drif 2018). The fact that actors from the global South are now admitted into the "humanitarian club" does not mean that their voices are truly welcome; they are expected to exhibit decorum and accept the rules of the club (Barnett 2021, 175).

While the humanitarian-development nexus remains a moot point among policymakers, with some indeed arguing that humanitarianism and development are practically a false dichotomy (Slim 2000), field operators have a pragmatic approach to this binary, either undercutting or blurring these ways of operating. Others have pointed to the different cultures and debates underpinning the politics of development and the politics of aid (Suhrke and Ofstad 2005). Discussions about the humanitarian-development nexus have questioned the presumption that the farther from the beginning of a crisis, the smaller humanitarian need becomes, instead prioritizing longer-term needs such as refugee employment. On the official agenda, a large segment of NGO and UN programs aim to make individuals employable and view displacement as an overarching disenfranchising condition that subtends the lives of both refugees and locals. The continuous hardship of refugee groups in Dahiye and Akkar seemingly points to the importance of establishing a common set of principles that integrates both approaches because the tyranny of emergency continues to drain development assistance resources. Indeed, development assistance fades to the background as soon as a new crisis is declared somewhere else or within Lebanon itself. For several NGOs operating in Lebanon, the possibility for development assistance directly springs from humanitarian relief. This paradoxically happens not only because crisis attracts funding in Lebanon but also because cyclic humanitarian need undermines longstanding forms of development. The improvisation or training of development actors as humanitarian workers enables them to access greater financial generosity in a world dominated by emergency-driven politics, which, through exceptional governance, implements measures that enhance economic inequality, political disenfranchisement, and social injustice.

In Lebanon, despite the apparent fragility of state sovereignty, development and humanitarianism have predominantly—although complexly—worked through a governmental politics of opportunistic absence or clear-cut repression. The discussions about how aid and development should be delivered in Lebanon are more relevant than ever after the blast at the Beirut Port on August 4, 2020. Bypassing the government to deliver aid was identified as one of the primary apparent causes of fragile state sovereignty (Fakhoury 2017), with international actors channeling resources to selected partners rather than the state. Recent campaigns to rebuild the areas of Beirut hit by the blast have advocated for direct delivery to local NGOs and the people affected. The August blast was, in fact, a turning point for the visibility of local actors and support networks; they received large parts of international funding directly rather than through global donors and INGOs. Local campaigns encouraged the international community to support local actors by donating money directly to social workers—and those identified as reliable gatekeepers—instead of the Lebanese government or political parties. Social media played a large role in Lebanon's civil society and diasporas in promoting the closure of Lebanese politicians' bank accounts worldwide to limit state corruption and incompetence. Nonetheless, according to Ziad Abdel Samad from the Arab NGO Network for Development,[1] managing and coordinating foreign funding without passing through accountable public administration has turned out to be difficult. Likewise, reconstruction after the civil war and the July War were largely led by private companies, with the state sidelined and smaller visibility for local civil actors.

During emergency, ambitious humanitarian sovereignties can replace a lax welfare state while upholding state power. In fact, a relief-oriented agenda enabled the political elites that form the state to survive and endure in times when large segments of Lebanon's society ask for the state to be dismantled. The message that emerged out of the August blast powerfully suggested that the humanitarian politics of crisis-making can indeed be effective in (more or less inadvertently) stifling political reforms and radical transformations. After August 2020, sidelining the state was promoted as effective political action to help the people hit by the blast and advocate for justice beyond the provision of humanitarian assistance. Local organizations like the Lebanese civil society knowledge platform *Daleel Madani* built a database of actors providing relief and other services to the displaced and those affected by the blast, with the database suggesting that local and private actors contributed most of the relief provision.[2] As Fawaz and Harb (2020) incisively put it, "the inspiring energy of hundreds of young individuals who flocked to the downtown districts affected by the blast, armed only with shovels and brooms, fueled hope in a city where time seemed to have stood still." A large community of ex or current Lebanon dwellers demonstrated their support, efficiency, and affection for Lebanon, securing international funding through digital platforms and carrying out social media campaigns. Many of these campaigns were explicitly aimed at raising money to rebuild the local shops, cafeterias, bars, and restaurants that previously proliferated in the areas heavily stricken by the blast (e.g., from the Beirut Corniche to the eastern districts of Jemmayze, Mar Mkhayel an-Nahr, and Karantina). People cared not only about the provision of relief and shelter to those affected by the blast but also the recreation of Beirut's spaces normally considered secondary to human survival. Local understanding of reconstruction, as in Dahiye in 2006, at a grassroots level, revolved around the preservation of intimate spatial memories, the debated opportunity for urban development and spaces of wellbeing, and the contested boosting of private, humanitarian, or political businesses.

The blast reasserted the need for the humanitarian system to hone its way of working in urban spaces. Crisis management in urban societies raises the issue of negotiating humanitarian presence and plans with local authorities. On the one hand, representatives from several INGOs and UN agencies I interviewed deemed collaboration with official authorities tiring and sensitive, believing that collaboration could incur the risk of politicization and shorten projects due to political issues. On the other hand, the biopolitical containment of refugees off the shores of most Western countries cannot function as a development incentive for local authorities in Lebanon or in other parts of the South where most displaced people presently live. While some mayors have been eager to collaborate with vibrant civil society actors to improve towns and cities across Lebanon (Harb and Atallah 2015, 199), that is not always the case when urban improvement is instrumentalized for geopolitical purposes and subject to refugee containment. In sum, the mainstream humanitarian discourse increasingly revolves around the need to include local governments rather than bypass them to implement quicker aid provision. Throughout the years, however, I observed a lack of interest in some Lebanese municipalities in improving infrastructure, as such improvements only seem to serve the foreign interest of containing human mobility within the region (Carpi and Boano 2018). Additionally, improved cities may attract larger numbers of refugees from less fortunate areas. The lack of incentive for local development questions the simplistic dictum of "working with local authorities," which nowadays overpopulates expert recommendations in policy briefs and humanitarian accounts. Nor can international actors remain unscathed from local politics or represent an apolitical system. Similarly, some local authorities struggle to envision forms of local development that can be implemented independently from foreign politics. In this sense, today's problem does not only reside in budget shortfalls, often used as a legitimate justification, as when refugee food rations were cut from Lebanon to Uganda and Kenya (Gladstone 2015 in Dunn 2017, 205); it also lies in the politics of feeding a crisis-making machine that does not physically need to halve resources and spaces with the displaced to whom it purportedly conveys solidarity.

The energy demonstrated by local initiatives in the aftermath of the Beirut blast points to the inescapable failure of a humanitarianism which deliberately ignores why an atrocity is happening and does not place blame on any side, acting as a historical anesthetizer. The alleviation of suffering cannot be the only answer and, as has been seen, is not effective. However, the politics of granting rights passes through compensatory humanitarianism because of a continually entropic state of life, where neither war-affected local people nor refugees are approached as unconditional rights bearers but rather as mere "beneficiaries of a humanitarian order" (Rodogno 2012, 254). The deep-seated need for relief in Lebanon's political history has led the general public to focus on the improvement of humanitarian and development policies within given structures. The unthinkability of a Lebanon that develops and thrives on the very basis of better public policies—rather than of effective humanitarian policies—is the greatest struggle. In the meantime, the crisis-driven logic of humanitarian governance problematically thrives on a deterministic ontology of conflict and the impossibility of a political resolution, while leaving aging—but still pulsing—humanitarian emergencies behind.

LOCALIZING AID?

Ignoring the implications of development-arianism—where humanitarianism and development seem to synchronize while local welfare is depleted—remains a structural issue international actors need to deal with. Against the vast domestic capacity of Lebanese aid, well financed foreign aid interventions have characterized Lebanese history. In this context, localization—"work that originates with local actors or is designed to support local emerging initiatives" (Wall and Hedlund 2016)—may make us think of quick solutions. In practice, humanitarian agencies have begun to enlarge their local staff. And yet, this is a partial and flawed understanding of localization. First, there is a lack of transformation at the institutional level, with donor agendas and unequal structures of work potentially implemented by holders of any nationality. Second, local recruitment has increased in Lebanon in the wake of tougher migrant labor policies also aimed at foreign professionals—generally labeled "expats" to grant them a higher social status. Thus, fewer job positions have become available in the country in such categories. From 2016, local recruitment has occurred as a result of budget shortfalls because local staff normally have lower pay scales (see chap. 5). Such tendencies certainly cannot mean greater international accountability in the eyes of displaced people. With the mobile international technocrat remaining the official professional authority in the sector, a radical revision of humanitarian recruitment policies—of which experts are those with an "easy passport" who can move from Latin America to the Middle East with prepackaged beliefs and standards—is a priority to counter epistemic failure. Moreover, local-international partnerships have received rhetorical attention as a more acceptable face of hegemonic humanitarianism. There is, however, evidence that foreign donors still prefer implementers from their regions (Ramalingam et al. 2012), who purportedly uphold higher professional authority (Carpi 2022). In similar ways, localization used as self-legitimization (De Waal

1997) is neither promising in settings where local-international partnerships are still exploitative and hierarchical nor where refugees and locals are included merely to facilitate foreign access to people in need (Fiddian-Qasmiyeh 2019). Localization does not have to be a "mission" to look radically different from the past.

Many NGOs and research institutions from the North and South speak about being "the voice of the South" regardless of where and how principles and knowledge are developed. A progressive step may start with more jobs assigned to researchers and humanitarians displaced from war themselves and with reliance on multilingual resources (Carpi and Fiddian-Qasmiyeh 2020). The priority, therefore, becomes allowing for a political economy of support (and of research) that makes room for developing such capacities, which requires enormous efforts.

Furthermore, there is a growing emphasis on the need for economic, cultural, and social inclusion. Frequently used in human rights, humanitarian, and development reports, inclusion is an all-encompassing word that inherently entails positive intentions and actions (Carpi 2018). Inclusion is simply employed as the opposite of isolation and marginalization. As a matter of fact, rethinking inclusion is as difficult as eradicating exclusion. Inclusion presumes the existence of an established situation that dares to either include or exclude external elements: the word "include" comes from the Latin *in* + *claudere*, meaning to enclose or incorporate something. A critical inclusion ends up preserving the key features and relationships that underpin the center (Carpi 2018). It is against this backdrop that entities such as the United Nations Office for South-South Cooperation (UNOSSC) emerged in the 1970s as a watchdog of Southern interrelations, where only a win-win strategy for Northern and Southern actors could pave the way for economic and political stability (Fiddian-Qasmiyeh 2019). While the geopolitics of powers that exclude and include certainly exists, it remains problematic to assume that those excluded desire to migrate from the periphery to the center. The inclusion principle is exemplified by humanitarian slogans such as the 2030 SDG "Leave No One Behind" pledge, for which Save the Children was one of the loudest advocates. The language of exclusion and inclusion risks whitewashing the persistence of an intact mainstream culture undergirding a civilizing form of humanitarianism. Introducing the logic and language of active coexistence—which demands all actors be mutually informed and contemplates the multiplicity of voices—would at least be an unprecedented act of historical honesty. For local actors to play a publicly acknowledged role in rehabilitating displaced people, we need to reclaim a space that cannot be approached in terms of outsides and insides but instead learns from the different actors. It should be a space liberated from the amnesiac workings of the politics of crisis-making, learning from forms of vernacular assistance that existed long before the mobilization of mainstream humanitarianism. In this framework, I find some current academic attempts to reconsign agency to the disenfranchised both heuristically sterile and neocolonial at a time when Southern agency is heralded as a human and intellectual conquest of the North's consciousness. This book has tried to unearth the polyphony of highly diverse political, social, and moral actors—with the humanitarian lifeworld located at their interface—who aspire to uphold the forms of assistance (and the geographies of aid) that really matter to them.

THE WAY FORWARD

The official emergencization of life in Lebanon and the subsequent turning of deprived social spaces into humanitarian spaces make people exist only as humanitarian victims. Foreign aid provision represents the minimum of what the international community can do. Aid as a "modern conscience given an alibi" (Rieff 2002) coalesces with the experience of nothingness that Dunn (2014) theorizes. The politicide of Syrian refugees and weak moral support for Lebanon from the Arab region itself during the July War—when Hezbollah received reproaches from Saudi Arabia, Jordan, and Egypt—unmask the alibi.

The Politics of Crisis-Making is a polyphonic, ethnographic account of how different cultures of assistance can coalesce or counter one another on societal, political, and moral grounds. While the July War in Dahiye was constructed by Hezbollah as a unifying experience, Syrians in Lebanon became "refugeed" and made Others to the local context via international humanitarianism. International humanitarianism, in turn, wants selected testimonies to tell the life stories of victims (Adams 1998), while the inheritance of victimhood in Dahiye could be resisted through everyday acts of giving. This does not mean that all of Dahiye's residents felt empowered by war, because territorial citizenship was acknowledged and protected by the ruling party as long as war victims used the grammar of local power.

Chronic uncertainty in Lebanon is compounded with the ineluctability of Dahiye's exposure to war and Akkar's poverty. From here comes the mantra that Lebanon cannot exist—or would be worse—without foreign aid. In this respect, I sympathize with Assaad Thebian from the Gherbal Initiative, who, in a Konrad-Adenauer event in Beirut after the 2020 blast, stated that foreign aid is the unquestioned incipit of all discourses around present solutions for Lebanon. Solidarity-driven help is not inherently problematic (this is what we should jealously preserve in contemporary times). Instead, foreign humanitarian actors should act as a springboard for joint collective action rather than proposing themselves as capacity builders or simply approaching humanitarianism as a career. Fueling international solidarity and active support into locally grown networks is a just point of departure.[3] For the time being, the practical necessity for hegemonic actors to gain local accountability is left unaddressed. The international humanitarian cannot keep indulging discontents by blaming the locals as well as the abstract decisional power of global donors.

The severity of injustice, impunity and deprivation in Lebanon is exasperating. By no means has this book drawn on expertise from the political economy: it cannot suggest in detail how the current collapse should be addressed, or if foreign aid should be dismantled once and for all. Whether or not humanitarianism should be there is an unhelpful and, fundamentally, an impossible question to answer. It would mean imagining decades of international politics and interventions fading away—a world that, historically, does not subsist. In this book, I have rather aimed to unpack the crisis rubric and its discursive and operational workings on individual and collective understandings of war, forced displacement, and the chronic hardships with which these become enmeshed.

I treasure the memory of Arabic students who frequented a Tripoli-based NGO led by Syrian refugees I had the fortune to be in touch with during February 2018. A couple of students were interested in volunteering, and one would visit the NGO to use the library when preparing for his Arabic exam. Spaces of solidarity can emerge through these encounters. Instead, such spaces are generally discouraged in UN agencies and many INGOs, which are bureaucratized and (physically, or only morally, as shown) securitized from the entrance to the upper floors. Despite the enduring tensions that underlie such moral economies (see chap. 5), it is in these untold spaces of encounter that an interactive politics of informed support can emerge: a politics that shifts our attention away from the mission-driven humanitarian impetus, lost in heavy digital records containing the names of people whose faces many providers have never seen, lost in metal detectors, eye-catching logos, and meetings held in five-star hotels throughout the world while chronic hardships keep barking outside. This should not remind us of the deafening urgency of humanitarian action, which has now been there for quite some time. This should rather remind us that the logic of urgent action can engender even larger inequalities and suffering. It should remind us of the need to end the violent dissonance that the politics of crisis-making cyclically wheels out. If anger is the emotion with the longest memory (Shafak 2020, 71), this book has been my own way of facing it constructively.

NOTES

1. Watch "Rethink Aid for Lebanon," sponsored by the Konrad-Adenauer-Stiftung Foundation, November 20, 2020. https://www.kas.de/en/web/libanon/veranstaltungsberichte/detail/-/content/beirut-debates.

2. See https://daleel-madani.org/beirut-blast-response.

3. "Rethink Aid for Lebanon" workshop, sponsored by the Konrad-Adenauer-Stiftung Foundation, November 20, 2020. https://www.kas.de/en/web/libanon/veranstaltungsberichte/detail/-/content/beirut-debates.

APPENDIX

Key Dates in Lebanon's Political History

1916	Sykes-Picot Agreement between France and Great Britain determines the partition of the Ottoman Empire. Lebanon and Syria are incorporated into France's sphere of influence.
1920–43	French mandate in Greater Syria, ending with Lebanon's independence on November 22. The National Pact in 1943 establishes Lebanon as a multiconfessional state.
1948	Palestinian *Nakba* from British mandate Palestine during Israel's foundation.
1958	Creation of the United Arab Republic between Egypt and Syria promoting pan-Arabism. Lebanese president Camille Chamoun supports the United States "Blue Bat Operation" in Lebanon, aimed at countering such politics.
1968	Israeli "Operation Gift" on Beirut Airport allegedly in response to attacks by the Lebanon-based Popular Front for the Liberation of Palestine.
1975	Beginning of the Lebanese Civil War (April 13).
1976	Phalangist militias, supported by Syrian president Hafez al-Asad's army, assault the Tel al-Zaatar Palestinian refugee camp. Fifteen hundred people are massacred.
1978	Israel launches "Litani Operation," invading southern Lebanon.
1982	Israeli invasion of southern Lebanon ("Peace for Galilee Operation"). Massacre of civilians by Phalangist militias in Sabra and Shatila refugee camps (September 16).

(Continued)

1985–88   "War of the Camps": Palestinian refugee camps in the southern suburbs of Beirut are besieged by the Amal Movement militias.

1989–90   End of Lebanese Civil War. The Ta'if Agreement establishes a regime based on sectarian power sharing. Syrian forces remain in Lebanon.

1996   One hundred six civilians are killed in Qana, South Lebanon, during Israel's "Grapes of Wrath Operation."

2000   Israel withdraws from South Lebanon (May 24).

2005   Assassination of ex-prime minister Rafiq al-Hariri (February 14) leads to Cedar Revolution (March 14) and Syrian withdrawal from Lebanon (April 26).

2006   July War: major conflict erupts between Israel and Hezbollah, causing thousands of victims and major displacements.

2007   Clashes between Lebanese army and al-Qaeda offshoot group Fatah al-Islam in the Nahr Al-Bared Palestinian refugee camp, North Lebanon.

2008   Clashes between Sunni and Shiite militias as a result of the government's decision to dismantle Hezbollah's telecommunication system (May 7).

2011–13   Syrian popular uprising (March 15), government repression, and exodus of millions of refugees toward neighboring countries.

2014   "Lebanon Crisis Response Plan": first official state response to displacement from Syria.

2015   "Garbage Crisis" leads to massive demonstrations ("You Stink" - "tala3t ri7tkon" - campaign) to demand better infrastructure and the end of the sectarian power system (August).

2019   "October Revolution": introduction of austerity plan sparks renewed protests against the post-Ta'if sectarian regime (October 17).

2020   Economic downturn and COVID-19 pandemic restrictions cause collapse of Lebanese economy. Blast at Beirut port kills hundreds and causes vast infrastructure damage (August 4).

2022   Parliamentary elections (May 15).

BIBLIOGRAPHY

Abi-Habib Khoury, Roula. 2012. *Rapid Assessment on Child Labour in North Lebanon (Tripoli and Akkar) and Bekaa Governorates*. Beirut: USJ and ILO.

AbiYaghi, Marie-Noëlle, and Léa Yammine. 2019. *Understanding the Social Protection Needs of Civil Society Workers in Lebanon. Towards Strengthening Social Rights and Security for All*. Beirut: Lebanon Support.

Abu Lughod, Lila. 1991. "Writing Against Culture." In *Recapturing Anthropology: Working in the Present*, edited by Richard Fox, 137–62. Santa Fe: School of American Research Press.

Achcar, Gilbert, and Michel Warschawski. 2007. *The 33-Day War: Israel's War on Hezbollah in Lebanon and Its Aftermath*. Berkeley, CA: Saqi Books.

Adams, Vincanne. 1998. "Suffering the Winds of Lhasa: Politicized Bodies, Human Rights, Cultural Difference, and Humanism in Tibet." *Medical Anthropology Quarterly* 12 (1): 74–102.

Agamben, Giorgio. 1998. *Homo Sacer: Sovereign Power and Bare Life*. Translated by Daniel Heller-Roazen. Stanford, CA: Stanford University Press.

Agier, Michel. 2003. "La Main Gauche de l'Empire: Ordre et Désordres de l'Humanitaire." *Multitudes* 11:67–77.

———. 2010. "Humanity as an Identity and Its Political Effects (A Note on Camps and Humanitarian Government)." *Humanity* 1 (1): 29–46.

Ajami, Fouad. 1986. *The Vanished Imam: Musa al-Sadr and the Shi'a of Lebanon*. New York: Cornell University Press.

Alamuddin, Hana. 2010. "The Reconstruction Project of the Southern Suburb of Beirut." In *Lessons in Post-war Reconstruction: Case Studies from Lebanon in the Aftermath of the 2006 War*, edited by Howayda Al-Harithy, 22–46. New York: Routledge.

ALEF-Act for Human Rights. 2013. *Two Years On: Syrian Refugees in Lebanon*. Beirut: IKV Pax Christi.

Al-Harithy, Howayda. 2010. "The Politics of Postwar Reconstruction in Lebanon: An Introduction." In *Lessons in Post-war Reconstruction: Case Studies from Lebanon in the Aftermath of the 2006 War*, edited by Howayda Al-Harithy, 1–20. New York: Routledge.

Allan, Diana. 2013. *Refugees of the Revolution: Experiences of the Palestinian Exile.* Stanford, CA: Stanford University Press.

Almeida, Paul. 2019. *Social Movements: The Structure of Collective Mobilization.* Oakland: University of California Press.

Anderson, Mary B. 1999. *Do No Harm: How Aid Can Support Peace—Or War.* Boulder, CO: Lynne Rienner.

Antze, Paul, and Michael Lambek. 1996. *Tense Past: Cultural Essays in Trauma and Memory.* New York: Routledge.

Arendt, Hannah. 1958. *The Human Condition.* Chicago: Chicago University Press.

Aretxaga, Begoña. 2003. "Maddening States." *Annual Review of Anthropology* 32:393–410.

Arif, Yasmeen. 2008. "Religion and Rehabilitation: Humanitarian Biopolitics, City Spaces and Acts of Religion." *International Journal of Urban and Regional Research* 32 (3): 671–89.

Ashkar, Hisham. 2015. "Benefiting from a Crisis: Lebanese Upscale Real-Estate Industry and the War in Syria." In "La société libanaise à l'épreuve du drame syrien." Special Issue, *Confluences Méditerranée* 1 (92): 89–100.

Aubin-Boltanski, Emma, and Leila Vignal. 2020. "Hosting and Being Hosted in Times of Crisis: Exploring the Multilayered Patterns of Syrian Refuge in the Dayr al-Ahmar Region, Northern Bekaa, Lebanon." In *Mobility and Forced Displacement in the Middle East*, edited by Z. Babar, 55–78. London: Hurst and Oxford University Press.

Azoulay, Ariella, and Adi Ophir. 2012. "Abandoning Gaza." In *Agamben and Colonialism*, edited by S. Svirsky and M. Bignall, 178–203. Edinburgh: Edinburgh University Press.

Bahram, Haqqi. 2020. "Kurdish Guests or Syrian Refugees? Identity, Belonging and Intra-Ethnic Displacement." *Routed Magazine*, Oxford Migration Conference paper. May 29, 2020.

Balanche, Fabrice. 2012. "The Reconstruction of Lebanon or the Racketeering Rule." In *Lebanon: After the Cedar Revolution*, edited by Are Knudsen and Michael Kerr, 145–62. London: Hurst.

Barnett, Michael. 2005. "Humanitarianism Transformed." *Perspectives on Politics* 3 (4): 723–40.

———. 2011. *The Empire of Humanity: A History of Humanitarianism.* Ithaca, NY: Cornell University Press.

———. 2021. "The Humanitarian Club." In *Global Governance in a World of Change*, edited by Michael N. Barnett, Jon C.W. Pavehouse, and Kaul Raustiala, 155–81. Cambridge: Cambridge University Press.

Baumann, Hannes. 2013. "The New 'Contractor Bourgeoisie' in Lebanese Politics: Hariri, Mikati and Fares." In *Lebanon: After the Cedar Revolution*, edited by Are Knudsen and Michael Kerr, 125–44. London: Hurst.

Bayeh, Jumana. 2015. *The Literature of the Lebanese Diaspora. Representations of Place and Transnational Identity.* London: I.B. Tauris.

Belloni, Roberto. 2005. *Is Humanitarianism Part of the Problem? Nine Theses.* Boston: Kennedy School of Government, Harvard University.

Bhaskar, Roy. 2000. *From East to West: Odyssey of the Soul.* London: Routledge.

Bhatt, Chetan. 2007. "Frontlines and Interstices in the Global War on Terror." *Development and Change* 38 (6): 1073–93. Oxford: Blackwell Publishing.

Biehl, João. 2005. *Vita. Life in a Zone of Social Abandonment.* Berkeley: University of California Press.

Blanford, Nicholas. 2011. *Warriors of God: Inside Hezbollah's Thirty-Year Struggle Against Israel.* New York: Random House.

Blondel, Jean-Luc. 1991. "The Fundamental Principles of the Red Cross and Red Crescent: Their Origin and Development." *International Review of the Red Cross* 31 (283): 349–57.

Bou Akar, Hiba. 2018. *For the War Yet to Come: Planning Beirut's Frontiers.* Stanford, CA: Stanford University Press.

Bourdieu, Pierre. 1986. *Distinction: A Social Critique of the Judgment of Taste.* London: Routledge.

Bouris, Erica. 2007. *Complex Political Victims.* Bloomfield, CT: Kumarian.

Boustani, Marwa, Estella Carpi, Hayat Gebara, and Yara Mourad. 2016. *Responding to the Syrian Crisis in Lebanon: Collaboration Between Aid Agencies and Local Government Structures.* London: International Institute for Environment and Development (IIED).

British Red Cross. 2012. *Learning from the City: British Red Cross Urban Learning Project Scoping Study.* London: British Red Cross.

Brković, Čarna. 2017. "Introduction: Vernacular Humanitarianisms." Allegra Lab. https://allegralaboratory.net/vernacular-humanitarianisms/.

Brun, Catherine. 2010. "Hospitality: Becoming 'IDPs' and 'Hosts' in Protracted Displacement." *Journal of Refugee Studies* 23 (3): 337–55.

———. 2016. "There Is No Future in Humanitarianism: Emergency, Temporality and Protracted Displacement." *History and Anthropology* 27 (4): 393–410.

Bruszt, Laszlo, and Ronald Holzhacker. 2009. *The Transnationalization of Economies, States and Civil Societies: New Challenges for Governance in Europe.* New York: Springer.

Butt, Leslie. 2002. "The Suffering Stranger: Medical Anthropology and International Morality." *Medical Anthropology* 21:1–24.

Calculli, Marina. 2018. *Hezbollah e la Mimesi Strategica.* Milan: Il Mulino.

Calhoun, Craig. 1993. "Nationalism and Civil Society: Democracy, Diversity, and Self-Determination." *International Sociology* 8 (4): 387–411.

———. 2004. "A World of Emergencies: Fear, Intervention, and the Limits of Cosmopolitan Order." *Canadian Review of Sociology and Anthropology* 41 (4): 373–95.

———. 2008. "The Imperative to Reduce Suffering: Charity, Progress, and Emergencies in the Field of Humanitarian Action." In *Humanitarianism in Question: Politics, Power, Ethics*, edited by Michael Barnett and Thomas G. Weiss, 73–97. Ithaca, NY: Cornell University Press.

Cammett, Melani. 2011. "Partisan Activism and Access to Welfare in Lebanon." *Studies in Comparative International Development* 46:70–97.

Cammett, Melani, and Sukriti Issar. 2010. "Bricks and Mortar Clientelism, Sectarianism, and the Logics of Welfare Allocation in Lebanon." *World Politics* 69 (3): 381–421.

Campbell, Leah. 2016. "Stepping Back: Understanding Cities and Their Systems." ALNAP Working Paper. London: ALNAP/ODI. https://climatecentre.org /downloads/modules/training_downloads/2e%20%20ALNAP%20urban -systems-stakeholders-2016.pdf.

Carpi, Estella. 2013. "The Alliance of Media and Humanitarianism in Lebanon." *Open Democracy*, April 2, 2013. https://www.opendemocracy.net/en /opensecurity/alliance-of-media-and-humanitarianism-in-lebanon/.

———. 2018. "Empires of 'Inclusion?'" *Southern Responses to Displacement*, July 2018. https://southernresponses.org/2018/07/30/empires-of-inclusion/.

———. 2019. "Winking at Humanitarian Neutrality: The Liminal Politics of the State in Lebanon." *Anthropologica* 61 (1): 83–96.

———. 2020a. "The Borderwork of Humanitarianism During Displacement from War-Torn Syria: Livelihoods as Identity Politics in Northern Lebanon and Southeast Turkey." In *Mobility and Forced Displacement in the Middle East*, edited by Z. Babar, 33–53. London: Hurst and Oxford University Press.

———. 2020b. "On Ethnographic Confidence and the Politics of Knowledge in Lebanon." *Contemporary Levant* 5 (2): 144–60.

———. 2020c. "Towards a Neo-cosmetic Humanitarianism: Refugee Self-Reliance as a Social Cohesion Regime in Lebanon's Halba." *Journal of Refugee Studies* 33 (1): 224–44.

———. 2022. "The Epistemic Politics of 'Northern-led' Humanitarianism: The Case of Lebanon." *Area* 54 (2): 330–34.

Carpi, Estella, and Camillo Boano. 2018. "Humanitarianism in an Urban Lebanese Setting: Missed Opportunities." *Legal Agenda*, February 7, 2018. http://legal -agenda.com/en/article.php?id=4211.

Carpi, Estella, and Chiara Diana. 2019. "The Right to Play Versus the Right to War? Vulnerable Childhood in Lebanon's NGOization." In *Disadvantaged Childhoods and Humanitarian Intervention: Processes of Affective Commodification and Objectification*, edited by Kristen Cheney and Aviva Sinervo, 135–56. New York: Palgrave Macmillan.

Carpi, Estella, and Elena Fiddian-Qasmiyeh. 2020. "A Sociology of Knowledge: Lebanon, Jordan, Turkey and Egypt." In *The Oxford Handbook of the Sociology of the Middle East*, edited by A. Salvatore, S. Hanafi, and K. Obuse, 689–710. Oxford and New York: Oxford University Press.

Carpi, Estella, Jessica A. Field, Sophie I. Dicker, and Andrea Rigon. 2020. "From Livelihoods to Leisure and Back: Refugee Self-Reliance as Collective Practices in Lebanon, India and Greece." *Third World Quarterly* 42 (2): 421–40.

Carpi, Estella, and H. Pınar Şenoğuz. 2018. "Refugee Hospitality in Lebanon and Turkey: On Making the Other." *Journal of International Migration* 57 (2): 126–42.

Catusse, Miriam with Joseph Alagha. 2008. "Les Services Sociaux du Hezbollah. Effort de Guerre, Ethos Religieux et Ressources Politiques." In *Hezbollah. Etat des Lieux*, edited by S. Mervin, 123–46. Paris: Actes Sud.

Chalcraft, John. 2006. *Syrian Migrant Workers in Lebanon: The Limits of Transnational Integration, Communitarian Solidarity, and Popular Agency*. EUI Papers, RSCAS, San Domenico di Fiesole (FI), Italy, 2006/26.

———. 2009. *The Invisible Cage: Syrian Migrant Workers in Lebanon*. Stanford, CA: Stanford University Press.

Chambers, Iain. 2002. "Citizenship, Language, and Modernity." *Publications of the Modern Language Association* 117 (1): 24–31.

Chatty, Dawn. 2011. "Bedouin in Lebanon: The Transformation of a Way of Life or an Attitude?" *International Journal of Migration, Health and Social Care* 6 (3): 21–30.

———. 2013. "Guest and Hosts." *Cairo Review of Global Affairs*, Spring 2013. https://www.thecairoreview.com/essays/guests-and-hosts/.

———. 2017. "The Duty to Be Generous (Karam): Alternatives to Rights-Based Asylum in the Middle East." *Journal of the British Academy* 5:177–99.

Chit, Bassem. 2014. "Nationalism, Resistance and Revolution." *International Socialism* 2 (145): 99–118.

Collaborative Listening Project. 2009. *Field Visit Report: Lebanon, May–July*. Cambridge, MA: Collaborative Listening Project.

Collier, Paul. 2000. "Doing Well out of War: An Economic Perspective." In *Greed and Grievance: Economic Agendas in Civil Wars*, edited by M. Berdal and D. M. Malone, 91–111. London: Lynne Rienner, IDRC.

Comaroff, John L., and Jean Comaroff. 2009. *Ethnicity*. Chicago: University of Chicago Press.

Corm, Georges. 2006. *Il Libano Contemporaneo. Storia e Società*. Milano: Jaca Book.

Cutts, Mark. 1998. "Politics and Humanitarianism." *Refugee Survey Quarterly* 17 (1): 1–15.

Daehnhardt, Madeleine. 2020. "Social Movement and Mobilisation Approaches: A Case Study of Tearfund." In *International Development and Local Faith Actors: Ideological and Cultural Encounters*, edited by K. Kraft and O. Wilkinson, 59–73. London: Routledge.

Daher, Joseph. 2016. *Hezbollah: The Political Economy of Lebanon's Party of God*. London: Pluto Press.

Daou, Alain, and Jennifer Ghazal. 2020. "Les ONGs Libanaises Entre Autonomie et Responsabilité." In *Transition Humanitaire au Liban*, edited by Marie-Noelle Abi-Yaghi and Virginie Troit, 41–58. Paris: Karthala.

Darling, Jonathan. 2014. "Asylum and the Post-political: Domopolitics, Depoliticisation and Acts of Citizenship." *Antipode* 46 (1): 72–91.

Das, Rupen, and Julie Davidson. 2011. *Profiles of Poverty: The Human Face of Poverty in Lebanon*. Mansourieh, Lebanon: Niamh Fleming-Farrell.

Davis, Mike. 2006. *Planet of Slums*. London: Verso.

De Chaine, Robert. 2002. "Humanitarian Space and the Social Imagery: Doctors without Borders and the Rhetoric of Global Community." *Journal of Communication Inquiry* 26 (4): 354–69.

Deeb, Lara. 2006. *An Enchanted Modern: Gender and Public Piety in Shi'i Lebanon*. Princeton, NJ: Princeton University Press.

———. 2009. "Emulating and/or Embodying the Ideal: The Gendering of Temporal Frameworks and Islamic Role Models in Shi'a Lebanon." *American Ethnologist* 36 (2): 242–57.

Deeb, Lara, and Mona Harb. 2012. "Sanctioned Pleasures: Youth, Piety and Leisure in Beirut." *Middle East Report*. www.merip.org/mer/mer245/sanctioned-pleasures.

Derrida, Jacques. 2000. "HOSTIPITALITY." *Angelaki* 5 (3): 3–18.

De Waal, Alex. 1997. *Famine Crimes: Politics and the Disaster Relief Industry in Africa*. London: Africa Rights.

Dewachi, Omar. 2017. *Ungovernable Life. Mandatory Medicine and Statecraft in Iraq*. Stanford, CA: Stanford University Press.

Diamond, Todd. 2010. "Do Military and Development Mix?" *Foreign Policy in Focus*, March 18, 2010. https://fpif.org/do_the_military_and_development_mix/.

Di Peri, Rosita. 2014. "Re-defining the Balance of Power in Lebanon: Sunni and Shiites Communities Transformations, the Regional Context and the Arab Uprisings." *Oriente Moderno* 94 (2): 335–56.

Doraï, M. Kamel, and Olivier Clochard. 2007. "Non-Palestinian Refugees in Lebanon: From Asylum Seekers to Illegal Migrants." In *Migration and Politics in the Middle East*, edited by François de Bel-Air, 127–43. Beirut: IFPO.

Drif, Leila. 2018. "Être Réfugié et 'Volontaire': Les Travailleurs Invisibles des Dispositifs d'Aide Internationale." *Critique Internationale* 81 (4): 21–42.

Duffield, Mark. 2014. *Global Governance and the New Wars: The Merging of Development and Security*. London: Zed Books.

———. 2015. "From Immersion to Simulation: Remote Methodologies and the Decline of Area Studies." *Review of African Political Economy* 41 (1): 75–94.

Duffield, Mark, and Nicholas Waddell. 2004. *Human Security and Global Danger: Exploring a Governmental Assemblage*. ESRC Report, New Security Challenges Program, University of Lancaster, UK.

Dunn, Elizabeth C. 2012. "The Chaos of Humanitarian Aid: Adhocracy in the Republic of Georgia." *Humanity* 3 (1): 1–23.

———. 2014. "Notes Towards an Anthropology of Nothing: Humanitarianism and the Void in the Republic of Georgia." *Slavic Review* 73 (2): 287–306.

———. 2017. *No Path Home: Humanitarian Camps and the Grief of Displacement.* Ithaca, NY: Cornell University Press.

El-Mufti, Karim. 2014. "Official Response to the Syrian Refugee Crisis in Lebanon, the Disastrous Policy of No-Policy." *Civil Society Knowledge Centre, Lebanon Support,* January 2014. http://civilsociety-centre.org/paper/official-response -syrian-refugee-crisis-lebanon-disastrous-policy-no-policy.

Fakhoury, Tamirace. 2017. "Governance Strategies and Refugee Response: Lebanon in the Face of Syrian Displacement." *International Journal of Middle East Studies* 49 (4): 681–700.

———. 2021. "Echoing and Re-echoing Refugee Policies in the International System: The Lebanese State and Its Political Imaginary." *Digest of Middle East Studies* 30 (4): 262–69.

Fassin, Didier. 2005. "Compassion and Repression: The Moral Economy of Immigration Policies in France." *Cultural Anthropology* 20 (3): 362–87.

———. 2007. "Humanitarianism as a Politics of Life." *Public Culture* 19 (3): 499–520.

———. 2011. *Humanitarian Reason: A Moral History of the Present.* Berkeley: University of California Press.

———. 2013. "Why Ethnography Matters: On Anthropology and Its Publics." *Cultural Anthropology* 28 (4): 621–46.

Fassin, Didier, and Richard Rechtman. 2009. *The Empire of Trauma: An Inquiry into the Condition of Victimhood.* Princeton, NJ: Princeton University Press.

Fawaz, Leila T. 1994. *An Occasion for War: Civil Conflict in Lebanon and Damascus in 1860.* Berkeley: University of California Press.

Fawaz, Mona. 2005. "Agency and Ideology in Community Services: Islamic NGOs in the Southern Suburbs of Beirut." In *NGOs and Governance in the Arab World,* edited by S. Ben-Nefissa, N. 'Abd al-Fattah, S. Hanafi, and C. Milani, 229–56. Cairo: AUC Press.

———. 2017. "Exceptions and the Actually Existing Practice of Planning: Beirut (Lebanon) as Case Study." *Urban Studies* 54 (8): 1938–55.

Fawaz, Mona, and Mona Harb. 2010. "Influencing the Politics of Reconstruction in Haret Hreik." In *Lessons in Post-war Reconstruction: Case Studies from Lebanon in the Aftermath of the 2006 War,* edited by Howayda Al-Harithy, 21–45. New York: Routledge.

———. 2020. "Is Lebanon Becoming Another 'Republic of the NGOs?'" Arab Center, Washington DC, October 13, 2020. https://arab.org/blog/lebanon -a-republic-of-ngos/.

Fayyad, Ali. 2008. *Fragile States: Dilemmas of Stability in Lebanon and the Arab World.* London: INTRAC.

Feldman, Allen. 2004. "Memory Theatres, Virtual Witnessing, and the Trauma-Aesthetic." *Biography* 27 (1): 163–202.

Feldman, Ilana. 2007. "Difficult Distinctions: Refugee Law, Humanitarian Practice, and Political Identification in Gaza." *Cultural Anthropology* 22 (1): 129–69.
———. 2012a. "The Challenge of Categories: UNRWA and the Definition of a
Palestine Refugee." *Journal of Refugee Studies* 25 (3): 387–406.
———. 2012b. "The Humanitarian Condition: Palestinian Refugees and the Politics of Living." *Humanity* 3 (2): 155–72.
———. 2018. *Life Lived in Relief: Humanitarian Predicaments and Palestinian Refugee Politics.* Oakland: University of California Press.
Ferguson, James. 1994. *The Anti-politics Machine: Development, Depoliticization, and
Bureaucratic Power in Lesotho.* Minneapolis: University of Minnesota Press.
Ferris, Elizabeth. 2011. "Faith and Humanitarianism: It's Complicated." *Journal of
Refugee Studies* 24 (3): 606–25.
Fiddian-Qasmiyeh, Elena. 2011. "Invisible Refugees and/or Overlapping Refugee-
dom? Protecting Sahrawis and Palestinians Displaced by the 2011 Libyan Upris-
ing." *International Journal of Refugee Law* 24 (2): 263–93.
———. 2014. *The Ideal Refugees: Gender, Islam, and the Sahrawi Politics of Survival.*
Syracuse, NY: Syracuse University Press.
———. 2016. "Refugees Hosting Refugees." *Forced Migration Review* 53:25–27.
———. 2019. "Southern-led Responses to Displacement. Modes of South-South
Cooperation?" In *The Routledge Handbook of South-South Relations*, edited by
Elena Fiddian-Qasmiyeh and Patricia Daley, 239–55. Abingdon and New York:
Routledge.
Fiddian-Qasmiyeh, Elena, and Yousif M. Qasmiyeh. 2017. "Refugee Neighbours
and Hospitality." *Critique*, January 5, 2017. http://www.thecritique.com/articles
/refugee-neighbours-hostipitality-2/.
Fisher, William F. 1997. "Doing Good? The Politics and Antipolitics of NGO Prac-
tices." *Annual Review of Anthropology* 26:439–64.
Fourn, Léo. 2017. "Turning Political Activism into Humanitarian Engagement:
Transitional Careers of Young Syrians in Lebanon." Power2Youth, Working
Paper No. 28. April 2017. http://www.iai.it/sites/default/files/p2y_28.pdf.
Fregonese, Sara. 2020. *War and the City. Urban Geopolitics in Lebanon.* London: I.B.
Tauris.
Gabiam, Nell. 2016. *The Politics of Suffering: Syria's Palestinian Refugee Camps.*
Bloomington: Indiana University Press.
Gilsenan, Michael. 1985. "Law, Arbitrariness and the Power of the Lords of North
Lebanon." *History and Anthropology* 1 (2): 381–98.
———. 1986. "Domination as Social Practice: Patrimonialism in North Lebanon,
Arbitrary Power, Desecration, and the Aesthetics of Violence." *Critique of An-
thropology* 6 (1): 17–37.
———. 1996. *Lords of Lebanese Marches: Violence and Narrative in an Arab Society.*
Berkeley: University of California Press.
Graham, Stephen. 2003. "Lessons in Urbicide." *New Left Review* 19 (19): 63–77.

Guilhot, Nicolas. 2012a. "The Anthropologist as Witness: Humanitarianism between Ethnography and Critique." *Humanity* 3 (1): 81–100.

———. 2012b. *The Democracy Makers: Human Rights and the Politics of Human Order.* New York: Columbia University Press.

Gupta, Akhil, and Aradhana Sharma. 2006. *The Anthropology of the State: A Reader.* Oxford: Blackwell Publishing.

Hadath Municipality Publication. 2012. *an-Nashra al-Baladiyya 2012 (Aiyar 2010–Aiyar 2012) Sanatani min ajl Hadath Afdal* [Two Years for a Better Hadath (May 2010–May 2012), title translated by author].

Hage, Ghassan. 1996. "Nationalist Anxiety or the Fear of Losing Your Other." *The Australian Journal of Anthropology* 7 (2): 121–40.

———. 2015. *Alter-Politics: Critical Anthropology and the Radical Imagination.* Melbourne: Melbourne University Press.

Hanafi, Sari. 2012. "Explaining Spacio-cide in the Palestinian Territory: Colonization, Separation and State of Exception." *Current Sociology* 61 (2): 190–205.

Hanf, Theodore. 1993. *Coexistence in Wartime Lebanon: Decline of a State and Rise of a Nation.* Translated by John Richardson. London: Center for Lebanese Studies in association with I. B. Tauris.

Hanieh, Adam. 2015. "Shifting Priorities or Business as Usual? Continuity and Change in the Post-2011 IMF and World Bank Engagement with Tunisia, Morocco and Egypt." *British Journal of Middle Eastern Studies* 42 (1): 119–34.

Hannerz, Ulf. 1996. *Transnational Connections: Culture, People, Places.* Hove, UK: Psychology Press.

Hannig, Florian. 2018. "The Power of the Refugees: The 1971 East Pakistan Crisis and Origins of the UN's Engagement with Humanitarian Aid." In *The Institution of International Order: From the League of Nations to the United Nations,* edited by Alanna O'Malley and Simon Jackson, 111–35. Abingdon and New York: Routledge.

Harb, Mona. 1995. *Politiques Urbaines dans la Banlieue au Sud de Beyrouth.* Beirut: Arnaud, Institut d'Urbanisme de l'ALBA, Université de Balamand.

———. 2006. "La Dahiye de Beyrouth: Parcours d'une Stigmatisation Urbaine, Consolidation d'un Territoire Politique." In *Les Mots de la Stigmatisation Urbaine,* edited by J. Depaule, 199–224. Paris: UNESCO.

———. 2010. *Le Hezbollah à Beirut (1985–2005): De la Banlieue à la Ville.* Paris: Karthala.

Harb, Mona, and Sami Atallah. 2015. "Lebanon: A Fragmented and Incomplete Decentralization." In *Local Governments and Public Goods: Assessing Decentralization in the Arab World,* edited by Mona Harb and Sami Atallah, 189–228. Beirut: Lebanese Center for Policy Studies.

Harrell-Bond, Barbara. 1999. "The Experience of Refugees as Recipients of Aid." In *Refugees: Perspectives on the Experience of Forced Migration,* edited by A. Ager, 136–68. London and New York: Continuum.

Harvey, Paul, and Sarah Bailey. 2015. *Cash Transfer Programming and the Humanitarian System: Background Note for the High-Level Panel on Humanitarian Cash Transfers*. London: Overseas Development Institute.

Hassan, Ismael Sheikh, and Sari Hanafi. 2010. "Insecurity and Reconstruction in Post-conflict Nahr al-Bared Refugee Camp." *Journal of Palestinian Studies* 40 (1): 27–48.

Hayden, Patrick, and Natasha Saunders. 2019. "Solidarity at the Margins: Arendt, Refugees, and the Inclusive Politics of World-Making." In *Arendt on Freedom, Liberation, and Revolution*, edited by K. Hiruta, 171–99. London: Palgrave Macmillan.

Hein, Jeremy. 1993. "Refugees, Immigrants, and the State." *Annual Review of Sociology* 19:43–59.

Hermez, Sami. 2017. *War Is Coming: Between Past and Future Violence in Lebanon*. Philadelphia: Pennsylvania University Press.

Hilal, Nancy. 2008. "Governance and Public Participation in Post-war Reconstruction Projects: Haret Hreik, Beirut as a Case Study." MA diss., American University of Beirut.

Hoffman, Peter J., and Thomas G. Weiss. 2017. *Humanitarianism, War, and Politics: Solferino to Syria and Beyond*. London: Rowman and Littlefield.

Hourani, Guita. 2007. "Lebanese Diaspora and Homeland Relations." Paper presented at the American University of Cairo Conference, Cairo, Egypt, October 23–25, 2007.

Houri, Nadim. 2010. "Impossible Choices for Iraqi Refugees in Lebanon." *Human Rights Watch*, March 25, 2010.

HRW (Human Rights Watch). 2007. "Rot Here or Die There: Bleak Choices for Iraqi Refugees in Lebanon." *Human Rights Watch*, August 19, 2007.

———. 2011. "Stop Detaining Syrian Refugees." *Human Rights Watch*, May 20, 2011.

Humphrey, Michael. 1993. "Migrants, Workers and Refugees: The Political Economy of Population Movements in the Middle East." *Middle East Report* 181:2–7.

———. 2002. *The Politics of Atrocity and Reconciliation: From Terror to Trauma*. London: Routledge.

International Crisis Group. 2020. "How Europe Can Help Lebanon Overcome Its Economic Implosion." *International Crisis Group*, October 30, 2020.

Janmyr, Maya. 2016. "The Legal Status of Syrian Refugees in Lebanon." Working Paper. Beirut (Lebanon): AUB Policy Institute.

Janmyr, Maya, and Lama Mourad. 2018. "Modes of Ordering: Labelling, Classification and Categorization in Lebanon's Refugee Response." *Journal of Refugee Studies* 31 (4): 544–65.

Jawad, Rana. 2009. "Religion and Social Welfare in the Lebanon: Treating the Causes or Symptoms of Poverty?" *Journal of Social Policy* 38:141–56.

Jelin, Elizabeth. 2007. "Public Memorialization in Perspective: Truth, Justice and Memory of Past Repression in the Southern Cone of South America." *International Journal of Transitional Justice* 1 (1): 138–56.

Joseph, Souad. 1997. "The Public/Private. The Imagined Boundary in the Imaged Nation/State/Community: The Lebanese Case." *Feminist Review* 57:73–92.

———. 1999. "Descent of the Nation: Kinship and Citizenship in Lebanon." *Citizenship Studies* 3:295–318.

Jurdi Abisaab, Rula. 2017. *The Shi'ites of Lebanon: Modernism, Communism, and Hizbullah's Islamists—Middle East Studies beyond Dominant Paradigms.* Syracuse, NY: Syracuse University Press.

Karam, Karam. 2006. *Le Mouvement Civil au Liban: Revendications, Protestations et Mobilisations Associatives dans l'Après-Guerre.* Paris: Karthala.

Kasfir, Nelson. 1979. "Explaining Ethnic Political Participation." *World Politics* 31 (3): 365–88.

Kenyon-Lischer, Sarah. 2003. "Collateral Damage: Humanitarian Assistance as a Cause of Conflict." *International Security* 28 (1): 79–109.

Khalaf, Samir. 2002. *Civil and Uncivil Violence in Lebanon: A History of the Internationalization of Communal Conflict.* New York: Columbia University Press.

Khalili, Laleh. 2006. "The Refugees Who Give Refuge." In "The Sixth War: Israel's Invasion of Lebanon," edited by Reinoud Leenders, Amal Ghazal, and Jen Hanssen. Special Issue, *MIT Electronic Journal of Middle East Studies* 6:57–67.

Khater, Akram Fouad. 2001. *Inventing Home: Emigration, Gender, and Middle Class in Lebanon, 1870–1920.* Berkeley: University of California Press.

Khazen, Farid E. 2000. *The Breakdown of the State in Lebanon: 1967–1976.* Boston: Harvard University Press.

Khosravi, Shahram. 2007. "The 'Illegal' Traveller: An Auto-Ethnography of Borders." *Social Anthropology* 15 (3): 321–34.

Kimmerling, Baruch. 2002. "The Politicide of Palestinian People." *Dissident Voice*, June 11, 2002.

Knudsen, Are J. 2016. "Camp, Ghetto, Zinco, Slum: Lebanon's Transitional Zones of Emplacement." *Humanity* 7 (3): 443–57.

———. 2018. "Decades of Despair: The Contested Rebuilding of the Nahr al-Bared Refugee Camp, Lebanon 2007–2017." *Refuge* 34 (2): 135–49.

Knudsen, Are J., and Sari Hanafi. 2011. "Nahr el-Bared: The Political Fall-out of a Refugee Disaster." In *Palestinian Refugees: Identity, Space and Place in the Levant*, edited by Are J. Knudsen and Sari Hanafi, 97–110. London and New York: Routledge.

Kobeissi, Ola I. 2009. "Rural-Urban Migration of the Shi'a of South Lebanon to Beirut Southern Suburbs." MA diss., American University of Beirut.

Kraft, Kathryn, and Olivia J. Wilkinson, eds. 2020. *International Development and Local Faith Actors: Ideological and Cultural Encounters.* London: Routledge.

Krever, Tor. 2011. "'Mopping-Up': UNHCR, Neutrality and Non-Refoulement Since the Cold War." *Chinese Journal of International Law* 10 (3): 587–608.

Kumin, Judith. 2008. "Orderly Departure from Vietnam. Cold War Anomaly or Humanitarian Innovation?" *Refugee Survey Quarterly* 27 (1): 104–17.

Lavalette, Michael, and Barrie Levine. 2011. "Samidoun: Grassroots Welfare and Popular Resistance in Beirut During the 33-Day War of 2006." In *Social Work in Extremis: Lessons for Social Work Internationally,* edited by Michael Lavalette and Vasilios Ioakimidis, 31–50. Bristol: Policy Press.

Lebanon Support. 2016. *The Basic Guidebook for Emerging Collectives, Cooperatives and NGOs in Lebanon.* Beirut: Civil Society Knowledge Centre. https://civilsociety-centre.org/resource/basic-guidebook-emerging-collectives-cooperatives-and-ngos-lebanon-en-ar.

Lebuhn, Henrik. 2013. "Local Border Practices and Urban Citizenship in Europe: Exploring Urban Borderlands." *City* 17 (1): 37–51.

Lehmann, Christian, and Daniel Masterson. 2014. *Emergency Economies: The Impact of Cash Assistance in Lebanon.* New York: International Rescue Committee.

Levine, Mark, and Rachel Manning. 2013. "Social Identity, Group Processes, and Helping in Emergencies." *European Review of Social Psychology* 24 (1): 225–51.

Loescher, Gil. 1992. "Refugee Movements and International Security." Adelphi Paper 268, International Institute of Strategic Studies. London: Brasseys.

Mačák, Kubo. 2015. "A Matter of Principle(s): The Legal Effect of Impartiality and Neutrality on States as Humanitarian Actors." *International Review of the Red Cross* 97 (897/898): 157–81.

Mac Ginty, Roger, and Christine Sylva Hamieh. 2010. "Made in Lebanon: Local Participation and Indigenous Responses to Development and Postwar Reconstruction." *Civil Wars* 12 (1–2): 47–64.

Makdisi, Ossama. 2000. *The Culture of Sectarianism: Community, History and Violence in Nineteenth Century in Ottoman Lebanon.* Berkeley: University of California Press.

Makdisi, Saree. 1997. "Laying Claim to Beirut: Urban Narrative and Spatial Identity in the Age of Solidère." *Critical Inquiry* 23 (3): 664–705.

Makkouk, Farah el-Jam. 2008. "Assessment of Airborne Particulate Matter Elevation in Haret Hreik (Beirut) After the Israeli Bombardment of July 2006." MA diss., American University of Beirut.

Malkki, Liisa H. 1995. "Refugees and Exile: From Refugee Studies to the National Order of Things." *Annual Review of Anthropology* 24:495–523.

———. 2015. *The Need to Help: The Domestic Arts of International Humanitarianism.* Durham, NC: Duke University Press.

Mauss, Marcel. 1969. *Forms and Functions of Exchange in Archaic Societies.* London: Cohen and West.

Maxwell Hart, Maddie, Kamel Mohanna, and Virginie Lefebvre. 2020. "Localisation de l'Aide au Liban: Plaidoyer Pour une Feuille de Route Nationale." In

Transition Humanitaire au Liban, edited by Marie-Noëlle AbiYaghi and Virginie Troit, 59–69. Paris: Karthala.

Meier, Daniel. 2016. *Shaping Lebanon's Borderlands. Armed Resistance and International Intervention in South Lebanon.* London: I.B. Tauris.

Mercer, Claire, and Maia Green. 2013. "Making Civil Society Work: Contracting, Cosmopolitanism, and Community Development in Tanzania." *Geoforum* 45:106–15.

Mertens, Donna M. 2005. *Research Methods in Education and Psychology: Integrating Diversity with Quantitative and Qualitative Approaches.* 2nd ed. Thousand Oaks, CA: Sage.

Minear, Larry. 2002. *The Humanitarian Enterprise.* Bloomfield, CT: Kumarian.

Moghnie, Lamia. 2021. "Infrastructures of Suffering: Trauma, *Sumud* and the Politics of Aid and Violence in Lebanon." *Medicine Anthropology Theory* 8 (1): 1–26.

Mosel, Irina, and Simon Levine. 2014. *Remaking the Case for Linking Relief, Rehabilitation and Development: How LRRD Can Become a Practically Useful Concept for Assistance in Difficult Places.* HPG Commissioned Report. London: ODI.

Mosse, David. 2006. "Anti-social Anthropology? Objectivity, Objection, and the Ethnography of Public Policy and Professional Communities." *Journal of the Royal Anthropological Institute* 12 (4): 935–56.

Mostowlansky, Till. 2019. "Humanitarian Affect: Islam, Aid and Emotional Impulse in Northern Pakistan." *History and Anthropology* 31 (2): 236–56.

Mouawad, Jamil. 2023. "Lebanon's Wadi Khaled and the Challenge of Sovereignty." In *Altered States. The Remaking of the Political in the Arab World,* edited by S. Haugbolle and M. Levine, 173–92. Abingdon and New York: Routledge.

Mouawad, Jamil, and Hannes Baumann. 2017. "'Wayn al Dawla?' Locating the Lebanese State in Social Theory." *Arab Studies Journal* 25 (1): 66–90.

Mourad, Lama. 2021. "Brothers, Workers or Syrians? The Politics of Naming in Lebanese Municipalities." *Journal of Refugee Studies* 34 (2): 1387–99.

Moushref, Aicha. 2008. *Forgotten Akkar: Socio-economic Reality of the Akkar region.* Beirut: Mada Association, UNDP, Handicap International and EU Humanitarian Aid.

Nandy, Ashis. 2002. *Time Warps: The Insistent Politics of Silent and Evasive Pasts.* London: Hurst.

Nicholson, Beryl. 2017. "Poor Albanians who Hosted Displaced Kosovars." *Forced Migration Review* 55:55–56.

Norman, Kelsey P. 2020. *Reluctant Reception: Refugees, Migration and Governance in the Middle East and North Africa.* New York: Cambridge University Press.

Norton, Augustus Richard. 1985. "Changing Actors and Leadership among the Shiites of Lebanon." *Annals of the American Academy of Political and Social Science* 482 (1): 109–121.

Nye, Joseph S. 1990. *Bound to Lead: The Changing Nature of American Power.* New York: Basic Books.

Omaka, Arua Oko. 2016. *The Biafran Humanitarian Crisis, 1967–1970: International Human Rights and Joint Church Aid*. Vancouver, CA: Farleigh Dickinson University Press.

Ophir, Adi. 2010. "The Politics of Catastrophization: Emergency and Exception." In *Contemporary States of Emergency*, edited by Didier Fassin and Mariella Pandolfi, 59–88. New York: Zone Books.

Otto, Ralf, and Lioba Weingärtner. 2013. *Linking Relief and Development: More Than Old Solutions for Old Problems? IOB Study*. Ministry of Foreign Affairs, The Netherlands. https://www.government.nl/documents/reports/2013/05/01/iob-study -linking-relief-and-development-more-than-old-solutions-for-old-problems.

Pandolfi, Mariella. 2000a. "The Humanitarian Industry and Supra-colonialism in the Balkan Territories." Paper presented at the Seminar in Postcoloniality, Subjectivity and Lived Experience, Friday morning seminar on Medical Anthropology and Cultural Psychiatry, Harvard University, Boston, October.

———. 2000b. "L'Industrie Humanitaire: Une Souveraineté Mouvante et Supra-coloniale. Réflexion sur l'Expérience des Balkans." *Multitudes* 3:97–105.

Petran, Tabitha. 1987. *The Struggle Over Lebanon*. New York: Monthly Review Press.

Pitt-Rivers, Julian. 2012. "The Law of Hospitality." *Journal of Ethnographic Theory* 2 (1): 501–17.

Polman, Linda. 2011. *War Games: The Story of Aid and War in Modern Times*. New York: Viking Press.

Potvin, Marianne. 2013. "Humanitarian Urbanism under a Neoliberal Regime: Lessons from Kabul (2001–2011)." Paper presented at the International RC21 Conference, Berlin, Germany, August 29–31, 2013.

Prendergast, John. 1996. *Frontline Diplomacy: Humanitarian Aid and Conflict in Africa*. Boulder, CO: Lynne Rienner Publications.

Presidency of the Council of Ministers in Lebanon. 2007. *Lebanon: On the Road to Reconstruction and Recovery*. Second Issue. May 4, 2007. http://www.pcm.gov.lb /Admin/DynamicFile.aspx?PHName=Document&PageID=3916&published=1.

Pupavac, Vanessa. 2004. "War on the Couch: The Emotionology of the New International Security Paradigm." *European Journal of Social Theory* 7 (2): 149–70.

———. 2005. "Human Security and the Rise of Global Therapeutic Governance." *Conflict, Security and Development* 5 (2): 161–81.

Quilty, Jim. 2006. "Politics and Business, State and Citizenry: Preliminary Thoughts on the Response to Lebanon's Humanitarian Crisis." In "The Sixth War: Israel's Invasion of Lebanon," edited by Reinoud Leenders, Amal Ghazal, and Jen Hanssen. Special Issue, *The MIT Electronic Journal of Middle East Studies* 6:80–95.

Ramalingam, Ben, Bill Gray, and Giorgia Cerruti. 2012. *Missed Opportunities: The Case for Strengthening National and Local Partnership-Based Humanitarian Responses*. London: Christian Aid, CAFOD, Oxfam, Tearfund, and Action Aid.

Redfield, Peter. 2010. "The Verge of Crisis: Doctors without Borders in Uganda." In *Contemporary States of Emergency*, edited by Didier Fassin and Mariella Pandolfi, 173–95. New York: Zone Books.

———. 2012. "The Unbearable Lightness of Ex-pats: Double Binds of Humanitarian Mobility." *Cultural Anthropology* 27 (2): 358–82.

Rieff, David. 2002. *A Bed for the Night: Humanitarianism in Crisis. With an Afterword on Iraq*. New York: Simon & Schuster.

Rodogno, Davide. 2012. *Against Massacres: Humanitarian Intervention in the Ottoman Empire, 1815–1914*. Princeton, NJ: Princeton University Press.

Rosello, Mireille. 2002. *Postcolonial Hospitality: The Immigrant as Guest*. Stanford, CA: Stanford University Press.

Roy, Ananya. 2009. "Civic Governmentality: The Politics of Inclusion in Beirut and Mumbai." *Antipode* 41 (1): 159–79.

Rozakou, Katerina. 2012. "The Biopolitics of Hospitality in Greece: Humanitarianism and the Management of Refugees." *American Ethnologist* 39 (3): 562–77.

Saad, Amal. 1996. "An Analysis of the Factors Conducive to the Group Cohesion and Political Mobilization of the Lebanese Shiites." MA diss., American University of Beirut.

Safa, Oussama. 2006. "Lebanon Springs Forward." *Journal of Democracy* 17 (1): 22–37.

Said, Edward. 1978. *Orientalism*. London: Routledge.

Salamey, Imad, and Paul Tabar. 2008. "Consociational Democracy and Urban Sustainability: Transforming the Confessional Divides in Beirut." *Ethnopolitics* 7 (2–3): 239–63.

Salih, Ruba. 2020. *The Political Cultures of Palestinian Refugees: Right to Rights and Right to Return*. Cambridge: Cambridge University Press.

Sassoon, Joseph. 2009. *The Iraqi Refugees: The New Crisis in the Middle East*. New York: I. B. Tauris.

Schininà, Guglielmo. 2008. *Assessment of Psychological Needs of Iraqis Displaced in Jordan and Lebanon*. International Organization of Migration. https:// migrationhealthresearch.iom.int/assessment-psychosocial-needs-iraqis -displaced-jordan-and-lebanon.

Schiocchet, Leonardo. 2014. "Palestinian Refugees in Lebanon: Is the Camp a Space of Exception?" *Mashriq & Mahjar* 2 (1): 130–60.

Schmelter, Susanne. 2019. *Gulf States' Humanitarian Assistance for Syrian Refugees in Lebanon*. Beirut: Civil Society Knowledge Centre, Lebanon Support.

Schuller, Mark. 2012. *Killing with Kindness: Haiti, International Aid, and NGOs*. New Brunswick: Rutgers University Press.

Sen, Amartya. 1981. *Poverty and Famines: An Essay on Entitlement and Deprivation*. Oxford: Oxford University Press.

Shafak, Elif. 2020. *How to Stay Sane in an Age of Division*. London: Wellcome Collection.

Shearer, David. 2000. "Aiding or Abetting? Humanitarian Aid and Its Economic Role in Civil War." In *Greed and Grievance: Economic Agendas in Civil Wars*, edited by Mats Berdal and David M. Malone, 189–203. London: Lynne Rienner, IDRC.

Shryock, Andrew. 2004. "The New Jordanian Hospitality: House, Host, and Guest in the Culture of Public Display." *Society for Comparative Study of Society and History* 46 (10): 35–62.

———. 2008. "Thinking About Hospitality with Derrida, Kant, and the Balga Bedouin." *Anthropos* 103:405–21.

Simone, AbdouMaliq. 2008. "The Politics of the Possible: Making Urban Life in Phnom Penh." *Singapore Journal of Tropical Geography* 29:186–204.

Slaughter, Amy, and Jeff Crisp. 2009. "A Surrogate State? The Role of UNHCR in Protracted Refugee Situations." Research Paper No. 168, New Issues in Refugee Research. Geneva: UNHCR.

Slim, Hugo. 2000. "Dissolving the Difference Between Humanitarianism and Development: The Mixing of a Rights-Based Solution." *Development in Practice* 10 (3–4): 491–94.

Slyomovics, Susan. 2009. "Financial Reparations, Blood Money, and Human Rights Witness Testimony: Morocco and Algeria." In *Humanitarianism and Suffering: The Mobilization of Empathy*, edited by R. Wilson and R. D. Brown, 265–84. Cambridge: Cambridge University Press.

Smirl, Lisa. 2015. *Spaces of Aid. How Cars, Compounds and Hotels Shape Humanitarianism*. London: Zed Books.

Smith, Anthony D. 1981. *The Ethnic Revival in the Modern World*. Cambridge: Cambridge University Press.

Spivak, Gayatri Chakravorty. 1999. *A Critique of Postcolonial Reason: Towards a History of the Vanishing Present*. Cambridge, MA: Harvard University Press.

———. 2004. "Righting Wrongs." *The South Atlantic Quarterly* 103 (2–3): 523–81.

Stoler, Ann Laura. 2013. *Imperial Debris: On Ruins and Ruination*. Durham, NC: Duke University Press.

Suhrke, Astri, and Arve Ofstad. 2005. "Filling 'the Gap': Lessons Well Learnt by Multilateral Aid Agencies." CMI Working Paper 2005:14. Bergen: CMI.

Tajfel, Henri. 1978. *Differentiation Between Social Groups*. London: Academic Press.

Tanielian, Melanie. 2017. *The Charity of War: Famine, Humanitarian Aid, and World War I in the Middle East*. Stanford, CA: Stanford University Press.

Terry, Fiona. 2002. *Condemned to Repeat? The Paradox of Humanitarian Action*. Ithaca, NY: Cornell University Press.

Thorleifsson, Cathrine M. 2016. "The Limits of Hospitality: Coping Strategies among Displaced Syrians in Lebanon." *Third World Quarterly* 37 (6): 1071–82.

Ticktin, Miriam. 2006. "When Ethics and Politics Meet: The Violence of Humanitarianism in France." *American Ethnologist* 33 (1): 33–49.

———. 2017. "Humanity as Concept and Method: Reconciling Critical Scholarship and Empathetic Methods." *Comparative Studies of South Asia, Africa and the Middle East* 37 (3): 608–13.

Traboulsi, Fawwaz. 2007. *A History of Modern Lebanon*. London: Pluto Press.

Trad, Samira, and Ghida Frangieh. 2007. "Iraqi Refugees in Lebanon: Continuous Lack of Protection." *Forced Migration Review*, 35–36. https://www.fmreview.org /iraq/trad-frangieh.

Trombetta, Lorenzo. 2014. "Le Liban, Entre Révoltes Arabes et Conflit Syrien: Un Exercice de Flexibilité." *Oriente Moderno* 94 (2): 317–34.

Tueni, Ghassan. 1985. *Une Guerre pour les Autres*. Paris: Lattes.

Turner, John C., Michael A. Hogg, Penelope J. Oakes, Stephen D. Reicher, and Margaret C. Wetherell. 1987. *Rediscovering the Social Group: A Self-Categorization Theory*. New York: Basil Blackwell.

Turner, Lewis. 2020. "'#Refugees Can Be Entrepreneurs Too!' Humanitarianism, Race, and the Marketing of Syrian Refugees." *Review of International Studies* 46 (1): 137–55.

UNDP. 2010. *ART-Gold Lebanon, Linking Communities for Local Development (April–December 2010)*. Program Newsletter.

UNHCR. 2018. "UNHCR: Who We Are and What We Do." https://www.unhcr .org/lb/wp-content/uploads/sites/16/2018/04/Who-we-are-and-what-we-do _Apr18_EN.pdf.

Valbjorn, Morten, and André Bank. 2012. "The New Arab Cold War: Rediscovering the New Arab Dimension of Middle East Regional Politics." *Review of International Studies* 38 (1): 3–24.

Vazquez-Arroyo, Antonio Y. 2013. "How Not to Learn from Catastrophe: Habermas, Critical Theory, and the 'Catastrophization of Political Life.'" *Political Theory* 41 (5): 738–65.

Wall, Imogen, and Kerren Hedlund. 2016. *Localisation and Locally-Led Crisis Response: A Literature Review*. Bern, Switzerland: Swiss Agency for Development and Cooperation.

Warde, Alan. 2014. "After Taste: Culture, Consumption, and Theories of Practice." *Journal of Consumer Culture* 14 (3): 279–303.

Watenpaugh, Keith D. 2015. *Bread from Stones: The Middle East and the Making of Modern Humanitarianism*. Oakland: University of California Press.

Weiss, Thomas G. 2006. "Principles, Politics and Humanitarian Action." *Ethics and International Affairs* 13 (1): 1–22.

Weizman, Eyal. 2011. *The Least of all Possible Evils: Humanitarian Violence from Arendt to Gaza*. New York: Verso.

Wigger, Andreas. 2005. "Encountering Perceptions in Parts of the Muslim World and Their Impact on the ICRC's Ability to be Effective." *International Review of the Red Cross* 87 (858): 311–26.

Wildeman, Jeremy, and Alaa Tartir. 2014. "Unwilling to Change, Determined to Fail: Donor Aid in Occupied Palestine in the Aftermath of the Arab Uprisings." *Mediterranean Politics* 19 (3): 431–49.

Wimmer, Andreas. 2008. "Elementary Strategies of Ethnic Boundary Making." *Journal of Ethnic and Racial Studies* 31 (6): 1025–55.

Yiftachel, Oren. 2009. "Critical Theory and 'Gray Space': Mobilization and the
    Colonized." *City* 13 (2–3): 240–56.
Yiftachel, Oren, and Haim Yacobi. 2003. "Urban Ethnocracy: Ethnicization and
    the Production of Space in an Israeli 'Mixed City.'" *Environment and Planning D:
    Society and Space* 21:673–93.
Zakharia, Leila and Sonya Knox. 2014. *The International Aid Community and Local
    Actors: Experiences and Testimonies from the Ground*. Beirut: Civil Society Knowl-
    edge Centre, Daleel Madani-Lebanon Support.
Zakhour, Faraj T. 2005. *Halba fy Nifs Qarn 1900–1950*. Halba, Lebanon: Dar
    Zakhour.
Zenker, Olaf and Karsten Kumoll. 2010. *Beyond Writing Culture. Current Intersec-
    tions of Epistemologies and Representational Practices*. Oxford: Berghahn Books.

INDEX

Italicized page numbers refer to tables.

Danish Refugee Council (DRC), 43, 66,
  72, 101, 105, 126, 133
Darling, Jonathan, 101
decentralization, 21, 84; administrative,
  16, 55, 100; of power, 85, 95
Deir ez-Zor, 72, 153
depoliticization, 93–94, 96, 97, 101;
  strategies, 13, 81
deprivation, 3, 21, 31, 46n12, 92, 117, 127,
  134, 150, 159, 167, 168
detention, 114, 115, 116, 139n2, 140n20
develop-manitarianism, 7, 82, 159
development, 6, 10, 20, 28, 29, 40, 56, 57,
  82, 85, 129, 152, 161, 162, 166; actors,
  8, 41, 160, 161, 162; decentralization,
  55; economic, 58, 59, 85, 127;
  humanitarian-development nexus, 7,
  161, 162; international, 91; investment
  in, 55; local, 160, 164; organizations,
  56, 78n50, 149; policies, 6, 165;
  programs, 18; projects, 7, 15, 58, 84;
  urban, 163. See also Akkar Network
  for Development; Arab Fund for
  Economic and Social Development;
  Development Initiatives; develop-
  manitarianism; Local Development
  Office; Network for Development;
  UN Development Fund for Women;
  United Nations Development
  Program; United Nations Sustainable
  Development Goals
Development Initiatives, 77n42
Diana, Chiara, 138
diasporas, 53; Iraqi, 118; Lebanese, 55,
  163; Levantine, 55; Syrian, 137
discrimination: in aid distribution,
  41; in identity politics, 83, 90;
  material, 142, 144, 145, 146, 147;
  racial, 121; in state policies, 92, 93;
  and Syrians, 95
distance, 2, 3, 121, 154; emotional,
  128; moral, 3, 142, 152; physical,
  146; political, 3, 155; social, 3, 82,

160; socioeconomic, 142. See also
  humanitarianism, humanitarian
  distances
Dom people, 87, 88, 108nn24–25
Domari language, 87, 108n25
donors, 67, 85, 102, 137, 151, 161; donor
  agendas, 165; donorship, 7, 155;
  external, 52; foreign, 49n75, 58, 135,
  160, 165; global, 162, 168; Gulf, 73–74,
  103; international, 24, 53, 78n51, 84,
  160; private, 51, 77n42; regional, 73;
  Western, 60, 62, 94
drug dealers, 89
Dunant, Henry, 81. See also
  humanitarianism, Dunantist
Dunn, Elizabeth, 73, 133, 167

economic status, 126, 136, 143
economy, 24, 52; domestic, 21; global,
  5; labor, 34, 35, 36, 83, 148; laissez-
  faire, 64; local, 30, 122; moral,
  152; national, 19; political, 15, 33,
  166, 168; relational, 142. See also
  humanitarianism, humanitarian
  economies
Egypt, 1, 5, 56, 75n6, 167; Egyptians, 88
elites, 19, 51; political, 21, 33, 57, 107, 163
Elyssar Project (1996), 21
emergency, 2, 14, 61, 63, 70, 74, 87,
  90, 102, 132, 144, 150, 158, 162, 163;
  actors, 12; areas, 151; chronic, 45;
  emergencization, 13, 14, 159, 161, 167;
  imaginary, 159, 160; state of, 10, 58,
  83, 92, 124; tyranny of, 159, 161, 162
empowerment, 20, 64, 92, 95, 99, 100,
  109n31, 167; social, 62. See also Global
  North, empowerment of
ethnicity, 112, 135, 136; ethnic identity,
  113; ethnocracy, 13, 111, 113, 120, 133,
  138, 159; ethnopolitics, 111
ethnicization, 5, 13, 111, 112–113, 117,
  120, 122, 124, 125, 132, 135–36, 139;
  neoethnicization, 138

whiteness, 120, 121, 122, 156; white identity, 121; white savior, 3

World Bank Group, 46n21

World Food Program (WFP), 69, 70, 78n63, 94, 134, 141n47

World Humanitarian Summit (2016), 53, 149

World Vision, 78n66

World War I, 57

Worldwide Refugee Day, 18

Yarmouk, 44, 133, 133, 135

Young Turks Revolution, 57

Zaatari camp, 44

Zabadani, 38

Zahle, 135

Zakhour, Faraj, 35

Zeinab, 61

zu'ama' (local village leaders), 33, 52

Estella Carpi is Assistant Professor in Humanitarian Studies in the Institute for Risk and Disaster Reduction at University College London. She is author of *Specchi Scomodi: Etnografia delle Migrazioni Forzate nel Libano Contemporaneo* (in Italian).

FOR INDIANA UNIVERSITY PRESS

Lesley Bolton, Project Manager
Brian Carroll, Rights Manager
Allison Chaplin, Acquisitions Editor
Sophia Hebert, Assistant Acquisitions Editor
Brenna Hosman, Production Coordinator
Katie Huggins, Production Manager
Rachel Rosolina, Marketing Manager
Pamela Rude, Book Designer

www.ingramcontent.com/pod-product-compliance
Lightning Source LLC
Chambersburg PA
CBHW030328270326
41926CB00010B/1550